Authoritarianism and the Evolution of West European Electoral Politics

Authoritarianism and the Evolution of West European Electoral Politics

ERIK R. TILLMAN

OXFORD
UNIVERSITY PRESS

OXFORD
UNIVERSITY PRESS

Great Clarendon Street, Oxford, OX2 6DP,
United Kingdom

Oxford University Press is a department of the University of Oxford.
It furthers the University's objective of excellence in research, scholarship,
and education by publishing worldwide. Oxford is a registered trade mark of
Oxford University Press in the UK and in certain other countries

First Edition published in 2021

Impression: 1

Published in the United States of America by Oxford University Press
198 Madison Avenue, New York, NY 10016, United States of America

British Library Cataloguing in Publication Data
Data available

Library of Congress Control Number: 2020951754

ISBN 978-0-19-289622-3

DOI: 10.1093/oso/9780192896223.001.0001

Printed and bound by
CPI Group (UK) Ltd, Croydon, CR0 4YY

Preface

This book is the product of many years' efforts to understand the changing shape of electoral behaviour in Western Europe. In 2004, while still a doctoral student, I published an article in which I showed that the proximity between voters and parties on the issue of European integration correlated with party support in the 1995 wave of member states. Catherine de Vries termed the phenomenon 'EU issue voting' in a more complete study of the topic, and it led to a collaboration on two articles as well as others by her and colleagues on the topic. The study of EU issue voting was important, as it challenged ideas about the limited relevance of EU attitudes to voting behaviour and suggested that the EU had become more relevant to national politics. Yet I struggled with how to make sense of this finding in a broader sense for a number of years.

Surprisingly, perhaps, the breakthrough for me came by reading about US politics. Hetherington and Weiler's *Authoritarianism and Polarization in American Politics* reintroduced me to the research on authoritarianism in political psychology. More importantly, though, their book's argument of a worldview evolution in US politics suggested for me the idea that something similar might be occurring in Western Europe. In one respect, it seems obvious. Western societies have experienced broadly similar developments in recent decades: the shift from industrial to post-industrial 'knowledge' economies, the growing liberalization of mainstream values, and higher levels of immigration generating increasingly polarized debates about multiculturalism. And yet there are obviously many differences between US politics and those of the various Western European states. In this book, I have attempted to develop an argument whose genesis is in the study of US politics but that is situated in an understanding of West European politics.

During the course of writing this book, I have relied on the support and feedback of many individuals and organizations. Now it is my pleasure to thank all of them for their generosity. The research reported in this book would not have been possible without the financial support of the University Research Council at DePaul University, which supported the survey experiment reported in Chapter 7 with a Competitive Research Grant and this book project with a Global Engagement Grant and a Paid Leave. Similarly, two Faculty Summer Research Grants and Undergraduate Research Assistant Program grants from the College of Liberal Arts and Social Sciences at DePaul University supported early work on this project. I am further grateful to the German Longitudinal Election Study and the Swiss Election Study (Selects) for providing access and funding to include survey questions used in this book, and to Qualtrics for fielding the survey experiments in Ireland reported in Chapter 7. Finally, the University of Koblenz and Landau provided an ideal intellectual and physical environment in which to pursue this project during a research leave in the spring of 2017.

I was fortunate to have the opportunity to present parts of this book in progress to audiences at the University of Amsterdam; Birkbeck, University of London; University of Koblenz and Landau; the European Union Center at the University of Illinois; the 'Campaigning for Europe' workshop in Annweiler, Germany; and Loyola University Chicago. My thanks to Bert Bakker, Sarah de Lange, Eric Kaufmann, Michaela Maier, Molly Melin, and various others for facilitating these talks and providing helpful feedback.

Many other individuals have been generous in sharing feedback and providing advice and support. I particularly want to thank Jessi Bishop-Royce, Meghan Condon, Catherine de Vries, Fernando De Maio, David Doherty, Ben Epstein, Alexandra Filindra, Sara Hobolt, Petia Kostadinova, Matthew MacWilliams, Duncan McDonnell, Sibel Oktay, Christine Reyna, Dan Slater, Wayne Steger, and David Williams for their help and advice. In addition, I have presented earlier versions of this research at numerous conferences along the way; I am grateful to the comments and questions from the many discussants and audience members. I am particularly grateful to Dominic Byatt at Oxford University Press for his support and efficient stewardship of this project, and to the anonymous reviewers whose feedback helped me to strengthen the manuscript. Finally, I am grateful to Ina Ajazi and Nick Aliotta for their research assistance during the early stages of this project. Though I am grateful to these many individuals for their support, I remain responsible for the interpretations and evidence presented throughout.

There are many others whose friendship and support has helped me through this project. Even though I do not have the space to name you all, please know that I am grateful. There are a few I want to mention. I thank Tom Lancaster, my PhD advisor at Emory University, for many years of professional guidance and support. Robert Baker has been a great source of insight and guidance over the past decade. Cathy May was a great friend and colleague in the Department of Political Science for ten years, and she embodied the ideals of the liberal arts educator. She left us too soon, but I want to thank her for her friendship and for encouraging me to do better as a teacher and a scholar. Finally, I am not the first author to divorce and remarry, but I am sure that I have been more fortunate than most during this process. I thank Özlem for her support during the formative years of this project and for her continuing friendship. But I am certain I would not have finished this project without Katie's love and patience, and I look forward to our shared future as I complete this book.

Contents

List of Figures

List of Tables

List of Abbreviations

AAA–PBP	Anti-Austerity Alliance/People Before Profit (Ireland)
AES	Austrian Election Study
AfD	Alternative for Germany
BES	British Election Study
CDA	Christian Democratic Appeal (the Netherlands)
CDU	Christian Democratic Union (Germany)
CHES	Chapel Hill Expert Survey
D66	Democrats '66 (the Netherlands)
DF	Danish People's Party
ESS	European Social Survey
EU	European Union
EVS	European Values Survey
FDP	Free Democratic Party (Germany)
FDP	Free Democratic Party (Switzerland)
FF	Fianna Fáil (Ireland)
FG	Fine Gael (Ireland)
FN	National Front (France)
FPÖ	Freedom Party of Austria
GFC	global financial crisis
GL	Green Left Party (the Netherlands)
GLES	German Longitudinal Election Study
IPP	Irish People's Party (Ireland, hypothetical)
KESK	Centre Party (Finland)
KOK	National Coalition Party (Finland)
LPF	Pim Fortuyn List (the Netherlands)
LR	Republican Party (France)
LREM	The Republic on the Move! (France)
ÖVP	Austrian People's Party
PG	Parties of the Left (France)
PRR	populist radical right
PS	Finns Party (Finland)/Socialist Party (France)
PTV	propensity to vote
PvdA	Labour Party (the Netherlands)
PVV	Party for Freedom (the Netherlands)
RN	National Rally (France)
RV	Social Liberal Party (Denmark)
RWA	Right-Wing Authoritarianism (Altemeyer)
SAP	Social Democratic Party (Sweden)
SD	Social Democratic Party (Denmark/Finland)

SDs	Sweden Democrats
SDP	Social Democratic Party (Finland)
SEM	structural equation modelling
SES	Swiss Election Study
SP	Socialist Party (the Netherlands)
SPD	Social Democratic Party of Germany
SPÖ	Social Democratic Party (Austria)
SPP	Socialist People's Party (Denmark)
SVP	Swiss People's Party
UKIP	UK Independence Party
VVD	People's Party for Freedom and Democracy (the Netherlands)

1

West European Politics in Turmoil?

A Populist Revolt?

The first two decades of the twenty-first-century have seen optimism replaced by a growing sense of crisis in the West European political mainstream. The first five years of the century saw the successful introduction of the common currency (the Euro) into circulation and the enlargement of the European Union (EU) into post-communist Europe. It was also a period of political moderation. Centre-left governments in states such as Germany and the United Kingdom signalled their comfort with increased market-oriented domestic reforms and regional economic integration, while 'rainbow' or 'purple' coalitions in states such as Finland or the Netherlands demonstrated a growing social liberal consensus. In short, it seemed that there was a growing convergence around market and social liberalism, ending the ideological fights of the twentieth century. Meanwhile, the successful enlargement promised a future in which the European continent would gradually unite in such a political and economic union.

That optimism did not last long. The early years of the century saw the first indications of the challenges it would soon be facing. After the 11 September terror attacks in the United States, European states were soon drawn into debates about military participation in US-led campaigns in Afghanistan and Iraq. The Iraq question in particular exposed foreign policy divisions among European leaders and generated intense public debates. West European societies also suffered terror attacks carried out by Islamic groups: in Madrid, Spain in 2004, and in London, UK in 2005. Along with these attacks, the assassinations of Dutch politician Pim Fortuyn in 2002 and Dutch filmmaker Theo van Gogh in 2004 intensified debates about immigration and multiculturalism in West European societies.

In the midst of this, West Europeans societies were also undergoing subtler changes. Rates of migration increased during the last decades of the twentieth century and into the twenty-first century, accelerated by conflicts in Iraq, Somalia, Rwanda, and the former Yugoslavia. EU enlargement in 2004 expanded possibilities for migration from post-communist to Western European societies. These changes led to growing debates about multiculturalism and citizenship.

These challenges started to manifest in politics as well. The rejection of the proposed EU constitution by Dutch and French electorates in 2005 was a setback to advocates of deeper European integration. Populist radical right (PRR) parties

Authoritarianism and the Evolution of West European Electoral Politics. Erik R. Tillman, Oxford University Press.
© Erik R. Tillman 2021. DOI: 10.1093/oso/9780192896223.003.0001

also experienced electoral successes, including the Freedom Party of Austria (FPÖ) in 1999, the National Front of France (FN) in 2002, and the Dutch Pim Fortuyn List (LPF) in 2002, but all three of these parties quickly regressed electorally. With the exception of FPÖ from 1999 to 2006, the radical right remained marginalized from governance. Moreover, it was possible to explain each development as a unique case, driven by public dissatisfaction with candidate quality or governing scandal. It was hard at the time to know whether these successes were an early sign of political change or aberrations.

In hindsight, the answer seems clearer. West European electoral politics is undergoing a transformation that is manifesting in changing voting behaviour and public attitudes. Mass Euroscepticism has grown more pronounced, prompting scholars to describe public opinion as a 'constraining dissensus' on European integration (Hooghe and Marks 2009). Growing Euroscepticism came to a head in the British EU referendum of 2016, in which the British public voted to become the first member state to quit EU membership. Electoral transformations have been equally profound. PRR parties have proliferated across national party systems, including in states such as Germany or Sweden that were presumed to be immune to radical right ideology. Moreover, PRR parties have gained electoral ground, becoming the third largest parties in a number of West European national parliaments. Their growing parliamentary strength has given them greater influence over policymaking. PRR parties have increasingly entered into coalition or confidence and supply agreements with governments led by centre-right parties, giving them power over national policy (de Lange 2012). Moreover, the perceived electoral threat of PRR parties has led established parties to emulate their messages and positions on salient issues such as immigration (van Spanje 2010). In short, mass politics in Western Europe is changing.

How should we understand these developments, and are they related? The remainder of this section examines three changes in more detail: growing mass Euroscepticism, increasing support for PRR parties, and growing acceptance of liberal values. Documenting these changes allows for the development of an argument explaining their relationship in the following section, which this book describes as the worldview evolution in West European politics. This chapter provides a brief overview of the main argument and its contrasts with rival explanations. The final section provides an overview of the book's structure.

Rising Euroscepticism

Increasing levels of Euroscepticism is one of the important trends of recent decades. Early research on public attitudes towards the EU described it as a 'permissive consensus' (Inglehart 1970; Lindberg and Scheingold 1970), meaning that EU citizens (then from West European states) were largely favourable towards

European integration without demonstrating much interest in the process. This environment gave European leaders wide latitude to pursue European integration as an elite project sheltered from popular debate. Scholarly interest in EU attitudes only began to increase in the 1990s as the evidence began to show eroding support for European integration (e.g. Eichenberg and Dalton 1993; Anderson 1998; Gabel 1998). Since then, public opinion towards the EU has become more polarized. More importantly, public opinion plays a greater role in the process of European integration. Treaties are subject to referenda in a growing number of member states, and growing attention to European integration raises the threat of an electoral backlash against governments for unpopular EU decisions.

Figure 1.1 shows the net positive image of the EU between 2000 and 2018 in Austria, Finland, Germany, and the United Kingdom. This chart uses responses in the Eurobarometer surveys fielded each spring asking respondents to indicate whether they have a positive, negative, or neutral image of the EU. This net positive image indicates the sum of respondents in each country choosing 'fairly positive' or 'very positive' minus the sum of respondents choosing 'fairly negative' or 'very negative'. Figure 1.1 highlights two important points. First, the image of the EU among its citizens is not uniformly positive. In each state but Germany, it veers below 0, indicating that more respondents had a negative image than a positive image at that time. Second, there are important temporal and cross-national differences in EU evaluations. The image of the EU is consistently (and

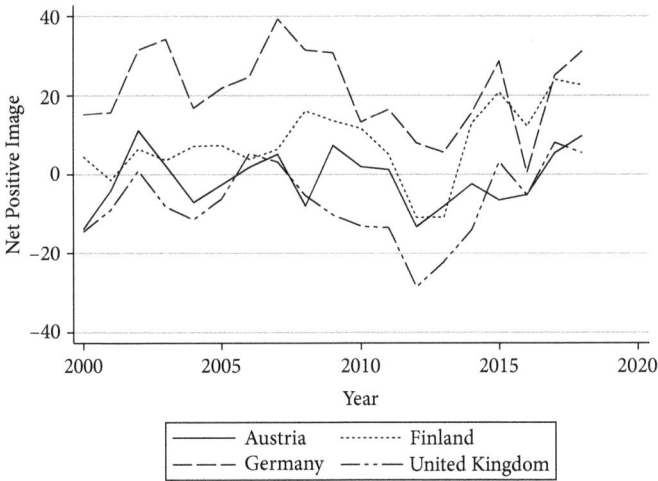

Figure 1.1 Net positive image of the European Union, 2000–18

Note: Lines show the net positive (fairly positive + very positive—fairly negative + very negative) image of the European Union for each state in the spring Eurobarometer survey for each year between 2000 and 2018.

Source: European Commission 2020.

unsurprisingly) higher in Germany than in the UK, but the image of the EU rises and falls in all four states in response to regional economic and political events. In short, Figure 1.1 shows that public opinion towards the EU is increasingly polarized.

Figure 1.2 shows the responses to a question asking respondents what the EU means to them. Respondents are presented with a number of choices, which they can (not) choose to indicate that the EU (does not) has that meaning to them. Among the options presented here, three items garner more than 30 per cent of the responses: the freedom to travel, work, or live anywhere in the EU; peace; and cultural diversity. European leaders often tout the importance of the EU in promoting regional peace and the weakening of national boundaries, and European citizens seem to have absorbed these messages. However, substantial minorities of Europeans also associate the EU with the loss of cultural identity (13 per cent), more crime (15 per cent), and a lack of external border controls (20 per cent). Thus, Europeans associate the EU with greater individual and cultural freedoms, but they also associate it with reduced national and cultural security. This book claims that these two sets of associations are important to understanding why public support for the EU is increasingly polarized. Chapters 4

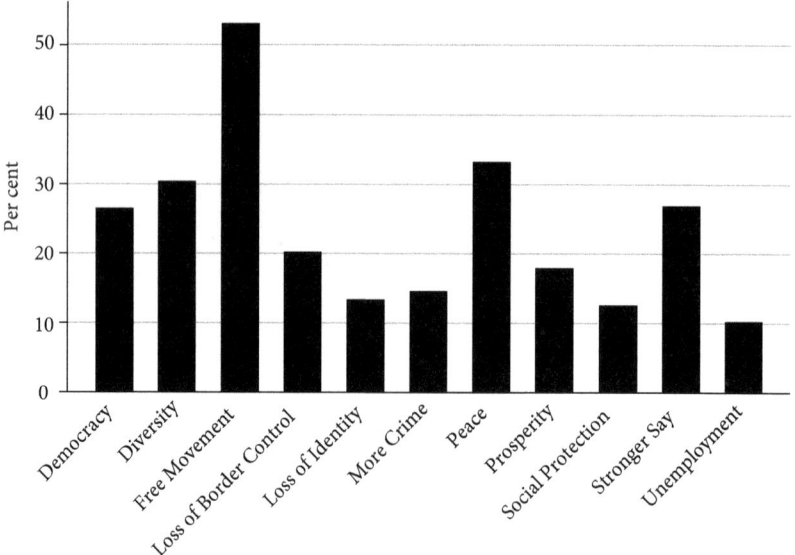

Figure 1.2 Public images of the European Union, 2018

Note: Each bar shows the percentage of respondents choosing that item in response to the question of what the European Union means to them. 'Free movement' means 'freedom to travel, study, or work anywhere in the EU'; 'Loss of border control' means 'not enough control at external borders'; 'Loss of identity' means 'loss of cultural identity'; and 'Stronger say' means 'a stronger say in the world'.

Source: European Commission 2020.

and 5 explain the structure of EU attitudes today and how they have evolved over the past thirty years.

Increasing Support for PRR Parties

Growth in electoral support for populist radical right parties is a second major trend of the twenty-first century. PRR parties share a core ideology based around nativism, populism, and authoritarianism (Mudde 2007). In practice, this ideology leads PRR parties to oppose immigration and multiculturalism, demand tougher 'law and order' policies against crime and terrorism, and to promote traditional Christian or 'Western' values. These positions have put PRR parties at odds with centre-left and liberal political parties, leading to debates about the appropriate responses for mainstream parties and generating new issue conflicts.

How much have PRR parties grown during the 21st century? Table 1.1 shows a basic comparison of electoral support for PRR parties in the last election of the 1990s and the most recent election prior to 2019 in seven West European states. The general pattern shows growth, with a few exceptions. In Austria, a PRR party was already established in national parliaments. The FPÖ had a breakthrough result in the 1999 parliamentary election, winning 26.9 per cent of the vote, which remains the party's electoral high-water mark. The intervening years saw swings in fortunes, but FPÖ again gained 26 per cent of the vote in the 2017 parliamentary elections. Denmark witnessed the entry of the Danish People's Party (DF) into parliament in 1999 after winning over 7 per cent of the vote. DF has subsequently expanded its support, and it won just over 21 per cent of the vote in the most recent national elections. Finland, Germany, the Netherlands, and Sweden experienced similar patterns. In the late 1990s, each country had a minor or non-existent PRR party. In the intervening period, this party either experienced

Table 1.1 Changing electoral support for PRR parties, 1997–2019

Country	End of 1990s (party)	End of 2010s (party)
Austria	26.9%	26.0%
Denmark	7.4%	21.1%
Finland	1.0%	17.7%
Germany	1.8%	12.6%
Netherlands	< 1%	13.1%
Sweden	< 1%	17.5%
United Kingdom	< 1%	1.8%

Notes: The first column shows the share of the national vote in the last general election before 2000; the second column shows the share of the national vote in the most recent general election before 2019.

an electoral breakthrough (the Finns Party in 2011; the Sweden Democrats in 2014), or a new PRR party achieved a breakthrough (the Party for Freedom (PVV) in the Netherlands in 2010; the Alternative for Germany (AfD) in 2017). The UK Independence Party has not grown into a relevant party in parliament, with the plurality electoral system hindering its chances (Norris 2005). However, its electoral threat to the Conservative Party in the early years of David Cameron's government influenced the decision to call the EU membership referendum (Clarke et al. 2017).

In most West European states, PRR parties have gained electoral support since 2000. These parties are often the third and occasionally second largest in national parliaments, giving them influence over cabinet formation and policy. What factors have driven this increased support? This book develops an argument linking the changing political and social climate to individual dispositions, with one's outlook towards the trade-off between individual autonomy and social conformity being central to this evolution in voting behaviour.

Growing Acceptance of Liberal Values

A third development, which is important to this book's argument, is that West European societies have experienced an ongoing values change over the past generation. There are various possible reasons for this values change, including increased prosperity, higher levels of educational attainment, and a shift in the structure of employment (Inglehart 1997; Norris and Inglehart 2019). Regardless of the specific causes, West Europeans tend to express greater social and cultural liberalism, as expressed in attitudes towards individual morality and cultural diversity. This values change has affected (and been reflected in) political discourse, popular culture, and the workplace. In short, liberal social and cultural attitudes are mainstream in West European societies, with prejudice towards religious, ethnic, or sexual outgroups being increasingly rejected.

One consequence of this values change is that previously mainstream ideas are now treated as unacceptable or 'backwards' in mainstream discourse. Individuals who hold such views—particularly those of older generations who were socialized when such views were considered mainstream—may find this shift unsettling. In particular, such voters may develop feelings of alienation towards the social and political mainstream or come to view themselves as 'left behind' in modern society (Ford and Goodwin 2014; Gest 2016). One possibility is that such voters are at the core of a 'cultural backlash' that is fuelling greater support for radical right politics (Norris and Inglehart 2019). Feeling abandoned by the political mainstream, perhaps older voters with traditional values have been receptive to PRR parties?

How much have values changed over the past generation? I illustrate the extent of values change by examining responses to two different questions between 1999

Table 1.2 Changes in social attitudes, 1999–2017

Question	1999	2017	Change in percentage points
Homosexuality is never justified	22.2%	8.4%	−13.8
Homosexuality is always justified	25.1%	49.2%	24.1
Natives should get preference over immigrants	54.1%	40.2%	−19.9

and 2017. These questions come from the European Values Survey and include respondents in Austria, Denmark, Finland, France, Germany, Italy, the Netherlands, Spain, and the United Kingdom. The first question asks respondents whether homosexuality is justified or not. Respondents can place themselves on a 10-point scale where 1 indicates 'never' acceptable and 10 means 'always' acceptable. The second question asks respondents, 'when jobs are scarce, employers should give priority to [members of the respondent's nationality] over immigrants'. Respondents can indicate whether they agree or disagree with this statement. Table 1.2 shows these comparisons.

The results in Table 1.2 show substantial levels of value change in less than two decades. In 1999, just over 22 per cent of respondents thought homosexuality is never justified while just over 25 per cent believed it is always justified, for a gap of just under 3 percentage points. By 2017, those believing that homosexuality is never justified had fallen by more than half to 8.4 per cent, but those believing it is always justified had nearly doubled to 49.2 per cent. The gap between 'always' and 'never' justifiable grew from just under 3 percentage points in 1999 to over 40 percentage points in 2017. The change in the percentage of respondents agreeing that employers should give natives preference over immigrants was more modest. Just over 54 per cent of respondents agreed with this statement in 1999, but that percentage fell to 40.2 per cent in 2017. As a result, the proportion of those agreeing with this claim declined from a majority in 1999 to a plurality in 2017. In short, an individual believing that homosexuality is never justified and natives should get job preference over immigrants would have been substantially closer to the mainstream in 1999, but this individual would have been distinctly in the minority in West European societies by 2017.

Understanding the Evolution of West European Electoral Politics

The three developments described in the previous section point to a major and ongoing reordering of West European politics. But these trends are well known, and many other scholars have observed and documented them. The value of this book must come from explaining why these trends are occurring, and the relationship among them. This section gives a brief overview of this book's argument in relation to that of other leading recent publications.

Prior Explanations

It is overly simplistic to describe the literature on the evolution of West European electoral politics as a debate between economic and cultural explanations. Recent scholarship examines the intersection of these phenomena to develop more nuanced accounts (e.g. Gest 2016; Norris and Inglehart 2019). Nonetheless, these two families of explanations have structured research on Euroscepticism and support for PRR parties.

Early research on PRR parties examined the claim that its supporters were the 'losers of modernity' who had suffered a loss of status as a result of the shift towards a post-industrial economy (e.g. Betz 1993; Kitschelt 1994). Because deindustrialization hit blue-collar, older, and male voters disproportionately, these voters formed the core of Eurosceptics and PRR party supporters. More nuanced accounts incorporate the role of social status and marginalization. The post-industrial shift has come with increased emphasis on education and cultural skills, which has left behind blue-collar workers. Working-class habits and values have also fallen out of favour, creating a sense of social marginalization (Ford and Goodwin 2014; Gest 2016). Rising Euroscepticism and PRR party support is the manifestation of a revolt against the political mainstream and its perceived abandonment of the working classes.

A second perspective argues that the evolution of West European politics is a response to changing social and cultural values. The post-war era has seen increased physical and economic security, triggering a series of values changes among younger generations (Inglehart 1977, 1997; Inglehart and Welzel 2005). Post-war generations who were socialized in an age of growing affluence and rising education developed new 'post-materialist' values emphasizing social justice, individual self-expression, and autonomy, rather than social order and security. Rising post-materialism led to growing social liberalism and multiculturalism and less acceptance of religious traditionalism and nationalism (Inglehart 1970, 1977, 1997). The growing influence of post-materialism has led to a 'cultural backlash' against these values (Ignazi 1992; Inglehart 2018; Norris and Inglehart 2019). As post-materialist values have become mainstream, Eurosceptical movements and PRR parties have attracted traditionalist voters by appealing to their values. In a related vein, fears about immigration and multiculturalism may drive Eurosceptical attitudes and PRR party support (Carey 2002; McLaren 2002; Ivarsflaten 2007).

Unresolved Questions

These different arguments have contributed greatly to our understanding, but questions remain. First, the arguments focusing on the losers of modernity provide important insights into the strength of PRR parties among working-class voters, but PRR parties derive support across class lines (Ford and Goodwin 2014), so these arguments only explain support for a certain portion of PRR party voters. In addition, research on PRR party behaviour shows that these parties only offer consistent messages on social and cultural issues like immigration, crime, or values, rather than economic issues (Ivarsflaten 2005; de Lange 2007). Indeed, Euroscepticism and support for PRR parties correlate more with cultural issues than economic position (McLaren 2002; Ivarsflaten 2007) and suggests that these concerns matter more than class.

Cultural arguments also leave certain puzzles unexplored. The 'cultural backlash' argument (Ignazi 1992; Norris and Inglehart 2019) suggests that PRR party supporters are predominantly older individuals, but many younger voters are Eurosceptical and support PRR parties. This argument might seem appealing to opponents of PRR parties, as it suggests their supporters will soon be replaced by younger generations, but it does not appear accurate. A second, bigger, question is why cultural issues divide voters in the first place. The argument that voters with anti-immigrant attitudes support anti-immigration parties is straightforward, but two questions remain. First, what explains why some voters gravitate towards anti-immigrant or nationalist positions while others do not? Second, considering that immigration has not been historically popular in West European societies, what explains the emergence of such issues in the contemporary era? Answering this question requires a theory drawing on political psychology.

The Argument

West European societies have experienced major economic and socio-cultural changes since the 1980s. From the early twentieth century until recent decades, issues of class and religion structured electoral politics in most West European states (Lipset and Rokkan 1967). The major issues of political conflict—such as taxation and the welfare state or the role of the Church in politics—fit within this structure of conflict. Electoral politics evolves when new issues emerge that do not fit comfortably within the existing dimensions of conflict. Enterprising political elites can exploit these new issues to attract voters from across party lines, leading to a shift of party loyalties and issue opinions (Carmines and Stimson 1989; Zaller 1992) that is aided by generational replacement. The shift to a post-industrial economy, increasing immigration, and social liberalization created a conducive environment for PRR parties to introduce new issues centred around identity and values that threaten older class and religious alignments.

This book argues that West European electoral politics is undergoing a worldview evolution. A worldview evolution occurs when the electoral change described in the previous paragraph is connected to fundamental psychological orientations about the organization of society (Hetherington and Weiler 2009). Rather than being connected to group interests or identities (such as class or religion), the issues driving the worldview evolution relate to basic social questions such as autonomy versus conformity, change versus stability, and sameness versus diversity. Voters and parties on either side of these issues are motivated by different orientations towards society, deepening the divide and making compromise or mutual understanding more difficult.

This book argues that this worldview evolution is driven by an individual personality trait called authoritarianism (Adorno et al. 1950; Altemeyer 1996; Feldman and Stenner 1997; Stenner 2005; Hetherington and Weiler 2009). Individuals who score high or low in authoritarianism ('high authoritarians' and 'low authoritarians', respectively) hold different worldviews on these basic social questions. High authoritarians have a fundamental orientation towards the preservation of social conformity and 'oneness', seeing increased diversity and change as a threat to the normative social order (Stenner 2005). Low authoritarians prefer to promote individual autonomy and difference, which leads them to view social and cultural institutions that enforce conformity and sameness as a threat.

This difference in worldviews leads high authoritarians and low authoritarians to view the social and political changes of recent decades differently. For low authoritarians, increasing social liberalism, diversity and multiculturalism, emphases on education and meritocracy, and the opening of national borders through European integration increase the potential for individual autonomy. Thus, low authoritarians tend to view these recent developments favourably. By contrast, high authoritarians view these same developments as undermining social cohesion and conformity—threatening the normative social order. As a result, they view these developments negatively.

These differences between high authoritarians and low authoritarians are at the heart of the ongoing worldview evolution. Low authoritarians view recent social and cultural changes favourably, so they are more likely to support the political mainstream (which has implemented or governed during these changes) or left-liberal parties that advocate for further diversity and autonomy. Additionally, they support the European Union and continued European integration, as it is consistent with their worldview. High authoritarians are a receptive audience for PRR parties, which emphasize the threat to society posed by social and cultural change. As a result, high authoritarians have become more likely to vote for PRR parties, abandoning the political mainstream in the process. In addition, high authoritarians have also become more likely to oppose the EU and European integration, which they view as threatening the normative social order (i.e. the sovereign nation state). Whereas authoritarianism had little relationship with voting behaviour or EU attitudes in the 1990s, it increasingly structures these political behaviours. This worldview evolution is transforming West European electoral politics, posing an increasing challenge for mainstream parties and the European project.

This book advances the novel argument that the worldview evolution affects both EU attitudes and voting behaviour. The common thread is the underlying threat to the normative order. European integration increasingly threatens national sovereignty and community. Radical right parties adopt Eurosceptical positions as part of a broader programme linking it to immigration and values change, all of which similarly threaten the established national community and culture. High authoritarians are more likely to perceive threats to the normative order and to support policies to stop those threats, while low authoritarians are more likely to view such developments favourably as enhancing autonomy. Thus, this book's worldview evolution argument can help us to understand the linkages between two important developments in West European politics of the twenty-first century: rising support for populist radical right parties and rising Euroscepticism.

Cross-national differences also shape the possibilities for a worldview evolution. Differences in political institutions affect the potential for new PRR parties to enter parliament (Givens 2005; Norris 2005), and historical factors have shaped the development of national party systems. Moreover, the strategic choices of political elites in each country will affect the path that a worldview evolution follows in each country. Therefore, the extent and nature of this worldview evolution will vary cross-nationally.

Overview of the Book

The following chapters develop the argument described above and test its implications. Chapter 2 presents the book's argument. After reviewing the changes in West European societies and economies, it evaluates different perspectives on changing electoral politics before detailing this book's argument that authoritarianism is the key to understanding the worldview evolution. While authoritarianism has always been distributed throughout West European electorates, it did not structure voting behaviour in earlier eras shaped by class conflicts because those conflicts did not threaten the normative social order. The result is an emerging political conflict fundamentally organized around rival worldviews: high authoritarians support parties committed to preserving social cohesion, maintaining the national culture, and enforcing security, while low authoritarians support parties committed to enhancing individual autonomy, choice, and social diversity.

Because established parties had organized around earlier class and religious divisions, they struggle to maintain support in this new era as left-liberal and radical right parties gain at their expense. The chapter concludes by describing hypotheses about the evolving relationship between authoritarianism and public support for the EU and voting behaviour, respectively.

Chapter 3 engages in a descriptive analysis of authoritarianism in Western Europe. The descriptive analysis highlights several important observations. First, authoritarianism is distributed normally throughout West European societies, though these societies have become slightly less authoritarian since 1990. Second, authoritarianism is related to education, as high authoritarians are consistently less likely to pursue post-secondary studies than low authoritarians. Finally, authoritarianism is strongly related to socio-cultural attitudes, occasionally related to political attitudes, but largely unrelated to economic attitudes. On social questions, high authoritarians are substantially more likely to hold traditionalist views on questions such as acceptance of same-sex marriage or endorsement of traditional gender roles. High authoritarians are much less accepting of immigration and are more likely to express national pride or ethnocentrism. On political questions, high authoritarians express less commitment to democracy and less trust in the political system. However, high authoritarians are not meaningfully different from low authoritarians on economic questions. These findings point to an important conclusion for this book's argument. Because high authoritarians vary from low authoritarians most on socio-cultural attitudes, the factors driving the worldview issue are socio-cultural rather than economic in nature.

Chapters 4 and 5 examine the relationship between authoritarianism and attitudes towards the European Union. The results in Chapter 4 show that high authoritarians are less likely to support European integration, to trust the EU, or to support enlargement of the EU's membership. To examine whether perceived threat to national community is the mechanism driving this relationship, the analysis uses a series of original survey questions fielded in Germany, which ask respondents about their fears concerning the EU. These results show that high authoritarians are consistently more likely to believe that the EU threatens Germany's culture and laws. Finally, authoritarianism accounts for part of the observed relationship between anti-immigration attitudes and opposition to the EU that has been observed in prior studies (e.g. McLaren 2002). Chapter 5 builds on these analyses to examine how the relationship between authoritarianism and EU attitudes evolved between 1990 and 2017. As public debates over European integration have shifted from economic to cultural concerns, the structure of EU attitudes has also changed during that era to reflect the activation of high authoritarians' perceptions of threat to the national community. The result is that a null relationship between authoritarianism and EU attitudes in the 1990s evolves to a significant and negative relationship in the twenty-first century. Moreover, this new relationship evolves faster in states with more party conflict over the EU, indicating that high authoritarians became more likely to oppose the EU in those countries where anti-EU parties were more successful in advancing the message that the EU threatens national community. Thus, the evolution of EU attitudes reflects the growing perception of threat to national community and sovereignty, which has been reinforced by political elites.

Chapters 6–9 examine the relationship between authoritarianism and voting behaviour. Chapter 6 considers whether high authoritarians are more likely to vote for PRR parties in recent elections, finding consistent evidence that they are. Moreover, high authoritarians with negative views of immigration are even more likely to vote for PRR parties. However, economic anxiety does not moderate this relationship. Taken together, the evidence suggests that concerns about threat to the normative social order (and not concerns about economic deprivation) are driving high authoritarians to support PRR parties. Chapter 7 builds on these analyses by considering the propensity of high authoritarians to vote for a PRR party in a country where one does not exist. Reporting the results of an original survey experiment conducted in the Republic of Ireland, the analysis shows that high authoritarians are significantly more likely to support a hypothetical new PRR party—but not a hypothetical new mainstream party. Moreover, high authoritarians are more likely to worry about the degradation of Irish society— expressed as a breakdown of shared values or as a more impersonal society—but not of another economic crisis. Importantly, these findings suggest that latent support for the radical right exists even in states lacking a PRR party, and that potential support reflects the same concerns about threats to the normative social order within Irish society.

Chapter 8 addresses a growing debate in the literature on the rise of the radical right, and an important question for this book's argument: are PRR party voters younger or older on average? One popular argument suggests that PRR parties have gained support by attracting older, high authoritarian voters. This 'cultural backlash' argument suggests that older voters have turned against the political mainstream in response to growing liberalism and multiculturalism (Norris and Inglehart 2019). Alternatively, this book's argument of a worldview evolution suggests that PRR party voters will be younger on average as they have weaker attachments to mainstream parties and have been socialized into politics in the present era. The evidence from various cross-national and national election studies is consistent with the latter argument. The relationship between authoritarianism and PRR party support is strongest among younger voters, and younger voters generally are more likely to support PRR parties in Western Europe. This finding points to a broader and more durable realignment of voting behaviour, indicating that support for PRR parties is not just the backlash of an ageing segment of the electorate that finds itself outside the political mainstream.

Chapter 9 tracks the evolving voting behaviour of high authoritarians and low authoritarians from the 1990s to the present. This analysis considers several important questions. First, is the relationship between authoritarianism and voting behaviour a new phenomenon, as this book argues? Second, which parties have lost voters to the radical right in recent years? The analysis finds support for this book's claim of a worldview evolution. There was no relationship between authoritarianism and party support in the 1990s. However, no clear pattern exists cross-nationally in terms of which parties have lost support. Instead, various patterns emerge across countries. Importantly, this finding suggests that a popular claim that social democratic parties have lost support to PRR parties is at best only partially correct. Instead, mainstream parties on the centre-left and the centre-right are both experiencing electoral challenges as a result of the ongoing worldview evolution.

Chapter 10 summarizes the findings of this book and suggests implications and directions for further research. Taken together, the evidence provided in this book supports the claim of an ongoing worldview evolution in the electoral politics of Western Europe. These developments share similarities to those in the United States and other Western democracies, though there are important unique contextual factors as well (in particular, the importance of the European Union). Crucially, this book's findings should counsel a rejection of claims that rising support for Euroscepticism and the radical right reflect a backlash of ageing voters that will soon fade, or that they are just the beginning of a long-term surge of right-wing populism. Instead, this book's findings indicate that Euroscepticism and PRR party support will remain durable but limited predominantly to high authoritarian voters as long as issues related to social cohesion and order remain salient in West European politics.

This Book's Focus

This book presents and tests a broader argument about an ongoing worldview evolution in West European electoral politics. The claim is that a voter's level of authoritarianism is increasingly relevant to understanding political behaviour. However, the empirical focus is primarily on the movement of high authoritarians towards anti-EU attitudes and support for PRR parties. Low authoritarians are equally important to this worldview evolution, but the book does not examine their behaviour as much. This may seem like an important oversight.

There are a few reasons for this asymmetry in the focus of the book. First, the growing influence of Euroscepticism and PRR parties constitute two of the most important developments in twenty-first-century West European politics, so it is crucial to understand them. By contrast, green and left-liberal parties have not seen such a dramatic rise in electoral support or participation in government. Second, the growing liberalization of mainstream attitudes over the past generation demonstrates the broader (if perhaps underemphasized) impact of these party families. Mainstream attitudes on European integration, immigration and multiculturalism, and social values have moved towards left-liberal positions in recent decades. Finally, while this broader shift in mainstream values reflects the influence of left-liberal movements (and their low authoritarian supporters), the rise of radical right movements is driving the ongoing worldview evolution. The movement of high authoritarian voters towards PRR parties (and their associated shift towards Eurosceptical attitudes) is an important facet of the worldview evolution, which may in turn further shift the behaviour of low authoritarian voters and left-liberal parties. Hence, this book focuses primarily on the changing behaviour of high authoritarians while hypothesizing (and presenting some descriptive evidence) about the behaviour of low authoritarians. Nonetheless, it is the hope that this book's argument will spur ongoing research into these developments, including how low authoritarians behave.

2

A Worldview Evolution in West European Politics

Introduction

On the morning of 24 June 2016, as the results of the British European Union membership referendum were trickling in via traditional and social media, a rather intense thunderstorm passed over Brussels. Although summer storms are not unusual, one could not help but see symbolism in nature. As the most intense part of the storm passed over Brussels, the results of the referendum had become apparent: the final count would show that the British had voted to leave the European Union (EU). Certainly, the results of the referendum hit European leaders like a thunderbolt. The result triggered fears about the potential for Eurosceptical movements to achieve similar results in other member states and about the growing electoral potential for populist radical right (PRR) parties in national and European elections.

One could also view the Brexit result as the culmination of a process unfolding over a decade or longer. Chapter 1 begins by noting how the optimism of EU leaders over the introduction of the common currency and the eastern enlargement gave way to pessimism over terrorism, the financial crisis, and right-wing populism. The political result was the growth of Euroscepticism and the rise of PRR parties, as they emerged and increased electoral shares in most West European parliaments. There were warning signs in the early years of the twenty-first century: the electoral breakthrough of the Austrian Freedom Party (FPÖ), National Front (FN) leader Jean-Marie Le Pen reaching the run-off of the 2002 French presidential election, and the Dutch and French rejection of the proposed EU constitution in 2005. At the time, it was also possible to see each as an aberration. Perhaps the period of grand coalitions in Austria during the 1990s fuelled support for the FPÖ, or France's continued struggles with high unemployment combined with political corruption scandals opened the way for FN leader Jean-Marie Le Pen to reach the run-off in the 2002 presidential election? And the Dutch and French rejections of the proposed EU constitution seemed to reflect domestic political frustrations as much or more than evaluations of the EU (e.g. Aarts and van der Kolk 2006; Hobolt 2009). For several years, observers of European politics debated whether growing Euroscepticism and right-wing populism constituted a threat or just a short-term phenomenon.

Authoritarianism and the Evolution of West European Electoral Politics. Erik R. Tillman, Oxford University Press.
© Erik R. Tillman 2021. DOI: 10.1093/oso/9780192896223.003.0002

Although the British EU referendum result also reflected a combination of domestic factors—including dissatisfaction with major party leaders (Clarke et al. 2017)—observers were in agreement that Brexit signalled a major change in West European politics and a threat to the European project.

How did this transformation of West European politics unfold? The first two decades of the twenty-first century have seen challenges to the political mainstream, the rise of PRR parties and Euroscepticism, and the increased salience of European integration, immigration, and multiculturalism as political issues. The argument of this book is that West European politics is undergoing a broad and long-term worldview evolution, in which traditional class- and religion-based political conflict is replaced by a broader conflict centred on one's worldview of society and politics. This chapter describes this worldview evolution and derives a series of predictions that subsequent chapters will develop and test empirically. To start, this chapter reviews the prior literature on the rise of Euroscepticism and PRR parties in order to document the gaps in our understanding.

Prior Explanations

The rise of the radical right has generated a large body of scholarly research since the 1990s, which in turn drew on earlier studies of support for far-right political movements in the early or middle of the twentieth century. Because PRR parties typically campaign on a mix of economic, cultural, and social themes, academic research has examined the effect of each set of factors on support for the radical right. Out of this research, several perspectives have emerged emphasizing different causes. One underlying claim is that PRR party supporters reject the economic, social, and cultural changes of the past several decades.

Public debate about support for PRR parties suffers from an interesting disconnect with academic research. While public commentary often emphasizes economic deprivation, or characterizes an 'economics versus culture' debate, most academic research has viewed economic causes as being entangled with social and cultural forces. Nonetheless, it is important to understand the arguments linking economic deprivation to PRR party support. Early research on PRR parties examined the claim that its supporters were the 'losers of modernity' who had suffered a loss of status as a result of the shift towards a post-industrial economy (e.g. Betz 1993; Kitschelt 1994). This perspective emphasizes the working-class nature of PRR party support, with these parties' voters being disproportionately blue-collar, older, and male. The shift to a post-industrial economy has rewarded education and cultural skills, while industrial workers have suffered job and income losses. Moreover, the concentration of industrial jobs exacerbates these effects in working-class communities. In its most basic form, this argument suggests that PRR parties succeed by appealing to working-class voters' sense of grievance by identifying globalization and immigration as the root causes. This line of research has produced mixed results. One conceptual problem with this argument is that it is not clear how the loss of industrial jobs would lead to support for parties campaigning against the threats posed by immigration and values changes.

More recent studies in this vein have developed more nuanced accounts emphasizing the role of social status and marginalization. The roots of PRR party support are not strictly economic; rather, there is also a social and cultural dimension. In particular, the shift towards a post-industrial economy has come with increased emphasis on education and meritocracy in which economic rewards (and greater social status) have gone to those with higher educational attainment and who work in creative, financial, or technological fields. One implication is that struggling members of the working class deserve their fate for failing to adapt to new economic and educational realities. More broadly, post-industrial societies have increasingly marginalized working-class habits and values as antiquated or even 'backward'. Members of the working class are left behind economically and socially. Blue-collar voters perceive this increasing social marginalization, and they have responded by shifting away from the political mainstream towards PRR parties (Ford and Goodwin 2014; Gest 2016). In this view, PRR party support constitutes a revolt against the political mainstream and its abandonment of the working classes.

These explanations focusing on the losers of modernity provide important insights into the strength of PRR parties among working-class voters. However, PRR parties derive support across class lines (Ford and Goodwin 2014), so these arguments only explain support for a certain portion of PRR party voters. Additionally, PRR parties offer consistent messages on social and cultural issues like immigration, crime, or values, but their economic messages are inconsistent (Ivarsflaten 2005; de Lange 2007). If PRR party support derived primarily from economically insecure voters, then one would expect PRR parties to emphasize economic rather than cultural messages (or, at least, to provide consistent economic messages focused on working-class grievances). The fact that PRR parties derive support on the basis of cultural appeals such as immigration rather than economic messages (Ivarsflaten 2007) suggests that their base of supporters extends beyond the working class. Finally, this view of PRR party supporters as members of a 'left behind' working class suggests that they are members of an ageing and increasingly marginal social group. If correct, PRR party support will fade away in the next few decades as these social groups die off.

A different perspective draws on the idea of PRR party supporters as 'losers of modernity' but emphasizes the effect of changing social and cultural values. Starting in the 1970s, a series of books by Ronald Inglehart and collaborators argued that the increased physical and economic security of post-war West European societies was fuelling a series of values changes among younger generations (Inglehart 1977, 1997; Inglehart and Welzel 2005). Because post-war generations grew up in an age of peace, growing affluence, and rising education, they developed new values that looked beyond the preservation of physical and economic security and the maintenance of order. These new 'post-materialist' values emphasized social justice, individual self-expression, and autonomy. Rising post-materialism led to growing social liberalism, acceptance of diversity and multiculturalism, the rejection of religious traditionalism, and declining nationalism (Inglehart 1970, 1977, 1997). As these newer generations entered the electorate, they provoked a political shift, leading to the rise of the 'new left' that emphasized their concerns rather than the traditional priorities of older, working-class voters.

The growing influence of post-materialism led to a counter-revolution against these values (Ignazi 1992; Inglehart 2018; Norris and Inglehart 2019). Individuals with materialist values, which include a preference for social order, economic and physical security, and tradition, reject post-materialism. In particular, materialists are opposed to the acceptance of new lifestyles, multiculturalism, and immigration, and the rejection of traditional religious values and sources of authority. As centre-left parties have embraced post-materialist values, PRR parties have attracted materialist voters by appealing to their values. This argument explains why a mix of economic and cultural issues shapes mainstream party conflict, but PRR parties compete primarily on cultural issues (Ivarsflaten 2005; de Lange 2007). Materialists do not necessarily share a common set of economic interests, but they oppose the growing influence of post-materialism in mainstream politics.

This argument provides a powerful perspective on rising support for PRR parties, but it falls short in identifying and explaining these parties' voters. This 'silent counter-revolution' (Ignazi 1992; Norris and Inglehart 2019) thesis suggests that PRR party supporters are predominantly older individuals who grew up in a less secure era. One implication of this claim is that generational replacement will reduce PRR party support as older, materialist voters are replaced by younger, post-materialist voters. Second, this argument relies on early life socialization as the causal mechanism. Various studies have challenged this aspect of the post-materialism thesis, arguing that post-materialism declines among adult voters during economic recessions, which suggests that voters respond to contemporary conditions rather than early life socialization (e.g. Clarke and Dutt 1991; Duch and Taylor 1993). Moreover, few members of those groups facing the greatest economic insecurity support PRR parties. Instead, support for PRR parties is typically higher among more economically secure members of the working class and small business owners (Kitschelt 1997; Givens 2005; Ford and Goodwin 2014). Although the post-materialism thesis has great intuitive appeal, it is hard to reconcile these facts with the claim that PRR party support comes from those whose early life experiences were shaped by economic insecurity, though it is possible to imagine that older generations who feel threatened by demographic and values changes are the core supporters of PRR parties.

Integrating the claims of these respective approaches, other scholars argue that the post-industrial economic and cultural changes are generating a new set of political cleavages. Political cleavages are major, durable social divisions about the proper sphere and goals of government, which structure party systems and voter alignments (Lipset and Rokkan 1967). The most significant political cleavage in most West European states is class: workers historically aligned with social democratic parties while owners and merchants aligned with conservative or liberal parties. While older political cleavages such as class have eroded in recent decades (Franklin et al. 2009), scholars have debated whether newer cleavages are forming to replace them (e.g. Dalton et al. 1984; Kriesi et al. 2008; Bornschier 2010).

One possibility is that a new 'integration-demarcation' cleavage is forming in the post-industrial, globalized context (Kriesi et al. 2008; Kriesi et al. 2012). This cleavage pits those who support and benefit from continuing economic and cultural integration against those who oppose it. In the former group are those with university education; professionals and workers in technology, financial, and cultural fields; and those who support multiculturalism. The latter group consists of those with lower education, blue-collar workers, residents of smaller towns or rural areas, and nationalists. As new left and centrist parties have moved to represent the former group of voters, PRR parties have emerged to represent the latter. The overlapping set of interests, values, and identities that divide these two groups structures a durable political cleavage, leading to a political realignment (Dalton 2018). One advantage of this approach is that it highlights the connections between the economic and socio-cultural changes of recent decades, rather than imposing an 'economics versus culture' distinction.

Each approach described above provides limited clarity about why these integration-demarcation issues divide voters into a new political cleavage. Namely, why would cultural issues concerning immigration, multiculturalism, and changing values divide voters into separate political camps? Answering this question requires a better account of what drives cultural attitudes. In other words, the evidence shows consistently that anti-immigration attitudes strongly correlate with PRR party support (Ivarsflaten 2007; Oesch 2008; Lucassen and Lubbers 2012). One can further understand how (to varying degrees) anti-immigration attitudes correlate with opposition to multiculturalism, values traditionalism, or nationalism. But it is less clear why some West Europeans hold anti-immigration attitudes and why these attitudes cluster together. A second question is how Euroscepticism relates to these phenomena. Research finds that anti-immigrant attitudes and exclusionary national identity correlate negatively with support for European integration (e.g. Carey 2002; McLaren 2002), and PRR parties frequently adopt Eurosceptical positions. However, prior scholarship has not identified the overarching link between traditionalist or exclusionary cultural attitudes, attitudes towards European integration, and party support. Explaining this requires a theory of political behaviour grounded in political psychology.

A Worldview Evolution in West European Politics

Issue Evolutions and Worldview Evolutions

The previous section describes major competing perspectives on the shift in support for the radical right and in Euroscepticism over the past two decades. These arguments attribute these shifts to changing social, economic, and political conditions, which have led to changes in individual attitudes and in party conflict. I propose an account that builds on these arguments, while emphasizing the role of individual personality differences and their interaction with the political context. This argument also draws on the arguments of Carmines and Stimson (1989) and Hetherington and Weiler (2009) to explain the evolution of West European electoral politics.

The background to this argument is the major economic and socio-cultural changes that have occurred in West European societies since the 1980s. At a given point in time, a country's electoral politics will likely be structured around one or two dominant axes of conflict—such as class interests, religious identity, or urban versus rural interests. These axes of conflict create ties between parties and voters and structure political identities. For example, a dominant class conflict will generate ties between workers and social democratic parties on one end, and owners and conservative/liberal parties on the other end. It will also structure party positions and mass opinion on political issues that fit comfortably into this axis of conflict (e.g. questions of taxation, collective bargaining, or welfare spending). As long as this axis of conflict remains dominant, it will continue to structure electoral politics.

In any society, there are multiple possible political identities and axes of political conflict, but most are not salient at a given time. Thus, the dominant axis (or axes) of electoral conflict privileges certain identities over others. For example, a dominant class conflict encourages workers to construct their political identity around their class identity, rather than their religious identity. As new political issues arise, political elites may successfully incorporate them into the dominant axis of conflict, producing an 'organic extension' (Carmines and Stimson 1989). Or political elites may attempt but fail to restructure political conflict to reflect a new issue, generating an 'unsuccessful adaptation' (Carmines and Stimson 1989). For a successful issue evolution to occur that will lead to the restructuring of political identities, the new issue(s) must cut across the existing axis of political conflict and be salient enough to shape voters' identities. Entrepreneurial political elites facilitate issue evolutions by introducing new political issues into political conflict and reshaping voters' understandings of their political identities. Depending on the permissiveness of electoral laws (Norris 2005), an issue evolution might occur either through the reorganization of existing parties or through the creation of a new challenger party.

Changing political or social conditions create a favourable environment for political entrepreneurs to trigger an issue evolution. The enterprising political elite takes a position on a new issue (or series of issues) that attracts voters from across existing party lines, challenging the dominant axis of conflict. These new elite messages attract the attention of voters, who in turn begin to shift their own attitudes and party loyalties to reflect this new structure of conflict (Carmines and Stimson 1989; Zaller 1992). Generational replacement contributes to the process: young voters who have no experience with the older structure of conflict form identities based on the newer dimensions of conflict. Over time and often unevenly, this shift in voter loyalties extends throughout the electorate, leading to a mass realignment of party loyalties organized along a new dimension of political conflict.

What types of issues are most likely to trigger such evolutions in political loyalties? Voters must be able to understand an issue at 'gut level' for it to trigger an evolution (Carmines and Stimson 1989). Such 'easy' issues are symbolic rather than technical and concern clearly defined policy ends rather than means, so voters are more likely to understand these issues independently of party cues (Carmines and Stimson 1980, 1989). By contrast, most voters struggle to understand technical issues surrounding the means of politics, making it easier for party elites to incorporate such issues into the existing dimension of conflict.

This distinction between 'easy' and 'hard' issues is a useful starting point to understand the worldview evolution in West Europe. Understood in this light, immigration is an easy issue at the heart of the ongoing evolution. Because it concerns questions about national identity and culture, voters can easily see and understand its symbolic content. And it presents clear policy alternatives, making it easy for voters to identify their own position on the issue and link it to party positions. Thus, immigration has been an important issue in the worldview evolution as political elites have campaigned on it alongside related issues (such as multiculturalism and values traditionalism). But what about European integration—another issue at the core of the ongoing evolution? For decades, political elites have defended the EU as bringing peace and prosperity. But in recent years, radical right politicians have criticized the EU as a threat to national sovereignty. Because the EU itself is a complex and technical issue (a hard issue), political elites have sought to 'translate' it into frames that voters can understand. The contrast between these two issues illustrates how the evolution unfolds. Attitudes towards the EU have not driven the worldview evolution described in this book. Instead, the structure of attitudes towards the EU has changed consistent with the worldview evolution argument as elite conflict over the EU has shifted from economic to cultural frames centred on the protection versus the opening of national borders and societies.

What makes a worldview evolution different from the issue evolution described here? Political elites can exploit a new issue to trigger a realignment of party conflict and mass voter alignments. This issue can be based on group interests, identity, or any other salient feature of politics. A worldview evolution is connected to fundamental psychological orientations about the organization of society (Hetherington and Weiler 2009). New issues are connected to this worldview divide, deepening the degree of party conflict. A worldview evolution is more powerful because the issues underlying it—and how voters perceive those issues—are not easily divisible. Voters on either side of the divide are motivated by different values or dispositions, making it hard for voters on either side to understand the position of their rivals or to find bases for compromise. Voters are approaching political and social issues with contrasting values. This contrasts with conflict based on interests (such as the traditional class conflict), which is more easily negotiated and in which it is easier to understand the rival position.

This new worldview evolution in Western Europe is being driven by an individual personality trait called authoritarianism. Because the worldviews of individuals scoring high and low in authoritarianism (respectively, 'high authoritarians' and 'low authoritarians') are distinct, they respond differently to the same political issues. The demographic, political, and values changes in Western Europe over the past two decades have provoked different reactions among high and low authoritarians, which are in turn reinforced by party conflict. High authoritarians find these changes a threat to their conception of the normative social order, increasing their receptivity to parties and messages promising to defend national community and sovereignty. Low authoritarians welcome these social and cultural changes, leading them to support parties promising to continue them. This evolution in attitudes and party loyalties is transforming West European politics.

Why are these changes occurring during this era and in these countries particularly? First, while there are several aspects to this worldview evolution that are unique to Western Europe, it is similar to patterns seen elsewhere. The concept of a worldview evolution is borrowed from Hetherington and Weiler's (2009) study of US electoral politics. There are certain similarities between their argument and that proposed in this book. Most importantly, authoritarianism is at the heart of this evolution. However, there are a number of differences. In Western Europe, the worldview evolution is occurring as a result of the emergence of a new party family—the populist radical right (PRR)—which is challenging established patterns of party conflict and creating broader dilemmas for mainstream centre-left and centre-right parties. Also, differences among West European electoral systems and party systems create variation in the opportunity structures for PRR parties in each country (Norris 2005). In addition, the issues driving the worldview evolution are different. While Hetherington and Weiler (2009) emphasize the role of civil rights and religiosity in the USA, immigration and values changes are the main drivers in Western Europe. Nonetheless, it is important to see this worldview evolution as part of a broader pattern occurring throughout the Western world in response to many of the same social and cultural changes.

A second question might be why this same change is not occurring in the Mediterranean or post-communist states in Europe. The political and social contexts are different in each region. Politics in the post-communist states has largely centred on the transitions since the collapse of Communism, leading to a different structure of conflict. The notable rise of PRR parties in several post-communist countries—especially Hungary and Poland—has occurred in that context. In addition, there has been relatively little immigration to post-communist countries in comparison to West European countries (Goodwin and Eatwell 2018), so the rise of PRR parties in that context is driven by other factors. A different account is needed to explain these developments, though it may be the case that high authoritarian voters support PRR parties in post-communist societies as well. Similarly, the Mediterranean countries have struggled with questions surrounding the post-2008 financial crisis and austerity, which have similarly produced a different structure of political conflict (Hooghe and Marks 2018). That conflict over economic policy has incorporated debates over national sovereignty, preventing a similar evolution as in Western Europe. Nonetheless, PRR parties have been successful in Italy, while the far-right Golden Dawn attracted international media attention along with a small share of votes in Greece. Because the social and political contexts are different in post-communist and Mediterranean Europe, this book's argument does not apply to those cases.

Authoritarianism

This book's argument focuses on the role of authoritarianism in the worldview evolution. This section provides an overview of the concept, and Chapter 3 explores the relationship between authoritarianism and political and social attitudes in greater detail. Scholars developed the concept of authoritarianism in the immediate post-war years as part of an effort to explain mass support for fascism. The puzzle was straightforward. What inspired large numbers of individuals to support a political movement and regime that promised to impose a dictatorial form of governance? One landmark study, *The Authoritarian Personality* (Adorno et al. 1950), provided an answer rooted in individual political psychology. Although this study soon fell out of favour due to conceptual and methodological critiques, the concept informed subsequent generations of political psychologists. While the works of Altemeyer (1981, 1996) helped to revitalize interest in the concept, a newer set of studies has provided a more useful conceptual and empirical framework for studying authoritarianism and its effects on attitudes.

Authoritarianism is an individual predisposition towards the maintenance of group uniformity, cohesion, and authority at the expense of individual autonomy and diversity (Stenner 2005: 14–15; see also Duckitt 1989; Feldman 2003). In this context, a predisposition describes a stable tendency to react similarly to particular stimuli (Rosenberg and Hovland 1960; Greenstein 1987). In this respect, authoritarianism describes a tendency to react towards various social or political stimuli in such a way as to preserve social cohesion. More importantly, individuals scoring high in authoritarianism will prefer social cohesion to individual autonomy, meaning that they would accept the suppression of the latter to protect the former. Further, high authoritarians will react with hostility towards sources of perceived threat to social cohesion, which may further inform a willingness to suppress the autonomy or group rights of those associated with that threat. Because one observes these tendencies across time and place, it suggests that authoritarianism is a predisposition rather than a product of culture or social learning (Stenner 2005).

One can observe various manifestations of authoritarianism in social and political attitudes, as well as cognitive style. High authoritarians display a greater need for order, which results in a tendency towards rigid, 'black-and-white' thinking (Hetherington and Weiler 2009) and a greater willingness to rely upon established sources of authority for answers to social or political questions (Adorno et al. 1950; Oesterreich 2005; Stenner 2005). High authoritarians display a greater preference for maintaining consistency in beliefs rather than obtaining accuracy (Lavine et al. 2005). This cognitive style extends to the social realm, with authoritarians being more ethnocentric and intolerant towards novel or unconventional ideas or behaviours (Altemeyer 1981, 1996; Stenner 2005). In short, authoritarianism describes a tendency towards reducing the complexity of social and political life through the maintenance of social cohesion and conformity, which leads to more reliance on established authorities for answers, identification with the in-group and distrust of out-groups, and a clearer demarcation between what is acceptable or trusted and what is not.

How does one get from an authoritarian *predisposition* to an authoritarian *attitude*? The object of that potential attitude—a social policy, a political party, or whatever—must pose an apparent threat to the established social or political order (i.e. it must threaten to undermine social cohesion). In other words, the effect of authoritarianism on political attitudes is *situational* with the perception of a threat being the key factor (Oesterreich 2005; Stenner 2005; Hetherington and Suhay 2011). An apparent threat to the social or political order activates the authoritarian predisposition. When faced with a threat to the established order or to social cohesion, high authoritarians are more likely to react with hostility and even aggression (Altemeyer 1996; Oesterreich 2005; Stenner 2005), being willing to support punitive behaviour towards the source of the apparent threat (Stenner 2005). In other words, the authoritarian predisposition will show up in generalized attitudes towards uniformity, diversity, and authority, but a threat to the normative order generates authoritarian attitudes towards specific political or social objects that threaten social cohesion. These latter attitudes are situational insofar as their existence depends on the perception of threat.

As a result, authoritarianism is only likely to predict political attitudes on certain issues and under certain circumstances. On issues unrelated to the established socio-political order, it is unlikely that high authoritarians will differ from low authoritarians in their attitudes. This situation describes most attitudes towards political or economic questions, which are typically too complex to trigger perceptions of threat or 'gut-level' reactions.[1] Authoritarianism is most relevant to understanding attitudes towards objects that pose an apparent threat to the existing social order. In such instances, the attitudes of low and high authoritarians diverge because the issue in question triggers different responses rooted in their rival dispositions (Feldman 2003; Stenner 2005; Hetherington and Weiler 2009). While the high authoritarian sees a threat to social cohesion, the low authoritarian may see an opportunity to enhance individual autonomy or to gain exposure to new ideas or experiences. In this case, one would observe a divergence in the attitudes of high and low authoritarians towards the object of that threat to the normative order and towards the appropriate policy responses.[2]

What About Low Authoritarians?

Most research has sought to understand and describe the behaviour of high authoritarians in contrast to the rest of the population, meaning that low authoritarians have been something of an afterthought. To an extent, this is reflected in terminology: while I use 'low authoritarians', Stenner (2005) uses 'libertarians', and others use 'non-authoritarians' (e.g. Hetherington and Weiler 2009). I prefer 'low authoritarians' because it better captures the notion that authoritarianism is a continuum rather than a binary distinction. In addition, low authoritarians may also display authoritarian attitudes under conditions of existential threat (Hetherington and Suhay 2011).

---

[1] However, the ongoing worldview evolutions in the US and Western Europe are leading to a structuring of economic attitudes by authoritarianism—but only in a contingent fashion. As high authoritarians move towards the Republican Party in the USA and PRR parties in Europe, the more politically attentive voters adopt the positions of their parties on the 'hard' economic issues (Malka et al. 2014; Johnston et al. 2017). However, the point is that there is no direct link between authoritarianism and economic attitudes. Rather, the link is contingent on the relationship between authoritarianism and party support, which is structured by socio-cultural issues.

[2] One recent study has found that existential threats (such as terrorism) may trigger authoritarian attitudes even among low authoritarians—leading to a convergence of attitudes between high and low authoritarians on those issues (Hetherington and Suhay 2011). Evidence of 'rally 'round the flag' effects (Mueller 1970), in which popular support for national leaders rises during the start of a war, would seem to be consistent with this interpretation. A similar result may arise due to a persistent threat of terrorism over a longer era (Peffley et al. 2015).

What distinguishes low authoritarians from the rest of the population? Recent scholarship argues that low authoritarians are motivated to protect individual autonomy, which distinguishes them from high authoritarians who prefer to enforce social cohesion (Feldman and Stenner 1997; Stenner 2005). That desire to protect autonomy leads to greater distrust of oppressive political or social institutions that govern behaviour, and it also leads to greater concern for maintaining diversity of thought and behaviour. Low authoritarians are less likely to defer to established authorities or to draw strong distinctions between members of in-groups and out-groups. One important theme in this book is that the ongoing worldview evolution reflects the shifting political attitudes and behaviour of low authoritarians as much as high authoritarians.

With that said, we know less about the behaviour of low authoritarians. Most research has focused on studying high authoritarians, given the normative concerns among many researchers that they may pose a threat to democracy and personal liberty (Adorno et al. 1950; Altemeyer 1996; Stenner 2005). As a result, many studies effectively treat low authoritarians as the reference category, which leads to some justifiable criticism that authoritarianism is treated as a pathology while low authoritarians are viewed as normal. Moreover, we know less about whether there is a similar dynamic by which low authoritarian predispositions are activated and can generate hostile attitudes towards threats to individual autonomy. Although this book does not address the latter question directly, the evidence shows that the attitudes and behaviour of low authoritarians have also shifted on several key dimensions.

Why Authoritarianism?

Why is authoritarianism at the centre of the ongoing worldview realignment occurring in Western Europe? High authoritarians are concerned with maintaining social cohesion. To that end, they are willing to subordinate individual autonomy and diversity in order to maintain social uniformity. By contrast, low authoritarians are motivated by a desire to preserve individual autonomy. A set of overlapping changes in the political and social context has provided a threatening context for high authoritarians and led to greater polarization in political attitudes and behaviour between high and low authoritarians.

Increased immigration and multiculturalism threaten high authoritarians' desire to maintain social cohesion. As a result, they are more likely to view growing diversity negatively and to favour reduced immigration, along with policies of assimilation designed to prevent multiculturalism (Stenner 2005). Recent decades have seen increased levels of immigration to West European societies. During the same period, social democratic parties adopted more favourable positions on multiculturalism as new left-liberal party families such as the greens also gained support and moved towards mainstream acceptance (Kitschelt 1994). Mainstream parties also supported efforts to expand the membership of the EU while strengthening its institutional powers (most visibly, through the adoption of the common currency). While high authoritarians would see these developments as a threat to social cohesion (through its weakening of national sovereignty), low authoritarians would be more likely to view them favourably because they increase individual autonomy. Thus, high authoritarians and low authoritarians would be likely to find themselves on opposite sides of these issues. As liberal positions on these issues became increasingly mainstream, PRR parties had an opening to attract dissatisfied voters with anti-immigration and nationalist programmes, particularly if centre-right parties also took more moderate positions (Ignazi 2003; Mudde 2007). PRR parties successfully attracted those high authoritarian voters who saw these developments as a threat. Meanwhile, low authoritarians rejected PRR parties and favoured centre-left and left-liberal parties that held liberal stances on immigration. Thus, these different stances towards immigration and multiculturalism resulted in high authoritarians and low authoritarians shifting towards different political camps.

High authoritarians also value traditional sources of authority and behaviour, which are at the root of social cohesion and the normative social order. Threats to the normative order are likely to motivate a response by high authoritarians (Stenner 2005). Changing social or cultural values constitute such a threat, particularly if these concern norms or behaviour based in traditional sources of authority such as religion or national identity. High authoritarians view liberalizing social values as a threat to social cohesion, while low authoritarians support them as enhancing individual autonomy by relaxing the restriction on personal behaviour and expression. Recent decades have seen a trend toward more liberal social and cultural values at the mass and elite levels (Dalton 2018). As mainstream parties embraced (or at least accepted) these changing social norms, PRR parties emphasized preserving traditional national values and customs. While low authoritarians favoured left-liberal parties' stances, high authoritarian voters found PRR parties' messages more attractive. Thus, these divergent stances on social values resulted in shifts in party support among high authoritarians and low authoritarians.

Finally, high authoritarians are sensitive to threats to social order. Perceptions of a loss of control or of rising disorder would be threatening to high authoritarians, and they would likely respond by endorsing authoritarian solutions to these problems (Altemeyer 1996; Stenner 2005). To some extent, the developments described in the previous two paragraphs could indicate growing disorder if the government is unable to manage immigration or to prevent a breakdown of social norms. A loss of national sovereignty or increasing threats of crime or terrorism would exacerbate this perception of declining order. In recent decades, West European states have transferred sovereignty to the European Union, with a resulting loss of national control over monetary policy, migration, and various legal and judicial policies. Events such as the European financial crisis, high-profile terror attacks, and the migrant crisis reinforce the perception of declining national control. Mainstream parties have broadly supported the deepening and widening of European integration, resulting in the transfer of sovereignty to a more powerful European bureaucracy and in shared governance among a more diverse set of member states. PRR parties and tabloid media have blamed EU membership for contributing to increased immigration, rising terror threats, and a loss of national products or industries. These messages have led high authoritarians to become less supportive of the EU and of the mainstream parties that have driven European integration, while low authoritarians tend to view the EU more favourably as opening opportunities for individuals. These divergent stances on national sovereignty and the EU have resulted in high authoritarians and low authoritarians moving apart on the EU and in party support.

Each of these changes pushed the ongoing worldview evolution in West European politics by driving high authoritarians towards PRR parties and low authoritarians towards left-liberal parties. The interaction between authoritarianism and the changing social and political context contributes to the worldview evolution by strengthening the political differences between high and low authoritarians. But have these changes in the political context actually occurred? The next section reviews evidence suggesting that West European societies have experienced a demographic, political, and social transformation. This transformation provided the context in which the political behaviour of high and low authoritarians transformed.

Sources of the Worldview Evolution

For the worldview evolution described in this chapter to have occurred, social and political conditions must have changed in ways to facilitate it. Conditions that are threatening to high authoritarians should have emerged, facilitating a shift in political behaviour among such voters. In the previous section, I argued that demographic change (via immigration), values change, and threats to the national order are at the heart of the worldview evolution. This section presents evidence relating to those shifts. First, a demographic shift driven by immigration has occurred since the 1990s. Second, there have been broad values changes on issues including traditional social norms, religion, and culture. Finally, shifting elite values towards liberalism and multiculturalism would further suggest that mainstream leaders were abandoning established social norms, increasing perceptions of threat.

West European societies have experienced demographic shifts over the past several decades. Since 1990, immigration rates have increased or remained at

Table 2.1 Average annual immigration per 10,000 residents

Country	1997–2000	2005–8	2013–16
Austria	77,808	89,909	128,490
	96.4	106.9	146.9
Denmark	51,517	57,805	70,394
	96.5	104.1	123.3
Finland	14,849	24,737	31,775
	28.6	46.1	57.8
Germany	839,568	683,030	1,037,827
	103.1	84.5	126.3
Ireland	50,719	110,610	76,259
	134.1	242.9	162.4
Netherlands	121,067	113,446	157,714
	76.0	68.0	92.9
Sweden	50,677	90,409	135,014
	57.1	96.3	137.3
Switzerland	101,474	148,947	154,843
	142.0	190.8	184.8

Notes: The top number for each country shows the average annual immigration total for that country and time period. The number below shows the average annual immigration total per 10,000 residents for that country and time period.

Source: Eurostat.

relatively high levels, leading to increases over time in the percentage of the foreign-born population. Such demographic shifts generate perceived threats to social cohesion due to increasing social, religious, and linguistic diversity. High authoritarians are more likely to perceive such increasing diversity as evidence that social cohesion is unravelling.

Using Eurostat data, I present two pieces of evidence on immigration and diversity. Table 2.1 shows average annual immigration totals and average immigration per 10,000 residents in four-year periods for eight West European states from 1997 to 2016. The data show a general pattern of stability or increase for each country. For example, average annual immigration more than doubled in Finland from just under 15,000 in 1997–2000 to just under 32,000 in 2013–16. Sweden experienced a similar increase of over 100 per cent during this period, while Austria, Denmark, Ireland, and Switzerland saw increases of about 50 per cent during this two-decade period. The Netherlands and Germany experienced somewhat slower growth in immigration numbers. The rate per 10,000 residents shows a general pattern of increase over time with more variability across countries. For example, Finland's rate of 57.8 per 10,000 residents is the lowest in the 2013–16 period, but it is a substantial increase on the rate of 28.6 per 10,000 residents in the 1997–2000 era. In the 2013–16 period, every country but Finland and the Netherlands has a rate of over 100 immigrants annually per 10,000

Table 2.2 Foreign-born share of population, 2009 and 2017

Country	2009	2017
Austria	15.11	18.80
Denmark	8.82	11.62
Finland	4.02	6.34
France	11.26	12.17
Germany	11.64	14.67
Ireland	16.27	16.65
Netherlands	10.88	12.51
Sweden	13.84	17.84
United Kingdom	11.06	14.12

Note: Figures show the foreign-born population as a percentage of the total population in 2009 and 2017.

Source: Eurostat.

residents. By contrast, only three of the eight countries had such a rate of immigration in the 1997–2000 period (though Austria and Denmark had rates over 96 per 10,000 residents). In short, immigration numbers increased in both absolute and relative numbers for most West European states in the two decades between 1997 and 2016.

One result of growing immigration is an increase in the share of the foreign-born population over time. Eurostat data were only available from 2009 to 2017 and are displayed in Table 2.2. As expected, the share of foreign-born population increases from 2009 to 2017 in each country. There are substantial differences across countries. Finland's share of foreign-born population remains below 7 per cent, while Austria, Ireland, and Sweden have shares above 15 per cent. All countries besides Finland have foreign-born population shares between 10 per cent and 18 per cent by 2017, indicating a substantial immigrant population. Moreover, the increases over this period hint at the rapidity of demographic change in each country. In Denmark, Germany, Sweden, and the United Kingdom, the share of the foreign-born population increases by more than 25 per cent, while it increases by more than 50 per cent in Finland.[3]

---

[3] One objection to these figures is that they fail to distinguish between immigrants who would be viewed as a threat to social cohesion versus those who would not. Broadly speaking, Europeans are more likely to favour fellow European (or Western), skilled, and educated immigrants (Hainmueller and Hangartner 2013). Thus, perceptions of threat are higher for non-Western and unskilled immigrants. However, matters can be more complicated as immigrants from some EU member states may still be viewed as threats to social cohesion by residents of West European states, and some individuals will simply view any evidence of an increased foreign-born population as a threat to social cohesion. Finally, data are more readily and consistently available showing foreign-born population shares without disaggregating for the national or regional source of the foreign-born population Thus, the tables presented here capture some amount of Western or European immigration, though West European societies experienced substantial levels of non-Western immigration during this era. Nonetheless, these tables should highlight the most important fact, which is that West European societies experienced increasing rates of immigration and correspondingly more diversity during the era from the 1990s to the present.

The evidence presented in Table 2.1 and Table 2.2 points to important demo-graphic changes in Western Europe during the early twenty-first century. High levels of immigration led to increasing diversity, reflected in the share of foreign-born residents. For high authoritarians, these demographic shifts represent a threat to social cohesion. Faced with the threat posed by rising changing demog-raphy, high authoritarians became more likely to support parties and policies designed to preserve social cohesion.

A second source of the worldview evolution is a shift in mass values. Changing values lead to perceptions among high authoritarians that shared, traditional social norms are under threat, provoking an authoritarian response to protect society. The 1990 and 2017 waves of the European Values Survey (EVS) contain a series of comparable questions on social values, making it possible to examine how responses have changed during this period in a group of common West European states.[4] Changes in the distribution of responses would be evidence of a values shift during the intervening years.

I examine questions measuring broad orientations towards social and cultural out-groups, gender roles, and religiosity. If West European societies liberalized between 1990 and 2017, attitudes should have shifted towards increased accept-ance of minorities, greater support for gender equality, and less religiosity. To examine orientations towards national in-groups and out-groups, I use a question asking respondents to indicate whether they agree or disagree that 'when jobs are scarce, members of [the nationality of that country] should get priority'. Fewer respondents should agree in 2017 than in 1990. A similar question asks whether men should get priority over women when jobs are scarce. There should be less support for this view in 2017 than in 1990. A third question asks respondents about their belief in God. If religiosity has dropped, then the percentage of respondents indicating a belief in God should likewise have fallen. Finally, a fourth question asks respondents to indicate whether they believe homosexuality is ever justified or not. The percentage of respondents indicating that homosexu-ality is never justified should have fallen from 1990 to 2017.

Figure 2.1 shows the results, which are consistent with expectations. The per-centage of respondents agreeing that members of one's nationality should get priority for scarce jobs declined from just over 62 per cent to about 40 per cent, while the percentage agreeing that men should get priority over women declined from around 30 per cent to under 9 per cent. The percentage of respondents indi-cating a belief in God dropped less dramatically from 76.6 per cent to 59.3 per cent. Finally, the percentage of respondents believing that homosexuality is never

---

[4] Those countries are Austria, Denmark, Finland, France, Germany, Italy, the Netherlands, Spain, Sweden, and the United Kingdom. Several countries are omitted because they were not included in the 2017 wave of the EVS.

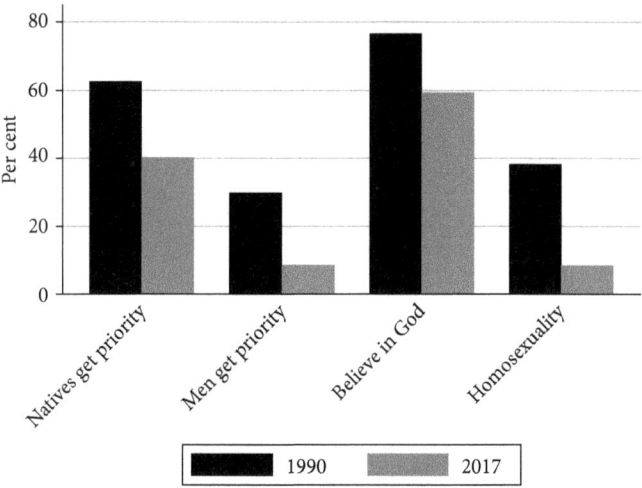

Figure 2.1 Socio-cultural values, 1990 and 2017
Source: EVS 2011a, 2019.

justified declined sharply from 38 per cent in 1990 to 8.4 per cent in 2017. In short, the mainstream of society shifted to display less hostility towards social and cultural out-groups, less gender traditionalism, and less religiosity between 1990 and 2017. All of these shifts are consistent with the view that social liberalism and multiculturalism increased during this era.

Importantly, this shift has taken mainstream West European mass opinion away from the positions held by high authoritarians. Figure 2.2 shows the percentages of high authoritarians and low authoritarians, respectively, agreeing with each statement. High authoritarians in 2017 are substantially more likely to respond to each question affirmatively. Just over 57 per cent of high authoritarians agree that members of the nation should get priority for jobs compared to 32 per cent of low authoritarians, while 20 per cent of high authoritarians think men should get priority compared to 4.6 per cent of low authoritarians. Just under 77 per cent of high authoritarians express belief in God compared to 51.6 per cent of low authoritarians. Finally, just over 20 per cent of high authoritarians think homosexuality is never justified, while fewer than 5 per cent of low authoritarians agree. In short, the changes that occurred between 1990 and 2017 shifted public opinion away from the positions held by high authoritarians, generating a potential sense of threat to the normative order. Chapter 3 examines the relationship between authoritarianism and a wide range of attitudes in detail.

Finally, I examine whether party positions shifted between the 1990s and 2010s in such a way as to threaten high authoritarians. I use the Chapel Hill Expert Survey data, which asks academic experts on each European country to place the

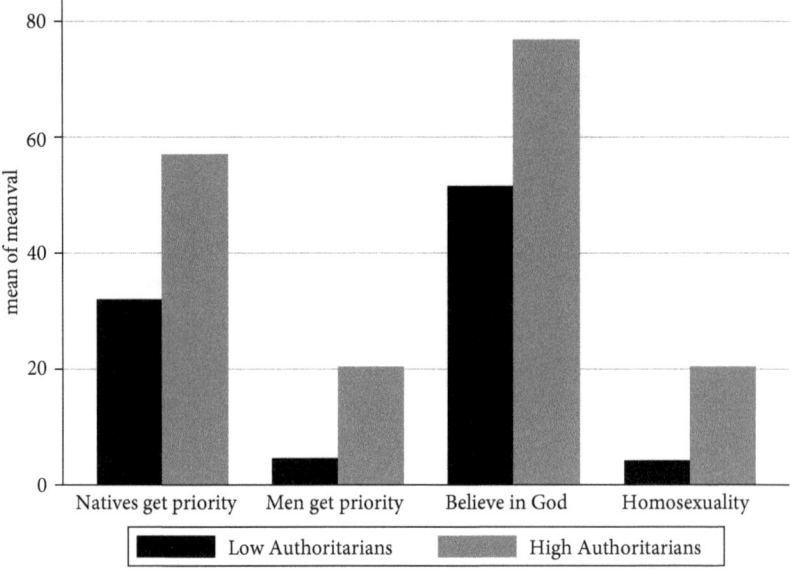

Figure 2.2 Authoritarianism and socio-cultural values, 2017

Note: Each bar shows the percentage of respondents answering each question affirmatively. See text for full details on question wording and answers.

Source: EVS 2019.

major political parties on scales measuring their positions on various issues and ideological scales (Bakker et al. 2015b). A team of researchers has administered this survey routinely since 1999 with the most recent version conducted in 2014, allowing for a comparison of expert party placements in those two years. I use survey questions asking expert respondents to place the party on scales measuring their positions on the economic left–right scale, a socio-cultural 'GAL-TAN' scale,[5] and a scale of support or opposition to European integration. I compare the positions of party families across West European countries.

Did the mean positions of each party family shift between 1999 and 2014? Party positions on the GAL-TAN scale are particularly important, as high authoritarians prefer policies closer to the TAN end of the scale. A shift in mean party positions away from the TAN end might provoke a perception of threat among high authoritarians. Finally, it is valuable to see how party positions on European integration have evolved over this same period. If mainstream party families have become (or remained) consistently pro-EU, then PRR parties would have more opportunity to attract Eurosceptical voters. For each scale, I examine

---

[5] GAL-TAN stands for 'Green-Alternative-Libertarian' and 'Traditional-Authoritarian-Nationalist' (Hooghe et al. 2002). It is roughly analogous to a 'libertarian-authoritarian' scale found in other surveys, and it broadly measures parties' positions on socio-cultural questions.

Table 2.3 Party positions on socio-cultural dimension and European integration, 1999–2014

Party Family	Socio-cultural dimension			European integration		
	1999	2014	Change	1999	2014	Change
Green	2.21	1.75	−0.46	4.35	5.46	1.11
Social Democratic	4.19	3.61	−0.78	6.10	5.81	−0.29
Christian Democratic	6.70	6.44	−0.26	6.35	6.10	−0.25
Liberal	4.01	3.87	−0.14	6.52	6.20	−0.32
Conservative	6.46	6.65	0.19	5.52	4.75	−0.77
Radical Right	8.51	8.77	0.26	1.97	1.67	−0.30

Notes: Socio-cultural (GAL-TAN) dimension is measured on a 0–10 scale in which 5 is the midpoint; European integration scale is measured on a 1–7 scale in which 4 is the midpoint.

Source: All data calculated using Chapel Hill Expert Survey trend file, 1999–2014.

the shifts in mean party position for six major party families (Conservative, Liberal, Christian Democratic, Social Democratic, Green, and Radical Right) in nine West European states (Austria, Belgium, Denmark, Finland, France, Ireland, the Netherlands, Sweden, and the United Kingdom). Table 2.3 displays the mean party family positions in 1999 and 2014 for the socio-cultural (GAL-TAN) and European integration dimensions.

What do the results show? Considering first the socio-cultural scale (where 0 represents the GAL end and 10 indicates TAN), there is evidence of increased party polarization between 1999 and 2014. While Conservative parties moved slightly towards the traditional-authoritarian-nationalist end (having already been towards the TAN side of the scale), Liberal, Christian Democratic, and Social Democratic parties moved towards the green-alternative-libertarian pole. Radical Right and Green parties remained strongly towards the TAN and GAL poles, respectively. The result was a general shift of the mainstream towards the left-liberal GAL end of the scale, with three of the four mainstream party families moving in that direction. For high authoritarians, this shift towards libertarian positions among mainstream parties might have reinforced the sense of threat to the normative order.

Party positions on European integration exhibit less movement. Here, the scale runs from 1 ('strongly opposed' to European integration) to 7 ('strongly in favour'). Though there was a slight shift away from the pro-EU end of the spectrum for most party families, the political mainstream remained broadly pro-EU, with every major party family besides the Radical Right on the pro-EU side of the scale in 2014. If high authoritarians perceived a threat from European integration, they had few mainstream parties that could represent their position.

In short, the evidence suggests a general trend towards the acceptance of libertarian-alternative social values by the political mainstream, combined with broad support for European integration. These two factors combined may have increased high authoritarians' perceptions that social cohesion was under threat.

Taken together, these three sets of evidence illustrate the context in which the worldview evolution unfolded around the start of the twenty-first century. Rising immigration and multiculturalism, combined with elite and mass values shifts away from traditional and authoritarian positions, have created the conditions for a potential worldview evolution in which high authoritarians turn away from the mainstream (i.e. traditional centre-left and centre-right) towards parties and positions that reflect their values. It is important to note that these analyses are illustrative; various other studies have demonstrated the demographic and attitudinal changes occurring in Western Europe during this time (e.g. Dalton 2018; Goodwin and Eatwell 2018; Norris and Inglehart 2019). Finally, it is important to emphasize that the worldview evolution does not only reflect the behaviour of high authoritarians; it is also a response to the movement of low authoritarians towards libertarian and cosmopolitan positions. In short, this section adds to the evidence that the conditions were increasingly favourable for an evolution in the political behaviour of high authoritarians. The remainder of the book will examine whether that shift is occurring.

The Worldview Evolution in Practice

The previous sections of this chapter have described the worldview evolution and traced its origins. This final section offers a series of predictions about the changes in political behaviour that are occurring because of the worldview evolution. Drawing on the logic of the argument described above, I suggest a series of observable outcomes as the worldview evolution occurs in each state. I develop and test these dynamics in the following chapters.

European Integration

The process of European integration accelerated during the 1990s and 2000s. In the post-Cold War era, the EU had the opportunity to enlarge into East Central Europe, a process that culminated in the 2004 wave of enlargement and subsequent accession of Bulgaria, Croatia, and Romania. The signing of the Maastricht Treaty paved the way for deeper economic and political integration, highlighted by the establishment of the common currency at the turn of the century. However, the rejection of the proposed European Constitution and the emergence of popular opposition to accession talks with Turkey followed these triumphs of European integration. During these two decades, the structure of public attitudes towards the EU has changed. This shifting structure of public opinion illustrates the ongoing worldview evolution.

For decades, the literature on public opinion towards the EU has emphasized its remoteness and complexity (e.g. Inglehart 1970; Lindberg and Scheingold 1970; Anderson 1998). The EU was established and expanded through a series of treaties and supranational law, and many of its functions are remote and technical. As a result, most European citizens remain relatively uninformed about the EU (Anderson 1998), and they continue to rely on elite messages to form opinions about the EU. During the early years of European integration until the early 1990s, mainstream parties in most member states took favourable positions, emphasizing the role of the EU in promoting peace and prosperity. This message helped to shape the 'permissive consensus' in which public opinion towards European integration was broadly favourable but also largely uninformed (Lindberg and Scheingold 1970).

The steps towards deepening and enlarging the EU starting in the 1990s have triggered more elite conflict and led to a restructuring of the debate over the EU. The permissive consensus has given way to a 'constraining dissensus' (Hooghe and Marks 2009) in which European publics are increasingly divided over the EU and use EU referendums and elections as a means to block further integration (Hobolt 2009). In this newly structured debate, anti-EU elites describe European integration as a threat to national sovereignty and community, while pro-EU elites argue that it increases individual opportunity for study, work, and travel. The structure of this debate fits with the worldview evolution. Anti-EU messages resonate with high authoritarians' desires to maintain social cohesion, while pro-EU messages will draw low authoritarians who seek to enhance individual autonomy.[6]

The result is a shift in the structure of public attitudes towards the EU. In the early 1990s, authoritarianism should have had little relationship with EU attitudes because elite messages did not clearly invoke high authoritarian or low authoritarian predispositions. As the debate shifted, the relationship between authoritarianism and EU attitudes should have as well, leading to the present situation in which high authoritarians oppose the EU and low authoritarians support it in Western Europe. Moreover, because the debate over the EU fits into a broader worldview, one would expect a concurrent shift in attitudes towards various manifestations of the EU: deeper integration, enlargement, the creation of a common foreign policy, the common currency, and so on. The result should be a transformation of EU attitudes from 1990 through the early twenty-first century to a new alignment structured by authoritarianism.

---

[6] Of course, many elite messages on the EU attempt to describe its (potential) economic effects or its effects on that member state's standing in the region or the world. Those messages do not align with the authoritarian worldview divide.

Populist Radical Right Party Support

Although various far-right parties were present throughout the post-war era in most countries, the contemporary radical right began to emerge as a serious force in the 1980s and 1990s (Mudde 2007). During that time, PRR parties have established themselves in most national party systems, becoming the third largest parties in vote share in many recent elections. Though their ability to translate votes into seats and government influence depends on electoral rules and the strategic behaviour of rival parties (Norris 2005), they now command substantial attention and influence in elections and political debate.

New parties face obstacles in their efforts to gain supporters. Voting is habitual, and many voters build a strong attachment to a party, which becomes part of their political identity (Campbell et al. 1960; Lipset and Rokkan 1967). Party attachment derives from a mixture of early-life socialization, group attachments, and congruence with issue positions, and it is typically durable once formed. As a result, many adult voters develop habitual patterns of party support, which are not easily changed. Moreover, because voters typically lack the political attention and sophistication to form opinions on most issues, they often follow party cues (Zaller 1992; Kinder and Kalmoe 2017). Still, voters often disagree with their preferred party on some issues, or they are simply unaware of their party's position on various issues. As a result, party attachments can remain strong even if the voter disagrees with the party on key issues, or if a new party emerges that better represents the voter. These factors make it difficult for new parties to gain voters, which means that patterns of party support will change slowly and unevenly.

New parties typically gain supporters through various mechanisms. First, generational replacement results in young voters who lack party attachments entering the electorate and replacing older generations with stronger party attachments. Those young voters are more likely to support a new party since they do not have prior attachments to established parties. Second, new parties can attract support from disengaged voters who were previously unattached to any of the existing parties, bringing new voters into the electorate. Finally, voters will shift their loyalties because of major political events, campaigns, or long-term processes of persuasion.

Populist radical right parties should gain support from high authoritarian voters. PRR parties' ideologies of populism, nativism, and authoritarianism (Mudde 2007) appeal to high authoritarians' predispositions. I expect that high authoritarian voters will be more likely to vote for PRR parties. However, this process of shifting party loyalties will occur unevenly across countries for several reasons. First, PRR parties have had more effective leadership in some countries than in others. Second, electoral rules and rival party strategies moderate the success of new PRR parties (Norris 2005). Finally, the strength of existing party attachments is greater in some countries, making party switching less likely.

Nonetheless, high authoritarians should be more likely to vote for PRR parties in each country, regardless of the electoral strength of that party.

What about low authoritarian voters? Many will have already shifted their party loyalties, forming the core support for New Left party families such as the Greens. During the time under consideration in this study, they are initially less likely to shift their party loyalties because changing social and political conditions do not threaten their worldviews. In particular, social democratic parties' adoption of liberal positions on socio-cultural issues helps to retain low authoritarians' support (Kitschelt 1994). The increasing adoption of liberal social and cultural positions by centre-left and some centre-right parties brings low authoritarian attitudes closer to the political mainstream. However, the ongoing worldview evolution leads to a shift in party conflict towards issues of national community and identity, which increases the salience of party messages concerning individual autonomy and diversity. This change in emphasis results in low authoritarians being more likely to vote for parties that take clearer liberal stances on cultural questions such as immigration, multiculturalism, and individual freedoms. Primarily, we should see low authoritarians move from established centre-left and centre-right parties towards Greens or other left-liberal parties in more recent years.

Finally, this argument suggests that high authoritarians would have a propensity to vote for a PRR party even if one did not exist in their country. As long as the threats to social cohesion exist that trigger the authoritarian response, high authoritarians should express a desire for policies that protect the normative order. In most West European states, a PRR party has successfully captured a major share of the high authoritarian vote. However, there are still countries in which no viable PRR party yet exists. I expect that high authoritarians would express a preference for voting for a PRR party even while being unable to do so in such contexts. I test this claim using an original survey experiment fielded in Ireland.

The result of this worldview evolution is an important shift in party loyalties. High authoritarian voters become more likely to support PRR parties (along with conservative parties that strategically adopt anti-immigrant or authoritarian rhetoric) in greater numbers. Low authoritarian voters should support left-liberal parties in greater numbers. The result is that older mainstream parties of the centre-left and centre-right suffer losses of both sets of voters due to the evolution of electoral politics towards issues of national community versus individual autonomy. While this trend should harm established social democratic parties, it should also cause vote losses among traditional centre-right parties as well.

It is important to keep in mind that the worldview evolution described in this book is partial and ongoing—and, as with all politics, subject to the strategic choices of political elites. Cross-national variation in political institutions and party system development produce different starting points for each country and condition the set of likely outcomes, and the actions of radical right and mainstream party elites further affect the development of electoral politics. As a result, cross-national variation in the evolution of electoral politics will likely continue, with some national systems experiencing a more extensive realignment than others. Chapter 9 explores these differences in greater detail.

Conclusion

This chapter has proposed a framework for understanding the ongoing evolution of West European electoral politics. This argument builds on previous analyses that examine value changes, demographic changes, and shifts in party conflict. Although these studies have contributed to our knowledge, none provides a clear explanation of why some voters are shifting towards Eurosceptical positions and towards PRR parties, while other voters are moving towards the other pole. Explaining that shift is crucial to our understanding of current electoral politics.

In this chapter, I propose an argument that blends insights from these prior studies with the study of political psychology. I argue that authoritarianism increasingly structures political behaviour in twenty-first-century Western Europe. High authoritarians have become more likely to oppose the EU and to support PRR parties, as they respond to perceived threats to the social order posed by immigration and value change. Low authoritarians are more likely to support the EU and to support left-liberal parties, as they support greater diversity and multiculturalism. These shifts are a response to changing social and political conditions, as well as the strategic choices of national political elites.

This argument yields a series of testable predictions about political attitudes and party support. Subsequent chapters provide analyses of survey data in which I test these different claims and find broad support for the arguments advanced in this chapter. Before advancing to tests of these arguments, I spend more time in Chapter 3 discussing authoritarianism and examining its relationship with economic, social, and political attitudes in Western Europe. Doing so provides greater perspective about its potential to reshape West European electoral politics. Chapters 4–5 then examine the evidence concerning EU attitudes, while Chapters 6–9 turn to the question of party support.

3
Authoritarianism in West European Electorates

Introduction

The previous chapter presented this book's argument, describing the evolving relationship between authoritarianism and political behaviour in Western Europe. The following chapters present and assess evidence of that argument. Before turning to that task, it is important to understand authoritarianism in greater detail. There has been a great deal of research on authoritarianism over the past six decades, but this has necessarily created some amount of disagreement among scholars about concept and measurement. Additionally, the prevalence of authoritarianism in contemporary West European electorates is unclear, along with its relationship to social, economic, and political attitudes.

This chapter examines the contours of authoritarianism in contemporary Western Europe electorates. It addresses the following questions in turn. First, what is authoritarianism, and how should we understand it? Second, how is authoritarianism distinct from other concepts, such as conservatism? Finally, how do we measure authoritarianism? The chapter then describes the survey evidence concerning authoritarianism and political behaviour in West European societies. How many high authoritarians are there in contemporary West European societies? Do they share a common set of economic, political, and social attitudes, and do these vary from low authoritarians? This chapter describes the attitudes held by high authoritarians and low authoritarians, showing when they are distinct from each other and when they are indistinguishable. This analysis improves our understanding of authoritarianism as a psychological construct, and it sets the stage for the analysis to follow.

Several important points emerge from the descriptive analysis that follows. First, authoritarianism is normally distributed among West European societies. Roughly equal amounts of West European respondents are high and low authoritarians, respectively. In this sense, high authoritarians are neither rare nor predominant. More importantly, most West Europeans are clustered closer to the centre on the authoritarianism scale. Relatively few individuals are strongly high or low authoritarian. Second, high authoritarians have distinctive attitudes on social and cultural issues compared to low authoritarians. On some questions,

Authoritarianism and the Evolution of West European Electoral Politics. Erik R. Tillman, Oxford University Press.
© Erik R. Tillman 2021. DOI: 10.1093/oso/9780192896223.003.0003

high authoritarians hold distinctive political attitudes. However, authoritarianism has little bearing on economic attitudes, where opinions are mixed across the authoritarianism scale.

The finding that high authoritarians hold distinctive cultural attitudes is important for the argument of this book. If authoritarianism distinguishes cultural and political attitudes but not economic attitudes, then it is likely that (perceived) changes in cultural or political conditions would trigger the shifts in (political) attitudes among high authoritarians that are the focus of this book. By contrast, it is unlikely that changing economic conditions would have such an effect if high authoritarians do not have distinctive economic preferences. In short, changing demographics, the rise of multiculturalism, increasing cultural liberalism, and the loss of national sovereignty are more likely to be drivers of changing behaviour among high authoritarians described in this book than are changing economic conditions.

Conceptualizing Authoritarianism

Over the course of six decades of research, scholars have developed competing conceptualizations of authoritarianism. As a result, the scholarship on authoritarianism today—and the associated measurement strategies—reflects these different conceptual approaches. The conceptual differences between different studies of authoritarianism tend to divide on two main questions. First, is authoritarianism a fixed personality trait, or is it a predispositional trait that is activated only under certain conditions? Second, what are the core traits of authoritarianism? The answers to each of these questions affect the corresponding measurement strategy.

Early research on authoritarianism described it as a set of fixed personality traits. The original model developed in *The Authoritarian Personality* highlighted nine clustered traits (Adorno et al. 1950), some of which were rejected by subsequent research. Altemeyer (1981, 1996) revitalized the study of authoritarianism by focusing on three traits that he termed Right-Wing Authoritarianism—conventionalism, authoritarian aggression, and authoritarian submission—while rejecting the other six traits. Conventionalism describes an adherence to traditional social norms and roles along with a belief that others should be compelled to adopt them. Authoritarian submission refers to a willingness to submit to established authorities and their values, while authoritarian aggression describes the willingness to use compulsion against those members of society (e.g. deviants, out-groups) who do not submit to established authorities. This conceptualization of authoritarianism as a relatively fixed set of personality traits implies that it can be measured using standard attitudinal questions.

Recent research conducted since the 1990s has moved towards viewing authoritarianism as a set of predispositional traits (Feldman and Stenner 1997;

Feldman 2003; Stenner 2005). This perspective describes the authoritarian predisposition as a motivation towards maintaining social conformity (Feldman and Stenner 1997; Feldman 2003; Stenner 2005), or towards maintaining order and security (Hetherington and Weiler 2009). In this framework, authoritarianism is dynamic and situational rather than fixed. The core characteristic of high authoritarians is a high sensitivity towards threats to the normative order—the beliefs and practices that maintain social cohesion. Threats to the normative order activate the authoritarian predisposition, leading to the expression of authoritarian attitudes directed at the source of those threats. When no such threat exists, then high and low authoritarians may not differ much in their attitudes.

Conceiving of authoritarianism as a predisposition has important consequences for measurement. While the underlying predisposition is stable according to theory, authoritarian attitudes are not. In this context, authoritarian attitudes refer to support for measures to enforce social cohesion or order—such as restrictions on civil liberties, enhanced scrutiny or discrimination against groups seen as posing a threat to society, and so on. Because authoritarian attitudes are conditional on the presence of a threat, survey questions that simply measure attitudes will not capture authoritarianism consistently. Rather, they will capture expressed authoritarian attitudes under conditions of perceived threat. Moreover, low authoritarians may also express authoritarian attitudes when faced with existential (rather than normative) threats, such as the possibility of violence or death (Hetherington and Suhay 2011). Instead, measures of authoritarianism must capture the predisposition rather than the attitudes. In practice, the distinction may be less important if normative threats exist to activate authoritarian predispositions. In addition, high and low authoritarians are likely to hold consistently different attitudes on questions measuring policy preferences towards social order or cohesion (such as questions on crime or immigration).

The second conceptual distinction concerns the set of traits in the authoritarian predisposition. While the earliest research theorized nine linked traits, recent research has tended to focus on a narrower—but perhaps more general—set of traits. In part, this focus reflects updated theorizing: the authoritarian predisposition captures a general desire for order, social cohesion, and security, which may manifest itself in attitudes such as conventionalism or authoritarian aggression when activated by threat. Measures designed to capture this more general predisposition cannot identify the different dimensions of the authoritarian disposition—making it hard to determine if an effect is driven by an aversion to difference or a fear of disorder, for example. However, more extensive questionnaires designed to measure different dimensions of the authoritarian personality are necessarily more costly to administer and may introduce additional problems of cross-national comparability.

Finally, authoritarianism is not binary in practice. Instead, authoritarianism ranges along a continuum. An individual might display a high level of authoritarianism, a low level, or something in between. In practice, authoritarianism is distributed normally among West European publics, with most individuals falling somewhere close to the middle of the scale while smaller numbers display very high or very low levels of authoritarianism. As a result, authoritarianism is relevant as a topic of study because many people have some degree of the predisposition, which can be activated by threats to the normative order. However, authoritarianism varies by individuals, meaning that each society contains a wide mix of high, medium, and low authoritarians. With that said, this book uses binary language (i.e. 'high authoritarian' and 'low authoritarian') for the sake of clarity in writing and to contrast the divergent attitudes and behaviours of individuals at each end of the spectrum.

What Authoritarianism Is Not

Before proceeding further, it is useful to consider some important boundaries to our definition—or what authoritarianism is not. This discussion accomplishes two important objectives. First, it provides greater conceptual clarity about authoritarianism and how it differs from related concepts. Second, it will help to elucidate the goals of this study, and in particular to address potential concerns about how authoritarianism is being conceptualized and applied.

Authoritarianism Is Not Pathological

One objection that might be raised is that authoritarianism appears to describe a pathological personality type. It is true that much of the literature on authoritarianism has treated it as problematic, as reflected in the concept's origins as an effort to explain mass support for fascism. However, it is important to clarify that the point of this study is not to demonize a group of individuals who hold certain political views. Rather, the aim is to explain the contemporary alignment of mass EU attitudes and party support, for which authoritarianism provides a powerful analytical tool. The goal of this study is to provide a faithful description and analysis of the evidence and ideas underpinning the analysis.

A better way of approaching a discussion of authoritarianism is to consider the broader role of dispositional traits. Living in a human society generates a range of individual and social dilemmas. Moreover, the human mind constantly receives and must interpret vast amounts of information, which requires the use of heuristics and other simplifications (Kahneman 2011). One might consider authoritarianism as a cognitive style or simplifying approach to making sense of the vast information and social dilemmas that confront individuals. A predisposition geared towards maintaining social cohesion, defending against out-groups, and preserving tradition and order provides a useful set of automatic answers for a wide range of novel social situations. High authoritarians will be more resistant to change or risk, and more distrustful of outsiders or of novelty. In a potentially dangerous world, authoritarianism is a safe and protective approach for members of a society to take.

Readers may also ask whether there is a 'good' side to authoritarianism. High authoritarians are more concerned about the security and protection of society against external (or internal) threats. As such, they may be more committed to the protection of their society (and its fellow members) than low authoritarians. Other evidence hints at this idea. For example, stronger in-group attachment (which correlates with authoritarianism) results in greater generosity towards fellow in-group members and a greater willingness to sacrifice oneself for society (Theiss-Morse 2009). This willingness to sacrifice may extend to other matters of social solidarity. In general, high authoritarians are motivated by a desire to protect the society in which they live.

Recent research also challenges the notion that prejudice or intolerance is itself particularly characteristic of authoritarianism (or related dispositions such as conservatism). Because many studies of prejudice focus on objects such as minorities or deviant groups, the apparent intolerance may reflect perceptions that such groups hold opposing political views. When potential targets of anger among low authoritarians—such as religious fundamentalists or members of the military— are included, respondents display equivalent levels of intolerance, including a willingness to deny political rights to members of those groups (Brandt et al. 2014; Crawford and Pilanski 2014; Brandt et al. 2015). In other words, the evidence suggests that individuals generally are intolerant towards those with whom they disagree or find threatening. Authoritarianism helps us to understand which groups one finds threatening, but high and low authoritarians may not vary in the level of intolerance they display towards groups they view as political adversaries. Further research is needed in this area, but it may be that authoritarianism is not a uniquely intolerant predisposition.

The argument of this book might be understood as follows. High authoritarians make up an important part of West European societies. Their style of processing information and forming political attitudes has certain predictable results, one of those being that they are less likely to accept rapid demographic, values, or political change. This reluctance is in large part the consequence of a heightened concern for maintaining social cohesion and solidarity, for which high authoritarians are willing to sacrifice more than low authoritarians. As a result, authoritarians' reluctance to support European integration and support for popular radical right (PRR) parties is motivated by a deeper concern to maintain national cohesion and sovereignty.

Authoritarianism Is Not Conservatism

One might be tempted to conclude at this point that authoritarianism is merely an alternative description of conservatism. This point is reinforced by the use of the term 'Right-Wing Authoritarianism' in other studies (e.g. Altemeyer 1981, 1996). And many studies of authoritarianism have sought to explore its relationship with various right-wing attitudes or loyalties (e.g. Adorno et al. 1950; Altemeyer 1981, 1996; Stenner 2005, Dunn 2015). In addition, some studies of personality and politics use the terms 'liberal' and 'conservative' to describe the different polar ends (e.g. Hibbing et al. 2013). Therefore, is authoritarianism just another way of describing conservatism?

The answer is that authoritarianism and conservatism are distinct, despite occasional overlapping usage. Consider attitudes towards economics and economic policy. Market-oriented policies are an integral part of contemporary conservatism, but they are not linked logically to authoritarianism. High authoritarians are likely to reject free-trade policies (Johnston and Wronski 2015), and the relationship between authoritarianism and economic attitudes is conditional on national context (Malka et al. 2014; Johnston et al. 2017; Federico and Malka 2018). In general, there is no compelling evidence that high authoritarians hold consistent right-wing attitudes on economics. Instead, authoritarian attitudes regarding economics are more likely to respond to elite cues, since most economic policies can be framed in a manner that emphasizes or de-emphasizes authoritarian values (Malka et al. 2014; Federico and Malka 2018). High authoritarians are more likely to be drawn to right-wing parties by social or cultural messages, and politically attentive high authoritarians may subsequently adopt those parties' economic positions (Johnston et al. 2017). Moreover, high authoritarians oppose free market policies when these are seen as being a radical change from the existing order, as during the collapse of communism in the former Soviet Union (McFarland et al. 1992; Malka et al. 2014). In short, there is no clear relationship between authoritarianism and conservative economic positions.

The conditional effect of authoritarianism on attitudes generates divergence from conservatism in other contexts. For example, members of ethno-religious minorities display higher levels of authoritarianism (Henry 2011). Members of minority groups are unlikely to support conservative political parties for reasons of group interest. Ethnic minorities may exhibit socially conservative attitudes in certain domains (e.g. religious practice) while favouring other liberal social policies (e.g. multiculturalism, positive discrimination). In short, the relationship between authoritarianism and conservative attitudes is conditional.

Finally, authoritarianism predicts a different political response than conservatism to changing social or cultural conditions (Stenner 2009). Conservatism is concerned with reducing or slowing the rate of social and cultural change, motivated by a general trust of tradition and established practices over social reform. However, as a broader political theory, conservatism can adapt to demographic or values change, while seeking to limit the rate of that change. By contrast, authoritarianism may see such change as dangerous, necessitating extreme methods to block it (see Stenner 2009). In this sense, theories of conservatism and authoritarianism would lead to different predictions about political behaviour during threats to the normative order. In short, authoritarianism is a distinct predisposition, but its study is important in order to understand those circumstances under which it leads to conservative political beliefs or party support.

About the Term 'Authoritarianism'

One final concern is that 'authoritarianism' has a clear negative connotation, and presumably few readers would be pleased to be described as 'high authoritarians' even if the description were accurate based on the definition. In some respect, this discussion revisits the point made above that authoritarianism does not describe a pathological tendency. But the problem may run deeper, as the negative connotations of the term creates the risk that some readers may simply disregard the book's argument as an effort to demonize a group of West European voters and parties. The comments section on a blog post I wrote describing my earlier research (Tillman 2013) made this accusation against me, which I understand but deny.

To put it as simply as possible, none of this book's message is designed to promote or criticize any worldview or set of attitudes over another. Instead, this book seeks to describe and explain an important political transformation that I argue is occurring in Western Europe. To that end, I adopt the existing language used in academic political psychology. For better or worse, political psychologists have used the term 'authoritarianism' to describe the set of attitudes or dispositions described here. Since I believe that it is important to be clear about the origins of one's ideas and their connection to broader fields of inquiry, I adopt the terminology and concepts already in use. Thus, I follow the academic convention that has developed since the 1950s in using this term.

A second concern that some readers might have is the confusion between how psychologists use 'authoritarianism' and how political scientists often use it. In political science, authoritarianism refers to a political system in which ruling elites are not accountable to the citizenry, and in which they rule without popular consent. These rival definitions create confusion, as it would seem to suggest that (psychological) authoritarians must support (political) authoritarianism. That is not necessarily the case. Although there are occasions when we would expect high authoritarians to support authoritarian political arrangements, I do not make that argument here. In fact, high authoritarians are typically quite attached to the established political order, which in Western Europe is representative democracy within the sovereign nation state. A core part of this book's argument is that high authoritarians believe that they are protecting this established political system in their country. How? European integration and immigration can be viewed as distinct threats to sovereignty and the nation state in that the first transfers power to the supranational level and the latter generates demographic change. Moreover, critics of the 'democratic deficit' in the European Union claim that it is not accountable to voters (see Hix 2008 for a discussion), which would suggest it threatens representative democracy. Regardless of how one views these criticisms of the EU and of immigration, what should be clear is that high authoritarians see them as a threat to sovereign national democracy. So it is not necessarily the case that high authoritarians support authoritarian political arrangements, and I do not argue that they do so in the West European context.

In short, my hope is to persuade readers that my research is motivated by a genuine social scientific desire to describe and understand the world while remaining faithful to the larger research traditions that have existed for decades. I believe that adopting the established term 'authoritarianism' is the best way to achieve those multiple goals. If one still objects to its use, then I note its close relationship to similar concepts. As described in the definition, two central characteristics of authoritarianism are a need for certainty and a need for security (or a higher sensitivity to threats). One can consider 'authoritarianism' as shorthand for a predisposition that describes these traits—along with a higher level of in-group identification. Other studies have found that the measures of authoritarianism used in this study correlate highly with similar measures of a need for closure or of an aversion to change (Kruglanski 1989; Jost et al. 2003; Malka et al. 2014; Johnston and Wronski 2015; Johnston et al. 2017; Federico and Malka 2018). If one remains uncomfortable with the use of the term 'authoritarianism', then one could substitute 'needs for security and certainty' instead.

Measuring Authoritarianism

Since the start of research into authoritarianism in the immediate post-war years (Adorno et al. 1950), scholars have developed several measurement approaches. In addition to the usual pitfalls facing the development of any valid and reliable measurement scale, the study of authoritarianism poses a further challenge. Scholars are usually interested in measuring authoritarianism in individual respondents in order to understand its effects on social and political attitudes. This goal requires the development of authoritarianism scales whose items do not measure the same attitudes that researchers hope to explain. In addition, the newer conceptualization of authoritarianism as a disposition has required a new measurement strategy.

The first attempt to measure authoritarianism was the California F-Scale, used in the landmark study *The Authoritarian Personality* (Adorno et al. 1950). Although this research and measurement strategy was pioneering in many respects, the F-Scale soon fell out of favour for several crucial reasons. Psychologist Bob Altemeyer developed the most important alternative called the Right-Wing Authoritarianism (RWA) scale (Altemeyer 1981, 1996). One important refinement of the RWA scale was to simplify the original nine-dimensional concept into three core dimensions (and measurement scales): conventionalism, authoritarian submission, and authoritarian aggression. The RWA scale includes items measuring social, cultural, and political attitudes, which is appropriate for measuring authoritarianism as a stable personality trait. However, its items are very close to the same sort of attitudes that authoritarianism researchers will wish to explain. Representative questions, all of which are measured on five-point Likert scales, from the RWA scale include:

- 'Our society desperately needs a mighty leader who will do what has to be done to destroy the radical new ways that are ruining us.'
- 'The majority of those who criticize proper authorities in government and religion only serve to create useless doubts in people's minds.'
- 'Obedience and respect for authority are the most important values that children should learn.'
- 'There is no one right way to live; everyone has to create their own way.' (Reverse coded.)

For all but the last item, stronger agreement with the statement indicates higher levels of authoritarianism.

The strength of the RWA measures is that they are conceptually linked to the core authoritarian traits (conventionalism, submission, and aggression), and they form a reliable scale. However, the problem with the RWA scale is that the items may measure the same attitudes that political scientists would be interested in explaining. For example, the second item listed above asks respondents to evaluate government critics, but scholars who study authoritarianism may wish to examine its relationship with support for anti-government protests. This item 'contaminates' the analysis because respondents who express opposition to public criticism of leaders will score higher on both the independent variable (RWA) and the dependent variable. In a similar way, other RWA items asking about alternative lifestyles or civil rights will correlate strongly with attitudes about those issues, but it will be difficult for an analyst to determine if authoritarianism predicts those attitudes or whether the RWA item is simply measuring those attitudes in a different way. This problem can be addressed by removing the items in question, though this may weaken the reliability of the RWA scale. The second conceptual problem with the RWA scale is that it measures fixed attitudes rather than dispositional traits. This measurement approach is not a problem in cases when the researcher wants to examine how activated authoritarian attitudes relate to other attitudes. It is a problem when one wants to observe the dynamics of how those attitudes are activated.

To address these concerns, an improved measure was proposed by political psychologists Stanley Feldman and Karen Stenner (Feldman 2003; Feldman and Stenner 1997; Stenner 2005). They identified that using items asking respondents to indicate preferences towards child-rearing values generates a scale that is a valid and reliable measure of authoritarianism while measuring values that are conceptually distinct and prior to the attitudes that authoritarianism should explain. Conceptually, the child-rearing items link to the original F-Scale and RWA scale, as highlighted by the third RWA item above measuring the need for obedience and respect for authority. The most common four-item scale is as follows:

'Although there are a number of qualities that people believe children should have, every person thinks that some qualities are more important than others. Below are four pairs of desirable qualities. Please choose which quality from each pair is more important for a child to have:

1. (a) Respect for elders OR (b) Independence
2. (a) Self-reliance OR (b) Obedience
3. (a) Good manners OR (b) Curiosity
4. (a) Being considerate OR (b) Being well-behaved'.

Respondents' answers to these questions reveal their preferences concerning the fundamental trade-off between individual autonomy and social conformity. The answers indicating a preference for individual autonomy (independence, self-reliance, curiosity, being considerate) reflect a preference for low authoritarian values, while the responses in favour of conformity (respect for elders, obedience, good manners, and being well-behaved) demonstrate a preference for high authoritarian values. These four items generate a scale of authoritarianism, which cross-national research has shown to be valid and reliable (Stenner 2005). This scale is appropriate because the questions about child rearing are causally distinct from socio-political attitudes, meaning that they will not contaminate analyses of the relationship between authoritarianism and political attitudes. Additionally, they come closer to measuring the predisposition towards social cohesion rather than expressed authoritarian attitudes.

In the section below, I analyse data drawn from four sources: the 1990 and 2017 waves of the European Values Survey (EVS) (EVS 2011a, 2019); the May

2014 wave of the German Longitudinal Election Study (GLES) (Rattinger et al. 2014); Wave 10 of the 2015 British Election Study (BES), fielded in November–December 2016 (Fieldhouse et al. 2019; and the 2015 Swiss Election Study (SES) (Lutz and Pekari 2015). Each includes a version of the child-rearing measure, with slight variations. The EVS measure varies the most from the others, as it is not measured using paired choices (i.e. choose between 'respect for elders' or 'independence'). Instead, respondents are presented with a list of eleven attributes and invited to choose up to five that are 'especially important'. These include three low authoritarian traits (independence, imagination, and tolerance and respect for other people) and three high authoritarian traits (good manners, religious faith, and obedience), along with five other traits that are not related to authoritarianism. Thus, respondents can choose any mixture of high and low authoritarian traits, or they can choose exclusively irrelevant traits. I calculate the number of high authoritarian traits and the number of low authoritarian traits chosen by each respondent and use these to create the measure of authoritarianism. The GLES measure contains only three items: respect for elders or independence, self-reliance or obedience, and good manners or curiosity. The BES and SES measures are as described above. These minor differences in measurement are worth noting, but they are unlikely to affect the inferences derived in this or the subsequent chapters.

Authoritarianism: Distribution and Demographics

This section describes the prevalence of authoritarianism and its relationship with other demographic variables. The goal in this analysis is to draw a broader picture of authoritarianism in Western Europe, which will provide an important context for the chapters to follow. The description will focus on the distribution of authoritarianism among respondents and the relationship between authoritarianism and political, economic, and social attitudes. If theorizing about authoritarianism and past analyses are correct, authoritarianism should structure political and social attitudes, but it should have no effect on economic attitudes. Additionally, authoritarianism should be normally distributed throughout the electorate, though it will be more common among less-educated and older respondents.

Distribution

How is authoritarianism distributed in West European electorates? I start by comparing EVS data from 1990 and 2017, along with more recent BES, GLES, and SES data from 2014–16. These comparisons will provide a sense of whether authoritarianism is normally distributed, as well as whether that distributed has shifted in the past several decades. We should expect to see a normal distribution, but it is possible that the population has become less authoritarian over time. There should also be no reason to observe major cross-national differences between the countries included here.

Figure 3.1 shows the results from the 1990 and 2017 waves of the EVS, including only the states that participated in both waves. The results are consistent with the expectation that authoritarianism is normally distributed, though there is a clear skew in responses in 2017. Importantly, rather few respondents are located at either extreme. In 1990, just under 40 per cent of respondents score on the low authoritarian side of the scale while just under 35 per cent are on the high authoritarian side. In 2008, these numbers are 54 per cent and 16 per cent, respectively. Just over 25 per cent of respondents in 1990 are at the midpoint, compared to just under 30 per cent in 2017. This evidence is consistent with a shift towards less authoritarianism between 1990 and 2017 (Norris and Inglehart 2019). High authoritarians are less common in West European societies in 2017, though they still comprise an important bloc of voters. Moreover, it is important to note that most respondents are clustered near the midpoint, suggesting that most voters hold a mix of high authoritarian and low authoritarian tendencies. As such, a majority of voters could be sensitive to threats to the normative order, though such voters are also likely to value individual autonomy.

Figure 3.2 shows the comparable results from the British, German, and Swiss election studies collected between 2014 and 2016. The results still hint at a broad distribution of authoritarianism in each country. In Germany, the inclusion of three child-rearing items resulted in very few respondents scoring at the midpoint

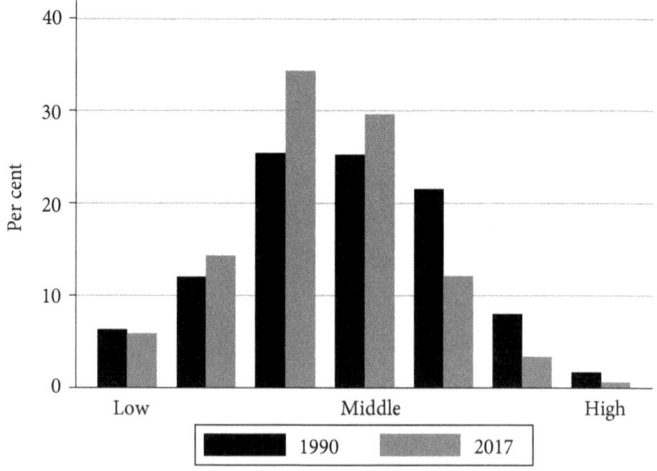

Figure 3.1 Distribution of authoritarianism in 1990 and 2017

Note: The figures show tabulated responses from the following countries: Austria, Denmark, Finland, France, Germany, Great Britain, Italy, the Netherlands, Spain, and Sweden.

Source: EVS 2011a, 2019.

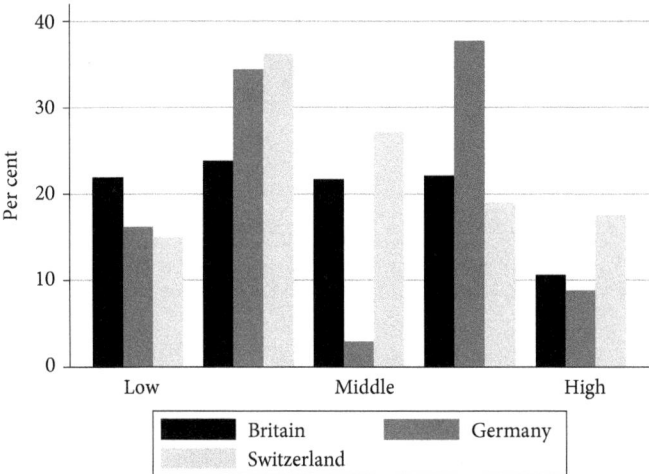

Figure 3.2 Authoritarianism in Germany, Great Britain, and Switzerland

Note: Each bar shows the percentage of respondents scoring at that level of authoritarianism in each election study.

Sources: British Election Study (Fieldhouse et al. 2014), German Longitudinal Election Study (Ratinger et al. 2014), Swiss Election Study (Lutz and Pekari 2015).

of the scale, as only those who failed to answer one of the three questions could do so. Given that limitation, respondents are otherwise broadly dispersed. In Great Britain, the distribution is flattened, with only the high authoritarian end of the scale having a lower number of respondents. In Switzerland, responses are skewed towards the low authoritarian end of the scale, with the second-lowest point having the largest number of responses. Although these data do not fully reflect a normal distribution, they show a broad distribution of responses. In short, high authoritarians make up a substantial minority of West European electorates, but the distribution of authoritarianism loosely follows a normal curve with some overrepresentation of low authoritarians.

Education

Does authoritarianism vary by educational attainment? Prior research has found a negative relationship between authoritarianism and education (Adorno et al. 1950; Altemeyer 1996), though the causality is less certain. It could be that higher education leads to the adoption of a low authoritarian outlook, with greater acceptance of ambiguity and tolerance of difference. However, authoritarianism may also predispose individuals towards avoiding post-secondary education. In other words, high authoritarians may choose not to pursue higher education because it promotes ambiguity and criticism (i.e. challenges to the normative order),

Table 3.1 Post-secondary education by authoritarianism

Survey	High Authoritarians	Low Authoritarians
EVS	19.6%	44.9%
Germany	21.6%	39.6%
Great Britain	24.4%	52.5%
Switzerland	14.6%	33.7%

Note: Figures show the percentage of respondents with post-secondary education among high authoritarians (score > 0) and low authoritarians (score < 0).

preferring to seek out career or educational tracks that offer greater certainty and order. Thus, low authoritarians are overrepresented in universities, but higher education does not necessarily have a liberalizing effect. Recent research showing that the association between higher education and liberal immigration attitudes is a result of selection rather than educational effects is consistent with this view (Lancee and Sarrassin 2015). While the direction of the causal effect is not crucial to this study, we should expect to see an association between higher authoritarianism and lower levels of educational attainment.

Table 3.1 shows the percentage of high authoritarians and low authoritarians, respectively, with post-secondary education. The measurement of post-secondary educational attainment varies slightly across each survey due to different measurement schemes. While it directly reflects reported educational attainment in the EVS, GLES, and SES, it is measured using the age at which the respondent finished full-time education in the BES. Respondents who finished school at age 20 or higher are coded as having post-secondary education, which possibly overestimates the proportion of British respondents with post-secondary education. However, there is no reason to expect that this would distort the relationship between authoritarianism and education. The results are consistent with expectations. In each survey, there is a gap of 15 percentage points or more between the proportion of low authoritarians and high authoritarians with post-secondary education. In short, high authoritarianism is associated with substantially lower levels of educational attainment. While only one-quarter or less of high authoritarians have obtained a university education, more than one-third— and in Great Britain and the EVS, closer to one-half—of low authoritarians have. Whether due to self-selection or a liberalizing effect, a significant educational gap exists between high and low authoritarians.

Age and Gender

Is there a relationship between authoritarianism and age or gender? There is reason to expect that older respondents may express more authoritarianism. One prominent argument suggests that the values change in West European societies has led to a major shift in which younger generations are less authoritarian than their older counterparts (Norris and Inglehart 2019). If correct, then older respondents should skew more towards the high authoritarian pole than younger respondents. Lifecycle effects could also produce higher levels of authoritarianism among older respondents by reducing tolerance for ambiguity or uncertainty as people grow older. In any case, we should expect to see higher levels of authoritarianism among older respondents.

Figure 3.3 shows the distribution of authoritarianism by age in the 2017 EVS sample. These results do not confirm expectations. Older respondents (defined as those aged 45 and over) display only slightly higher levels of authoritarianism than younger respondents. However, the difference between age groups is relatively minor, indicating that authoritarianism exists among all age groups. Importantly, a substantial portion of younger respondents are high authoritarians, which should lead to scepticism that authoritarianism is vanishing as a result of changing values in West European societies (Norris and Inglehart 2019). Instead, these results are consistent with the view that authoritarianism, as a dispositional trait, exists among a proportion of all populations, even as social norms have evolved.

What about gender? There may be reason to expect that men are more likely to endorse authoritarianism than women, but any gender differences should be minor. Indeed, this expectation is borne out by an examination of the data (not shown). There are slightly higher levels of authoritarianism among men than women. Roughly 48 per cent of female respondents fall on the low authoritarian

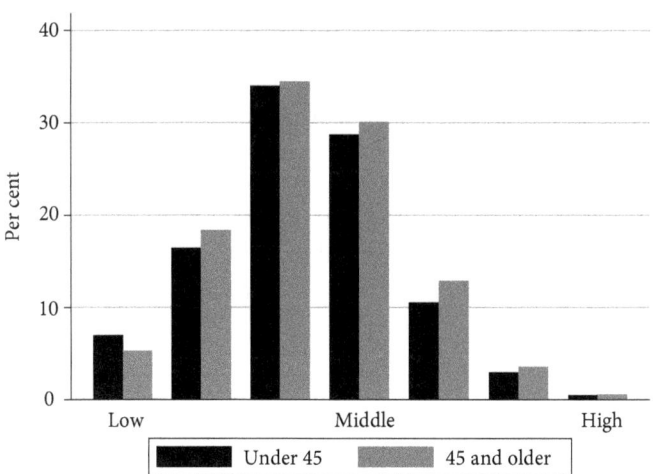

Figure 3.3 Age and authoritarianism

Note: The figures show tabulated responses from the following countries: Austria, Denmark, Finland, France, Germany, Great Britain, Italy, the Netherlands, Spain, and Sweden.

Source: EVS 2019.

side compared to 44.6 per cent of male respondents, while slightly fewer than 25 per cent of both male and female respondents score on the high authoritarian end of the scale. In short, female respondents are modestly more likely to score as low authoritarians, but there is no difference in the prevalence of high authoritarians by gender.

In summary, these results point to two conclusions. First, there are significant differences in authoritarianism by education. Without suggesting any causal direction, the results show that authoritarianism is more prevalent among those with secondary or less education, while those with post-secondary education are more likely to be low authoritarians. Second, there are limited differences in age, with older respondents being slightly higher in authoritarianism. However, there are no meaningful differences by gender. With these findings in mind, we turn to the relationship between authoritarianism and political, social, and economic attitudes.

Political Attitudes

This section examines the relationship between authoritarianism and political attitudes. There are several important questions meriting examination here. First, are high authoritarians more likely to identify with the left or the right politically? This question is important as it examines whether there has been ideological sorting by authoritarianism (e.g. high authoritarians being more likely to place themselves on the right). In the United States, high authoritarians have become more likely to vote for the Republican Party (Hetherington and Weiler 2009), so it is worth examining whether any evidence of such a pattern exists in Western Europe as well. Second, do high authoritarians exhibit reduced support for democracy? As discussed above, there has been scholarly interest in whether high authoritarians are more likely to support non-democratic regime types (e.g. Adorno et al. 1950; Altemeyer 1996). Recently, some observers have suggested that mass support for democracy is in decline (Foa and Mounk 2016). Finally, I examine whether high authoritarians express lower levels of political efficacy, which could similarly reflect less commitment to or less engagement with the political system. If high authoritarians are generally less tolerant of ambiguity or diversity, then they may be turned off by conflict and compromise that is inherent to democracy.

Ideology

I start by examining the relationship between authoritarianism and self-reported political ideology. In each survey, ideology is measured on a standard ten-point (in the EVS) or eleven-point left–right scale. One possibility is that high authoritarians are drawn towards the right, due to a natural affinity between authoritarianism and conservative ideology (Jost et al. 2003; see also Stenner 2005, 2009; Hetherington and Weiler 2009). Figure 3.4 shows the results from the EVS, while Table 3.2 shows the results from Germany, Great Britain, and Switzerland. The EVS data in Figure 3.4 show a modest tendency for high authoritarians to place themselves on the right relative to low authoritarians, while low authoritarians are more likely to place themselves on the left. This tendency has increased modestly since 1990 (not shown). In 1990, 45 per cent of high authoritarians placed themselves on the right compared to 35 per cent of low authoritarians—a gap of 10 percentage points. That gap in 2017 is 16 percentage points (53 per cent versus 37 per cent). Similarly, the gap between the per cent of low authoritarians placing themselves on the left versus high authoritarians increased from 13 percentage points to 18 percentage points between 1990 and 2017. Thus, there is modest evidence that high authoritarians are more likely to identify with the right and low authoritarians with the left, consistent with an ongoing worldview evolution of political identities and behaviours.

The same pattern holds in Germany, Great Britain, and Switzerland, with somewhat higher levels of intensity. In all three samples, high authoritarians are more likely to place themselves on the right, while low authoritarians identify more on the left. This difference is most pronounced and symmetric in Switzerland, which is likely the result of the long-term emphasis of the Swiss People's Party on national sovereignty and community. Because that party positions itself on the right culturally and economically, high and low authoritarians have more clearly

Table 3.2 Authoritarianism and ideology

	Germany		Great Britain		Switzerland	
	High	Low	High	Low	High	Low
Left	3.6	4.2	1.6	4.3	3.7	8.0
1	3.8	5.0	0.8	5.4	2.3	6.9
2	10.6	11.6	3.3	12.3	3.9	13.1
3	10.1	15.8	4.5	15.1	5.6	12.4
4	14.2	17.0	4.8	10.2	5.6	10.2
5	25.2	21.8	49.7	27.3	19.5	16.0
6	11.0	8.9	8.0	8.7	10.5	10.23
7	11.0	8.7	9.7	8.6	15.6	11.2
8	7.0	4.4	10.0	5.5	16.7	7.7
9	1.9	1.9	3.5	1.5	5.4	2.1
Right	1.7	0.8	4.1	1.1	11.2	2.2

Note: Figures show the percentage of respondents placing themselves at that ideological position among high authoritarians (those scoring above 0) and low authoritarians (those scoring below 0).

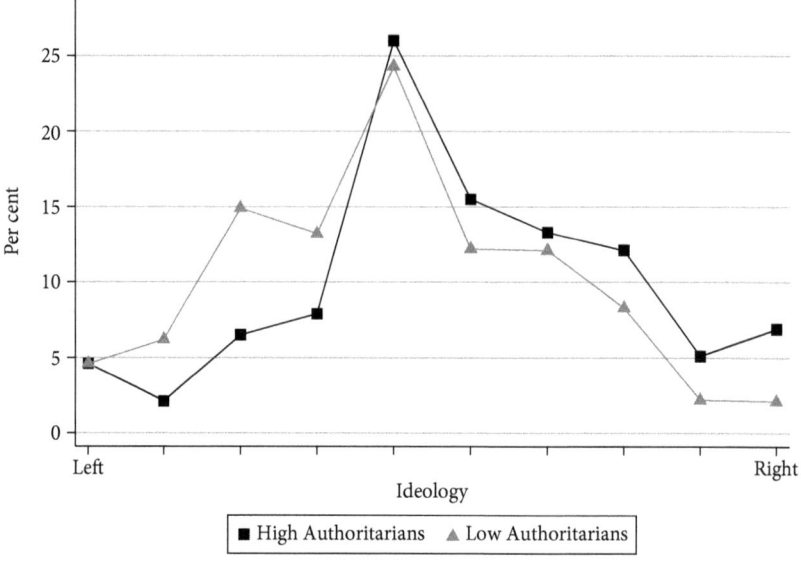

Figure 3.4 Authoritarianism and ideology

Note: The figures show tabulated responses from the following countries: Austria, Denmark, Finland, France, Germany, Great Britain, Italy, the Netherlands, Spain, and Sweden.

Source: EVS 2019.

sorted by ideology. A far more modest pattern of sorting exists in Germany, where the distinctions between the mainstream left and right parties on questions of national community have been relatively muted. Finally, Britain provides an interesting case in which high authoritarians are much less likely to place themselves on the left compared to low authoritarians, but the distinction on the right is much weaker. Instead, high authoritarians are far more likely to place themselves at the centre of the ideological scale. This tendency could reflect a sense of being cross-pressured between economic and socio-cultural preferences, but it could also reflect dissatisfaction or disengagement with party politics. In short, there is some positive but inconsistent association between authoritarianism and right-wing ideology. However, ideology may correspond weakly to issue positions or party support (Kinder and Kalmoe 2017).

Support for Democracy

Recent years have seen a growing interest in mass support for democracy in the advanced Western democracies, motivated by recent studies suggesting that it has fallen among younger generations (e.g. Foa and Mounk 2016). It is beyond the scope of this chapter to examine that debate fully, but it is important to understand if high authoritarians are less supportive of democracy. Declining support for democracy or a greater willingness to support non-democratic regime types could signal trouble for West European democracies if high authoritarians become increasingly sorted in certain political identities and activated by perceived normative threats. Here, I examine the relationship between authoritarianism and satisfaction with national democracy, as well as support for non-democratic alternative regime types.

To examine whether authoritarianism and satisfaction with democracy are related, I estimate a linear regression in which the latter variable is the dependent variable, authoritarianism is the independent variable, and education, income, gender, age, and left–right ideology are included as control variables. I estimate this regression on the EVS data. The results appear in Table 3.3. The results show that higher levels of education, higher income, and right-wing ideology have positive associations with support for democracy. In addition, authoritarianism is negatively associated with satisfaction with democracy. High authoritarians approve less of the performance of democracy in their countries than low authoritarians.

But are high authoritarians more willing to endorse non-democratic alternatives or to reject democracy itself? The EVS and BES contain questions probing these attitudes. One question is common to both: respondents are asked whether it would be preferable for their country to have a strong leader who does not have to bother with elections. Respondents answer on a five-point scale in the BES (four-point in the EVS), where higher values indicate more agreement that a strong leader would be better. The EVS includes a question asking respondents to evaluate the merits of living in a democratic system, with answers ranging from 'very good' (4) to 'very bad' (1). Finally, the BES asks respondents whether they believe that Britain needs to fundamentally change the way that society works. High authoritarians are normally less likely to endorse radical change, but they

Table 3.3 Authoritarianism and satisfaction with democracy

Variable	Coefficient	Standard Error
Authoritarianism	−.44*	.05
Ideology	.09*	.01
Education	.25*	.02
Income	.07*	.01
Gender	−.04	.04
Age	.09*	.01
Constant	3.7*	.10
N	17,557	
Root MSE	2.36	
Adjusted R^2	.04	

Note: Figures show unstandardized linear regression coefficients and standard errors, * p < .01.

(unlike conservatives) may be more likely to do so if they believe that society is threatened (Stenner 2009). Thus, either a negative coefficient or null finding could be expected here. Table 3.4 shows the results of these regression analyses, with the same control variables as the previous analysis.

The results show that authoritarianism has a significant effect in all four regressions. High authoritarians are more likely to agree that having a strong leader would be a good system, to evaluate democracy less favourably, and to agree that Great Britain needs fundamental social changes. Note that the coefficient for left–right ideology is not significant in Model 4 (Radical Change). This divergence illustrates Stenner's (2009) distinction between authoritarianism and conservatism. While high authoritarians and conservatives share misgivings about democracy due to its disorderly and messy nature, conservatives stop short of embracing radical social change. More generally, these findings point to a clear pattern of high authoritarians being less supportive of democracy than low authoritarians.

These findings illustrate the importance of understanding the partisan commitments of high authoritarians. If they become increasingly mobilized politically as a group, their willingness to support non-democratic rule could have profound effects upon their political systems. This is one important dimension on which high authoritarians and low authoritarians differ, and the name 'authoritarianism' seems apt to describe the disposition in this context.

Table 3.4 Authoritarianism and support for democracy

Variable	Strong Leader (EVS)	Democracy Good (EVS)	Strong Leader (BES)	Radical Change (BES)
Authoritarianism	.31*	−.17*	.50*	.07*
	(.02)	(.01)	(.03)	(.02)
Ideology	.06*	−.01*	.10*	−.10*
	(.00)	(.00)	(.01)	(.01)
Education	−.15*	.08*	−.22*	−.07*
	(.01)	(.01)	(.02)	(.02)
Income	−.02*	.01*	−.02*	−.02*
	(.00)	(.00)	(.01)	(.00)
Gender	.02	.04*	.18*	−.00
	(.01)	(.01)	(.03)	(.03)
Age	−.04*	.02*	−.07*	.01
	(.00)	(.00)	(.01)	(.01)
Constant	2.2*	3.3*	2.7*	4.5*
	(.04)	(.02)	(.11)	(.08)
N	15,801	16,047	4,636	4,636
Root MSE	.85	.54	1.1	.87
Adjusted R^2	.09	.06	.19	.06

Note: Figures show unstandardized regression coefficients with standard errors in parentheses, * p < .01.

Political Efficacy

If high authoritarians show a greater willingness to support non-democratic practices, is there also evidence that they are losing faith in their current democratic systems? To examine this, I rely on measures of political efficacy collected in the GLES and BES data. German respondents answered a series of questions measuring their perceptions of control over politics. These questions include prompts concerning whether politics is too difficult or confusing for the respondent to understand, whether politicians care about voters or just want their votes, and whether political participation makes a difference. All questions are coded on a one- to five-point scale, with higher values indicating higher levels of efficacy. I create an efficacy scale combining answers to those questions, and I regress it on authoritarianism and the usual control variables. The results appear in Table 3.5.

The results show that authoritarianism is associated with reduced political efficacy. High authoritarians are less likely to believe that their involvement in politics can make a difference, that they can understand complex political problems, or that politicians are concerned with solving major political problems. This finding is consistent with the interpretation that high authoritarians are turned off by democratic compromise and conflict, as they prefer order and social cohesion. Finally, ideology is not related with political efficacy, showing that authoritarianism has an effect distinct from political conservatism.

Table 3.5 Authoritarianism and political efficacy

Variable	Germany	Great Britain
Authoritarianism	−.20*	−.20*
	(.04)	(.02)
Ideology	−.00	−.01
	(.01)	(.01)
Education	.20*	.12*
	(.03)	(.01)
Income	.03*	.02*
	(.01)	(.00)
Gender	−.12	−.15*
	(.05)	(.02)
Age	.03	.04*
	(.02)	(.01)
Constant	2.1*	2.7*
	(.13)	(.06)
N	865	4,636
Root MSE	.69	.62
Adjusted R^2	.09	.12

Note: Figures show unstandardized regression coefficients with standard errors in parentheses; * p < .01.

High authoritarians show some distinctive patterns when it concerns political attitudes. They are somewhat more likely to identify on the political right, to support non-democratic alternative forms of government, and to express lower levels of political efficacy. As a result, high authoritarians should be more willing to support right-wing populist parties or candidates who promise dramatic political reforms designed to return political power to the people.

Economic Attitudes

Do high authoritarians have systematically different economic preferences than low authoritarians? Prior research provides conflicting expectations. First, high authoritarians are modestly more likely to place themselves on the right ideologically, so it is possible that they hold right-wing economic attitudes as a result. However, most voters struggle to connect abstract ideological principles to specific policies, so expressing a general right-wing orientation does not necessarily translate to right-wing issue positions (e.g. Converse 1964; Kinder and Kalmoe 2017). Second, having greater concern for social cohesion and security, high authoritarians might support state intervention into the economy more than low authoritarians. In particular, high authoritarians may support policies that protect workers from foreign competition (Johnston and Wronski 2015). These competing impulses suggest that authoritarianism may not relate to economic attitudes systematically. Instead, the relationship may be contingent, driven by political context and elite arguments (Malka et al. 2014; Johnston et al. 2017; Federico and Malka 2018).

The EVS includes a series of questions measuring respondents' economic views on ten-point scales. These questions include: (1) whether individuals should be responsible for providing for themselves or whether the state should take more responsibility for providing for citizens; (2) whether unemployed persons should be required to take any open job or lose their benefits, or whether they should be able to refuse jobs; (3) whether competition is harmful or whether competition is good for people; and (4) whether incomes should be made more equal or whether there should be greater incentives for individual effort. In each case, the latter option is coded as the higher value and corresponds to the more left-wing option (i.e. the option supporting greater state intervention in the economy or support of individuals). If high authoritarians are more likely to support state policy to ensure social cohesion and protection, we should observe positive coefficients in the regressions presented in Table 3.6. By contrast, a systematic preference for right-wing economic policies should lead to negative coefficients.

The results present a mixed picture. High authoritarians are more likely to agree that unemployed persons should be required to take an open job, which would

Table 3.6 Authoritarianism and economic attitudes

Variable	Individual or State	Unemployed	Competition	Equal Incomes
Authoritarianism	.08	−.43*	−.03	−.22*
	(.05)	(.05)	(.05)	(.05)
Ideology	−.23*	−.24*	−.14*	−.35*
	(.01)	(.01)	(.01)	(.01)
Education	−.13*	.11*	−.14*	−.10*
	(.02)	(.02)	(.02)	(.02)
Income	−.09*	−.10*	−.07*	−.11*
	(.01)	(.01)	(.01)	(.01)
Gender	−.12*	.01	−.38*	−.14*
	(.04)	(.03)	(.03)	(.04)
Age	−.07*	−.01	.03	.01
	(.01)	(.01)	(.01)	(.01)
Constant	7.3*	6.1*	5.5*	8.2*
	(.10)	(.11)	(.09)	(.11)
N	16,177	16,106	16,081	16,128
Root MSE	2.3	2.4	2.1	2.4
Adjusted R^2	.06	.06	.05	.11

Note: Figures show unstandardized regression coefficients with standard errors in parentheses, * $p < .01$.

be consistent with a right-wing economic position. However, high authoritarians also believe that there should be more effort to equalize incomes, consistent with a left-wing economic outlook. There is no significant relationship between authoritarianism and the other two economic variables. As such, high authoritarians show no clear lean towards left- or right-wing economic positions. The results may hint at a distinctive authoritarian view of the economy that limits individual autonomy to refuse work while making greater efforts to equalize incomes, which results in an economy in which society ensures an equitable outcome for those who 'pull their own weight' and in so doing strengthens social cohesion at the expense of individual autonomy.

While authoritarianism does not structure economic preferences, perhaps it affects perceptions of the national economy. Being more sensitive to threats to society, high authoritarians might display a negativity bias when thinking about the economy. To examine this question, I use the GLES, BES, and SES data. Each includes a question asking respondents to evaluate how the national economy has changed in the past year on a five-point scale where higher values indicate more positive evaluations. Figure 3.5 shows the difference in the percentage of high authoritarians and the percentage of low authoritarians choosing each option. The chart displays limited differences and no systematic pattern in evaluations of the national economy. Nor do high authoritarians express more concern about

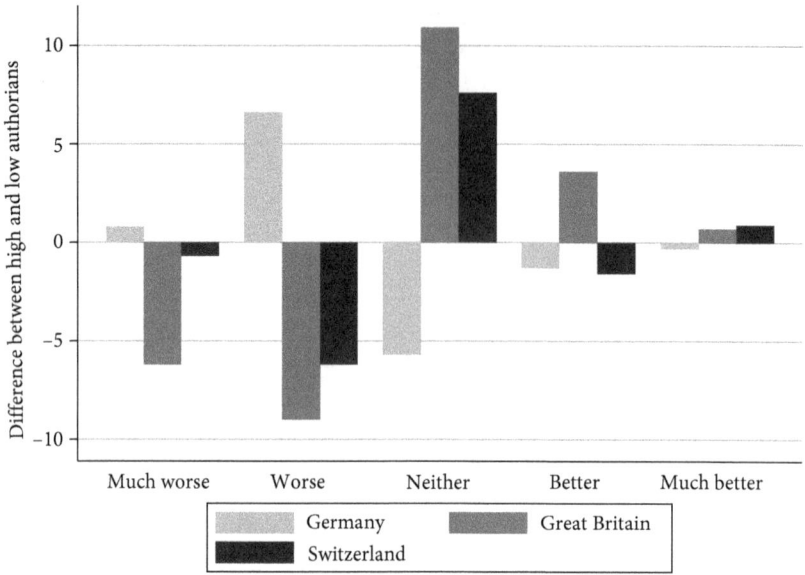

Figure 3.5 Authoritarianism and national economic evaluations

Note: The figure shows the difference in the percentage of high authoritarians and the percentage of low authoritarians who chose each response.

Source: British Election Study (Fieldhouse et al. 2014), German Longitudinal Election Study (Ratinger et al. 2014), Swiss Election Study (Lutz and Pekari 2015).

the state of the economy. The BES asks respondents three questions that can be used to measure economic anxiety. The first is whether the respondent considers it a good time to make a major household purchase. The second and third ask to what extent the respondent is worried about experiencing unemployment or poverty in the near future. Answers to these three questions are combined into a scale of economic anxiety. Figure 3.6 shows the distribution of economic anxiety among high and low authoritarians. The figure shows minimal difference between the two groups, with high authoritarians expressing slightly higher levels of concern about the economy. These findings should lead us to conclude that authoritarianism is not related to perceptions of the economy.

In short, authoritarianism has little relation to preferences about economic policy or perceptions of the economy. Despite expressing ideological leanings to the right, high authoritarians do not consistently support right-wing economic policies, nor do they lean to the left economically. Instead, it is more likely that economic preferences generally do not activate authoritarianism, so high authoritarians and low authoritarians form economic preferences on other considerations. Authoritarianism also is not related to perceptions of the national economy or of personal finances. In short, high authoritarians do not have systematically different preferences or perceptions concerning the national economy.

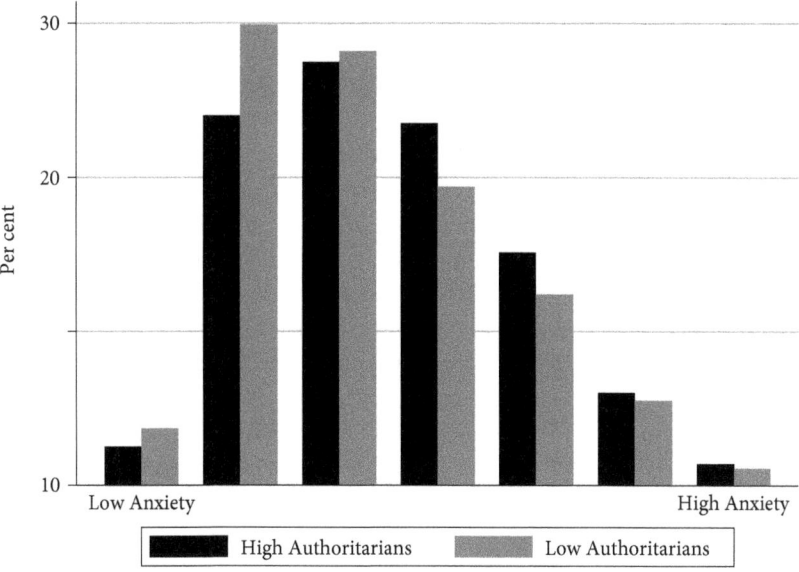

Figure 3.6 Authoritarianism and economic anxiety

Note: Each bar shows the per cent of respondents scoring at that level of economic anxiety among high authoritarians and low authoritarians, respectively. Economic anxiety is calculated as a scale based responses on three questions (see text for details).

Source: British Election Study (Fieldhouse et al. 2014).

Social Attitudes

We should expect to see the sharpest differences between high and low authoritarians in social attitudes. Given that authoritarianism is largely concerned with maintaining social cohesion at the expense of individual autonomy, high authoritarians are likely to have distinct attitudes concerning social identity, values and value change, and punitiveness. High authoritarians should be more likely to hold exclusionary views of social and national identity, to favour traditional social and moral values, and to support punitive measures against crime. I examine each set of attitudes below.

National Identity and Immigration

Theories of authoritarianism suggest that high authoritarians are more likely to hold exclusive social identities (Altemeyer 1996; Stenner 2005). Identifying more closely with members of their own social group, they are more likely to draw clear conceptual boundaries between members of their own group and outsiders who do not belong. There should be two observable manifestations in the survey data.

First, high authoritarians should identify more strongly with and express greater pride in their national group, which should extend to privileging members of their own group over outsiders. Second, high authoritarians should be less willing to support immigration or the naturalization of immigrant-descended residents.

The EVS includes a question asking respondents to indicate their level of national pride. For the sake of analysis, I collapse the response categories so that a value of 1 indicates being 'very proud' while 0 indicates being 'not at all', 'a little', or 'somewhat' proud of one's nation. I expect that high authoritarians are more likely to be 'very proud' than low authoritarians. The BES includes a series of questions measuring national identity. Respondents can place themselves on a scale between 1 ('not at all') and 7 ('very strongly') to indicate how strongly they feel as British and (as appropriate) English, Scottish, or Welsh. The BES also includes a series of questions measuring ethnocentrism. These questions ask respondents to indicate their level of (dis)agreement on a five-point scale to four statements on (1) whether Great Britain can learn from other countries, (2) whether it would be better if other countries were more like Great Britain, (3) whether the respondent feels ashamed to be British, and (4) whether people are too quick to criticize Britain. Answers are recoded so that higher values indicate stronger feelings of ethnocentrism. I estimate regressions on each of these variables (a logistic regression in the case of national pride), with authoritarianism and the usual controls as independent variables. I expect authoritarianism to have a positive coefficient in each analysis, indicating that authoritarianism is associated with higher levels of national pride. Table 3.7 shows the results of these analyses.

In each model, the coefficient for authoritarianism is positive and significant. High authoritarians are more likely to be proud of their nation, to identify with their nation, and to express ethnocentric views. These findings show that high authoritarians express more exclusive views of national identity, while low authoritarians express more inclusive views. There is an important caveat to these findings, which hints at the importance of context. While authoritarianism is significantly related to British identity and also English identity (not shown), the coefficients are not significant when examining Scottish or Welsh identity for respondents living in those nations. However, Scottish high authoritarian respondents are more likely to identify strongly as British. This difference highlights the fact that the link between authoritarianism and national identity is conditioned by political context and elite debate.

What about attitudes towards immigration? The GLES and BES ask respondents to place themselves on eleven-point scales where 0 indicates support for more immigration and 10 means opposition to further immigration. I estimate regression models for each country, and I expect authoritarianism to be positively signed. Table 3.8 shows the results of this analysis, and they are consistent with expectations. High authoritarians are more likely to oppose immigration.

Other surveys contain more specific questions. The EVS asks respondents whether native-born residents should have priority over immigrants when jobs

Table 3.7 Authoritarianism and national identity

Variable	National Pride (EVS)	British Identity (BES)	Ethnocentrism (BES)
Authoritarianism	.36*	.14*	.21*
	(.05)	(.04)	(.04)
Ideology	.15*	.15*	.14*
	(.01)	(.01)	(.01)
Education	−.18*	−.14*	−.06
	(.02)	(.03)	(.03)
Income	.00	−.00	.01
	(.01)	(.01)	(.01)
Gender	−.07	.11	.02
	(.03)	(.05)	(.05)
Age	.07*	.17*	.08*
	(.01)	(.02)	(.02)
Constant	−.66*	4.4*	1.9*
	(.09)	(.15)	(.15)
N	16,450	4,596	603
Root MSE	–	1.5	.56
Adjusted R^2	.04	.10	.34

Note: Figures show unstandardized regression coefficients (logistic regression coefficients in the National Pride model) with standard errors in parentheses, * $p < .01$.

Table 3.8 Authoritarianism and support for immigration

Variable	Germany	Great Britain
Authoritarianism	1.2*	.85*
	(.15)	(.05)
Ideology	.38*	.40*
	(.04)	(.02)
Education	−.82*	−.58*
	(.12)	(.04)
Income	−.00	−.04*
	(.03)	(.01)
Gender	.20	.14
	(.17)	(.07)
Age	−.18*	.19*
	(.06)	(.02)
Constant	7.5*	5.1*
	(.462)	(.21)
N	859	4,636
Root MSE	2.4	2.2
Adjusted R^2	.23	.31

Note: Figures show unstandardized regression coefficients with standard errors in parentheses, * $p < .01$.

are scarce. Responses are coded on a five-point scale with higher values indicating greater agreement that natives should get priority over immigrants. The Swiss Election Study asks a similar question. Respondents are asked to place themselves on a five-point scale where 5 means being 'strongly for' and 1 means being 'strongly against' the proposition that foreigners should have equal opportunities as Swiss natives. The SES also asks whether respondents believe it should be easier for third-generation immigrants to naturalize. Respondents place themselves on a four-point scale where 1 indicates opposition to naturalization and 4 indicates support. I expect that high authoritarians will be more likely to believe that natives should have priority for jobs, to be against equal opportunity for foreigners, and to oppose easing naturalization rules. I estimate linear regression models for each question. Table 3.9 shows the results of the analyses.

The results suggest that high authoritarians consistently hold more exclusionary views on immigration and naturalization. High authoritarians are more likely to believe that native-born residents should have priority over immigrants when jobs are scarce. They are also more likely to disagree that immigrants should have equal opportunities with native-born residents in Switzerland. Finally, they are less likely to agree that third-generation immigrants should have greater opportunities to naturalize. These findings show that high authoritarians express more exclusionary social attitudes on questions relating to national identity and inclusion.

Table 3.9 Authoritarianism and attitudes towards immigrant policies

Variable	Scarce Jobs (EVS)	Equal Opportunity (SES)	Naturalization (SES)
Authoritarianism	.50*	−.27*	−.15*
	(.03)	(.03)	(.03)
Ideology	.13*	−.21*	−.15*
	(.01)	(.01)	(.01)
Education	−.22*	.12*	.11*
	(.01)	(.02)	(.02)
Income	−.05*	.02*	.01
	(.00)	(.01)	(.00)
Gender	.02	−.04	.09*
	(.02)	(.04)	(.03)
Age	.04*	.01	.08*
	(.01)	(.01)	(.01)
Constant	3.2*	3.7*	3.1*
	(.05)	(.10)	(.08)
N	16,171	4,048	3,939
Root MSE	1.2	1.2	.903
Adjusted R^2	.15	.03	.22

Note: Figures show unstandardized regression coefficients with standard errors in parentheses, * p < .01.

Social Values

High authoritarians should be more likely to uphold traditional social values (Altemeyer 1996), meaning that they should differ from low authoritarians in their acceptance of non-conforming or novel social arrangements. In addition, high authoritarians should display greater willingness to employ punitive measures against lawbreakers or deviants. Finally, recent social and demographic changes may lead high authoritarians to express greater nostalgia about the past than low authoritarians.

The EVS and BES include several relevant questions to examine these relationships. First, the EVS asks respondents to indicate on a ten-point scale whether they believe various behaviours are never acceptable (1) or are always acceptable (10). I examine responses to the respective questions on homosexuality and euthanasia, each of which measures approval of non-traditional social behaviour. I also examine responses to the question on the death penalty, which measures support for punitiveness against lawbreakers. High authoritarians should be less likely to approve of homosexuality and euthanasia (which violate traditional norms) but more likely to approve of the death penalty (to punish criminals). The common thread across these three questions is a desire to uphold the normative social order. The BES has three questions, to which respondents indicate on a five-point scale whether they strongly disagree (1) or strongly agree (5). The first prompt is that same-sex couples should have the right to marry if they wish. The second question is whether it is a man's job to earn money and a woman's job to look after the home and family. The third statement asks whether things in Great Britain were better in the past. High authoritarians should be less likely to approve of same-sex marriage (a negative coefficient), more likely to approve of traditional gender roles (positive coefficient), and more likely to agree that things were better in the past (positive coefficient). I estimate regression models of the EVS questions, and the results appear in Table 3.10. Because the BES questions feature skewed distributions, I present these graphically in Figures 3.7, 3.8, and 3.9 without control variables.

The results presented in Table 3.10 are consistent with expectations. High authoritarians are less likely to approve of homosexuality or euthanasia, two behaviours that violate traditional social norms. But high authoritarians are more likely to approve of the use of the death penalty than low authoritarians, suggesting greater approval of harsh punishments against lawbreakers.

The results from the BES presented in Figures 3.7, 3.8, and 3.9 present a more nuanced picture. In each case, high authoritarians respond as expected: they are less likely to approve of same-sex marriage, and more likely to approve of traditional gender roles and to agree that things in the past were better. But these differences are driven more by the skewed distribution of low authoritarians rather than high authoritarians. Less than 10 per cent of low authoritarians

Table 3.10 Authoritarianism and social attitudes

Variable	Homosexuality (EVS)	Euthanasia (EVS)	Death Penalty (EVS)
Authoritarianism	−1.9*	−1.2*	.70*
	(.06)	(.06)	(.06)
Ideology	−.13*	−.05*	.23*
	(.01)	(.01)	(.01)
Education	.45*	.07	−.35*
	(.03)	(.03)	(.03)
Income	.12*	.05*	−.04*
	(.01)	(.01)	(.01)
Gender	−.69*	.23	.32*
	(.04)	(.04)	(.04)
Age	−.25*	−.11*	−.22*
	(.01)	(.01)	(.01)
Constant	7.4*	6.8*	4.1*
	(.11)	(.12)	(.12)
N	15,964	15,908	16,092
Root MSE	2.6	2.8	2.7
Adjusted R^2	.21	.05	.08

Note: Figures show unstandardized regression coefficients with standard errors in parentheses, * $p < .01$.

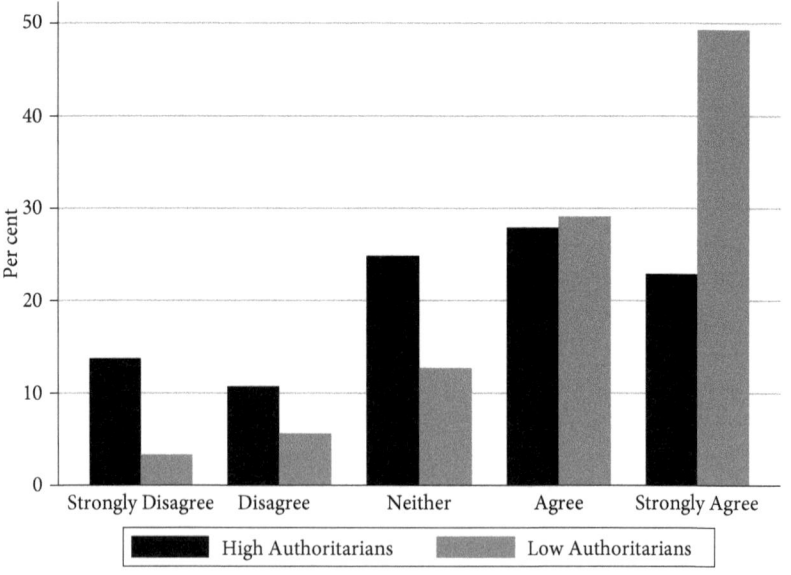

Figure 3.7 Authoritarianism and approval of same-sex marriage

Note: Each bar shows the percentage of respondents answering as indicated to whether same-sex couples should have the right to marry among high authoritarians and low authoritarians, respectively.

Source: British Election Study (Fieldhouse et al. 2014).

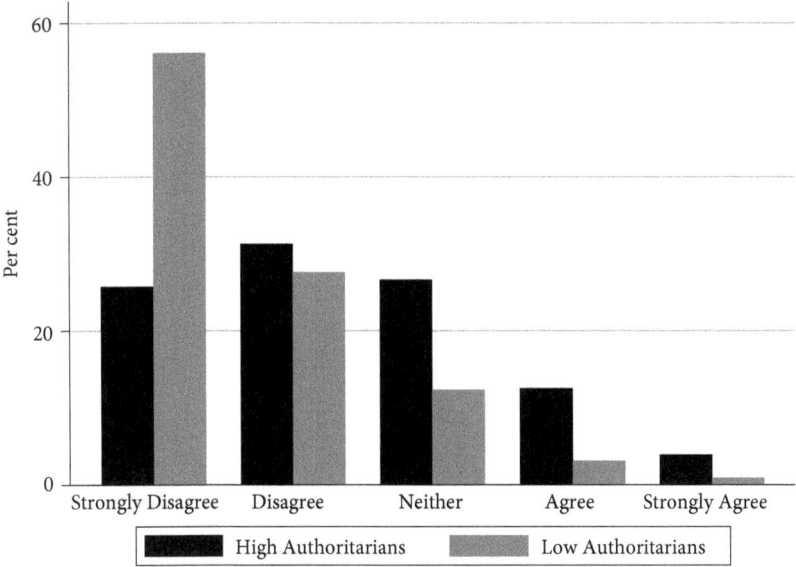

Figure 3.8 Authoritarianism and approval of traditional gender roles

Note: Each bar shows the per cent of respondents answering as indicated to the question of whether it is a man's job to earn money and a woman's job to look after the home and family.

Source: British Election Study (Fieldhouse et al. 2014).

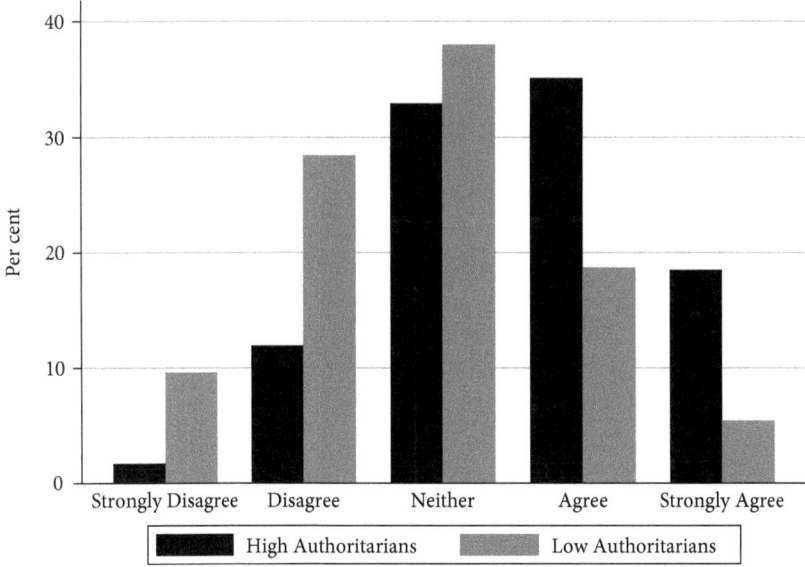

Figure 3.9 Authoritarianism and nostalgia for the past

Note: Each bar shows the percentage of respondents answering as indicated to the question of whether things were better in Britain in the past.

Source: British Election Study (Fieldhouse et al. 2014).

disagree that same-sex couples should be allowed to marry, while over 78 per cent agree. High authoritarians also lean towards approval of same-sex marriage, with about 50 per cent doing so, but there is more balance to their responses as around 24 per cent also disagree. This pattern is repeated for the question concerning traditional gender roles. Over 83 per cent of low authoritarians disagree with the statement, while about 56 per cent of high authoritarians do as well. In short, pluralities or narrow majorities of high authoritarians have adopted mainstream attitudes towards gender roles and same-sex marriage. By contrast, low authoritarians hold these views almost universally. In this sense, one might argue that low authoritarians are remarkable in how they have overwhelmingly adopted these attitudes (and, perhaps, driven broader mainstream acceptance).

Turning to the final question sheds further light on this dynamic. A slight majority of high authoritarians (53.6 per cent) agree that things in the past were better, compared to just less than 25 per cent of low authoritarians. In short, there has been a transition in social attitudes in the past few decades in which low authoritarians have overwhelmingly adopted (and likely driven the acceptance of) mainstream positions on major social and cultural questions such as same-sex marriage. Perhaps to a surprising extent, narrow majorities of high authoritarians have also adopted these values. But, perhaps because they have done so in reaction to changing social norms rather than because these values reflect their worldviews; high authoritarians express greater nostalgia for the past.

In contrast to economic and political attitudes, cultural attitudes vary consistently between high and low authoritarians. High authoritarians display exclusionary attitudes towards social identity, which manifest in greater opposition to immigration, higher levels of ethnocentrism, and support for privileging members of the national in-group over foreigners. High authoritarians are also more likely to support traditional moral and social values, leading to reduced acceptance of homosexuality, same-sex marriage, euthanasia, and non-traditional gender roles. As a result, high authoritarians also express more nostalgia for the recent past, presumably because it reflects a time before demographic and value changes that they view negatively.

The findings about social values raise an important question about the roots of the worldview evolution. Are high authoritarians 'out of touch' when it comes to contemporary social and cultural norms, or do they still hold values that low authoritarians have quickly abandoned in favour of more liberal values? As the British findings concerning same-sex marriage and traditional gender roles show, low authoritarians express virtual consensus in their support of same-sex marriage and rejection of traditional gender roles. Given that these cross-tabulations lump together low authoritarians of all classes, gender, religions, ages, and educational backgrounds, these are fairly remarkable findings. Many readers will likely share the view that these changing social norms reflect progress towards a more just and equal society. High authoritarians are more dispersed in their responses to these questions, indicating that many have accepted values changes that have quickly become mainstream while others hold more traditional beliefs. These results illustrate an important point about the conditions driving the worldview evolution: the political and social mainstream of West European societies has shifted away from values and priorities held by high authoritarians towards those favoured by low authoritarians. Not surprisingly, low authoritarians have quickly and broadly embraced these values while high authoritarians have not. But it should remind us that the worldview evolution—while manifesting in changing political behaviour among high authoritarians—is also at least partially a response to the growing mainstream dominance of low authoritarians.

Conclusion

This chapter has examined the distribution of authoritarianism in contemporary West European societies and compared the differences between high and low authoritarians on political, economic, and social attitudes. Several important results emerge from these analyses. First, authoritarianism is distributed relatively normally throughout West European societies, though there has been a gradual shift towards the low authoritarian pole since 1990. Second, while authoritarian has little relationship to age or gender, it is more clearly related to education. High authoritarians display lower levels of educational attainment on average than low authoritarians. It is beyond the scope of this analysis to uncover the reasons for this association, but this association is important to the extent that higher education is increasingly central to many occupations and social networks—which influence life opportunities and the transmission of political ideas. Finally, authoritarianism relates strongly to socio-cultural attitudes, to political attitudes on some dimensions, and relatively little to economic attitudes.

The fact that authoritarianism relates most strongly to socio-cultural attitudes hints at the possible reason for evolutions in political behaviour. Because high authoritarians vary from low authoritarians mostly in their views towards social identity and values, it is most likely that the factors leading high authoritarians to support the radical right and oppose European integration are related to those issues. By contrast, the relative lack of difference in economic attitudes makes it harder to envision how economic concerns could drive the evolution of political behaviour described in this book. Instead, value change and immigration would be more likely drivers of high authoritarians' increasing rejection of the European Union and support of populist radical right parties. The subsequent chapters explore these relationships and how they have evolved over the past several decades.

4

Threat to National Community?

Authoritarianism and Attitudes towards the European Union

The Puzzle of Rising Euroscepticism

'United in Diversity' is the motto of the European Union (EU). As a motto, it signifies several important features of the EU: its important role in promoting peace in post-war Europe; its success in expanding to include twenty-eight member states; the wide range of cultures, languages, and religions within its borders; and so on. Like any motto, it is also presumably intended to serve as an advertisement of sorts—a description of its virtues. But could this motto also inadvertently illustrate why the EU has become polarizing in the twenty-first century? If the idea of a continent of diverse nationalities becoming more unified appeals, then this motto and the project of European integration would resonate. However, many other Europeans find the idea of subordinating one's nation to a broader European community threatening. This motto and the project of European integration will repel such individuals. The argument presented in this chapter is that the former group of individuals—low authoritarians—are more likely to support the EU while the latter group—high authoritarians—are more likely to oppose it.

Developments in recent years have raised a variety of important questions for scholars of public opinion towards the EU. What structures mass EU attitudes in the present era, and how has that changed since the 1990s? Why have European publics become increasingly polarized over further European integration or EU enlargement? And why has this opposition become important enough to result in outcomes such as the rejection of the proposed Constitutional Treaty in 2005 by French and Dutch voters, or the British vote in 2016 to leave the EU?

Chapter 2 presents a theory arguing that mass attitudes and behaviour in West Europe is increasingly structured by authoritarianism. This theory argues that changes in the political-economic environment combined with the electoral strategies of political elites have made this shift in attitudes and party loyalties possible. One manifestation of this shift can be seen in the structure of EU attitudes. While existing scholarship on EU attitudes has tended to emphasize utilitarian (economic) or social identity (cultural) explanations, this chapter presents an argument and evidence that authoritarianism structures attitudes towards the EU.

Authoritarianism and the Evolution of West European Electoral Politics. Erik R. Tillman, Oxford University Press.
© Erik R. Tillman 2021. DOI: 10.1093/oso/9780192896223.003.0004

This chapter proceeds in several stages. First, it reviews existing research on EU support, evaluating the weaknesses of prior theories. The following section builds on the discussion in Chapter 2 to articulate the argument linking authoritarianism to EU attitudes and developing a series of predictions, tests of which are presented subsequently. The final analysis in this chapter tests a specific implication of this argument—that high authoritarians are more sensitive to the threats to social cohesion caused by the EU—using data collected in Germany. The findings of these analyses are consistent with expectations. High authoritarians are less likely to support European integration or enlargement of the EU, and they are more likely to perceive European integration as a threat to national culture and sovereignty. Moreover, high authoritarians are more likely to hold exclusionary social identities of the sort that previous studies have used to explain EU support (e.g. Carey 2002; McLaren 2002; Azrout et al. 2011; Hobolt et al. 2011; de Vreese et al. 2012).

Understanding EU Attitudes

Scholars of the European Union have been studying EU attitudes since the 1970s. Over the years, researchers have developed a number of arguments to explain EU support in response to changing conditions. There have been three main waves of the literature. Early scholarship developed the 'permissive consensus' argument, which described public opinion as mostly positive and weakly held (Lindberg and Scheingold 1970). A second wave in the 1990s emphasized utilitarian arguments based on perceived gains and losses from European integration (e.g. Eichenberg and Dalton 1993; Gabel 1998). Finally, a third wave in the twenty-first century has drawn on social identity theory to explain EU attitudes.

In the first several decades of European integration, public opinion was not considered important. In large part, this view reflected the overriding strategy of European integration as an elite project that was largely isolated from public view. Also, European integration had little visible effect on the lives of most citizens. Instead, state leaders tended to justify it as contributing to post-war peace and prosperity. Since there were relatively few dissenting voices in public debates, public opinion tended to follow the elite cues. As a result, public opinion was generally supportive of European integration, but these positive attitudes were held weakly—most Europeans had little knowledge or interest in European integration. This situation led scholars of the time to describe public opinion as providing a 'permissive consensus' in favour of continued elite-driven integration (Lindberg and Scheingold 1970).

The study of EU attitudes expanded in the 1990s in response to events. The controversies surrounding the adoption of the Treaty on European Union (Maastricht Treaty) along with increasing opposition in polls led to renewed interest in public opinion towards the EU. The Maastricht Treaty was significant because it established the common market, making it more visible to Europeans. A number of early studies highlighted the importance of utilitarian factors, suggesting that citizen evaluations of the EU were rooted in perceptions of economic gains or losses (e.g. Eichenberg and Dalton 1993). An important book emphasized human capital as a key explanatory factor (Gabel 1998). According to this argument, Europeans with higher education, occupational status, and income stood to benefit from economic integration, while less-educated, working-class Europeans stood to lose economically. Evidence in support of this argument suggested that West Europeans were evaluating the EU increasingly in terms of whether it benefited their personal economic fortunes (Gabel 1998)—and, to a lesser extent, their national economy (Gabel and Palmer 1995).

A rival set of studies during the following years emphasized the role of domestic political judgments as proxies for EU opinions. Citizens take cues from national political leaders (Anderson 1998), and they may also base their EU attitudes on their judgments of the democratic performance of national and EU institutions (Rohrschneider 2002; Sanchez-Cuenca 2000). As with the utilitarian studies, the key point of this research is that citizens base EU attitudes on *evaluations* of a political object (the EU, their domestic government, etc.). These models collectively assume that citizen opinion is driven primarily by cognitive processes and a cost–benefit model, both of which conflict with the observation that citizens lack knowledge about the EU or its policies (Anderson 1998).

A third wave of studies emerged in the twenty-first century that drew on various aspects of social identity theory (Tajfel 1978). While using different measures, these studies shared in common the core argument that individuals who hold exclusionary social identities are less likely to support European integration. This core finding has held up across a wide range of measures (which are typically examined in isolation from related social identity measures). Citizens who identify exclusively with their nation are less likely to support EU membership (Carey 2002; Christin and Trechsel 2002; Hooghe and Marks 2005) or the further expansion of EU powers (Luedtke 2005). Similarly, hostility towards members of outside cultures or nationalities also is associated with opposition to EU membership or further European integration (McLaren 2002; Elgün and Tillman 2007), as is opposition to immigration (de Vreese and Boomgaarden 2005), or hostility towards members of foreign religions and Islam in particular (Azrout et al. 2011; Hobolt et al. 2011; de Vreese et al. 2012). These findings have produced a strong body of evidence that 'attitudes toward the European Union tend to be based in great part on a general hostility toward other cultures' (McLaren 2002: 564).

This book's analysis builds on this last wave of research while attempting to provide a stronger theoretical basis. In particular, the argument linking authoritarianism to EU attitudes explains why this negative relationship exists in the current era but not in previous decades, which arguments based solely on social identity cannot offer. Moreover, it provides a better explanation of why various measures of social identity correlate with opposition to European integration. Thus, this chapter's argument builds on the existing literature while improving our understanding of the structure of EU attitudes.

Authoritarianism and EU Attitudes

The central argument of this book is that mass attitudes in the twenty-first century are increasingly structured by authoritarianism, a result of the shifting nature of political conflict in the past two decades. As party conflict is increasingly structured along a dimension of issues related to identity and demarcation, new parties organized around cultural issues appeal to high and low authoritarians in ways that earlier eras of party conflict did not. The shift in EU attitudes is one observable consequence of this worldview evolution.

High authoritarians are likely to perceive European integration as a threat to the normative social and political order. As the EU has expanded institutionally and geographically in its efforts to establish the common market and enlarge across the continent, critics argue that it undermines national sovereignty and cohesion. The creation of a new, supranational political organization threatens the established political order based on the traditional nation state. The establishment of European symbols, including the common passport and the common currency, reinforces this notion of a threat against national community and political order. Finally, the free movement of people within the EU threatens social cohesion. In short, the EU in the twenty-first century increasingly threatens traditional conceptions of the cohesive national community and the authoritative nation state.

These developments alone are not sufficient to generate opposition from high authoritarians. The reordering of EU attitudes by authoritarianism has occurred in response to increased elite conflict over Europe. Political entrepreneurs looking to expand their electoral support by restructuring party conflict have benefited from criticizing the EU as a threat to national cohesion and sovereignty. In doing so, they have contributed to the development of a two-sided information flow over European integration (Zaller 1992) and expanded the debate to include more anti-EU arguments. Whereas mainstream elite messages were previously more pro-EU (while not emphasizing the issue greatly), the emergence of Eurosceptical political elites has created a debate over Europe structured along a cosmopolitan/nationalist dimension (Hooghe and Marks 2009; Kriesi et al. 2012; de Vries and Hobolt 2012). These anti-EU messages, which are rooted in the defence of national community and sovereignty, appeal to high authoritarians who fear threats to social cohesion and tradition. Pro-EU elites have responded to these arguments by emphasizing the benefits of the EU for individual autonomy and diversity. These arguments appeal to low authoritarians but are threatening to high authoritarians. This structure of elite conflict has led to a similar development of mass attitudes towards the EU.

As a result, high authoritarians should be more likely to express negative opinions of the EU and to oppose efforts at further integration or enlargement. By contrast, low authoritarians are less likely to oppose the EU as they are not concerned about the threat to social cohesion. Instead, elite arguments emphasizing individual autonomy or diversity resonate with low authoritarians, increasing the probability that they support the EU.

The discussion thus far suggests that high authoritarians have become increasingly negative towards the EU—motivated by concerns emphasized by political elites of a threat to national cohesion and sovereignty. The result today is that authoritarianism structures EU attitudes in the current era. High authoritarians are likely to oppose further European integration, or further enlargement of the EU, while low authoritarians are more likely to support the EU. How does this argument relate to extant findings linking exclusionary social identities (e.g. national identity, hostility to foreign religions) to EU attitudes?

Contemporary theories of authoritarianism argue that high authoritarians seek to maintain social cohesion and security at the expense of individual autonomy (e.g. Feldman and Stenner 1997; Feldman 2003; Stenner 2005). As a result, high authoritarians are more likely to identify with the normative social order and to oppose threats to it. As such, high authoritarians should be more likely to hold exclusionary social identity attitudes, insofar as these reflect greater attachment to the normative social order and hostility towards threats to it.

Authoritarianism correlates positively with exclusionary social identities (Stenner 2005: 95–116; see also Hetherington and Weiler 2009), but it is not clear whether one is causally prior to the other. The expansive literature on authoritarianism does not provide clear guidance, with earlier scales of authoritarianism including measures of ethnocentrism (e.g. Adorno et al. 1950; Altemeyer 1996). However, recent studies have reconceptualized authoritarianism as a predisposition leading to the formation of worldview favouring the maintenance of social cohesion and order over individual autonomy (Feldman 2003; Stenner 2005; Hetherington and Weiler 2009). Moreover, recent studies use child-rearing measures, which are more likely to be causally distinct from the attitudes they should explain and less likely to be 'contaminated' by current political debates. As a result, there is reason to believe that the observed relationships between social identity variables and EU attitudes are at least partially endogenous to authoritarianism. High authoritarians should be more likely to express exclusionary social identities, and in turn to oppose the EU, while low authoritarians should be less likely to embrace exclusionary social identities and more likely to support the EU.

The preceding discussion generates four hypotheses. The first predicts a negative relationship between authoritarianism and attitudes towards the EU. The second hypothesis predicts that authoritarianism also affects attitudes related to social identity. Specifically, authoritarians should be more likely to express a strong national identity, pride in their nationality, opposition to immigration, hostility towards foreign religions, and resistance towards the adoption of a European identity. The third hypothesis predicts that authoritarianism should operate through these social identity variables to predict EU attitudes, indicating that these social identity variables are partially endogenous to authoritarianism. Thus, authoritarianism has both a direct effect and an indirect effect (through these social identity attitudes) on EU attitudes. Finally, high authoritarians should be more likely to fear the effects of European integration on national culture and sovereignty.

Hypothesis One: High authoritarians should be more likely to oppose the EU, efforts at further European integration, and efforts to enlarge the EU.

Hypothesis Two: Individuals scoring higher on measures of authoritarianism should be more likely to express exclusionary social identity—including pride in their nationality, opposition to immigration, and hostility towards outside religions.

Hypothesis Three: Authoritarianism has an indirect effect on EU support operating through the social identity variables.

Hypothesis Four: High authoritarians should express more fears about the loss of national culture and sovereignty due to European integration.

Authoritarianism, Social Identity, and EU Attitudes

The analysis includes data from cross-national and national election surveys. The choice of surveys is driven by the inclusion of appropriate survey questions—in particular, measures of authoritarianism. The analysis proceeds in three stages. The first set of analyses examines the relationship between authoritarianism and support for the EU. The second analyses examine the more complex relationship between authoritarianism, social identity attitudes, and EU attitudes. The final set of analyses draw on a unique set of questions to examine the relationship between authoritarianism and perceptions of threat from European integration. To preview the results shown below, the findings of these analyses are consistent with the hypotheses described above.

Authoritarianism and EU Support

The first analyses consider the direct relationship between authoritarianism and EU support. Data come from four national election surveys conducted in

Austria (2013) (Kritzinger et al. 2014), Finland (2011) (Finnish National Election Study 2015), Germany (May 2014 panel) (Rattinger et al. 2014), and Great Britain (February–March 2014) (Fieldhouse et al. 2019), along with the 2017 wave of the cross-national European Values Survey (EVS) (EVS 2019). All contain questions to measure EU support, authoritarianism, and other relevant factors. Due to differences in the design of each election study, there are minor variations in the questions and coding schemes used in each analysis. Of particular interest is the dependent variable. In Austria, Germany, and Great Britain, the dependent variable measures responses on an eleven-point scale to a question asking whether European integration has already gone too far (0) or should go further (10). In Finland, the dependent variable asks similarly whether it would be very good (0) or very bad (10) if Finland became *less* attached to the EU (hence, higher values indicate greater EU support). The EVS includes a different question asking respondents to indicate their level of trust in the EU on a four-point scale, with answers ranging from 'none at all' (1) to 'a great deal' (4). The EVS also includes a question asking respondents to indicate on a ten-point scale whether they believe enlargement of the EU has gone too far already (1) or should go further (10). The main independent variable measuring authoritarianism also varies between countries. In Germany, it is constructed from three items using the child-rearing scale. The EVS asks respondents to pick up to five desired qualities in children from a list including a mix of authoritarian, non-authoritarian, and irrelevant items. The measure of authoritarianism indicates the ratio of authoritarian to non-authoritarian items. In Austria, Finland, and Great Britain, it is constructed using several items measuring authoritarian values. There are minor differences in the wording and measurement of control variables, but I include a common set of variables including attitudes towards immigration (higher values mean more opposition to immigration), left–right ideology, preferences towards economic policy, and evaluations of the national economy. I also include demographic variables measuring respondent income, educational attainment, age, gender, and whether the respondent is a student or retiree.

I start by examining descriptive patterns, which appear in Figures 4.1, 4.2, and 4.3. Figure 4.1 shows the mean level of EU trust by authoritarianism among the respondents in the EVS sample. Low authoritarians indicate about 0.18 points more trust in the EU (on a 1–4 scale) compared to high authoritarians. This negative pattern is in the expected direction, but the strength of this relationship is very modest. In part, this modest association probably reflects the use of EU trust, rather than a more direct measure of support for integration. Figure 4.2 shows the same relationship among German respondents, with the use of the child-rearing measures of authoritarianism and a measure of support for European integration. Here, the relationship is stronger, with high authoritarians being substantially less likely to support further European integration than low authoritarians. Finally, Figure 4.3 shows the relationship between authoritarianism

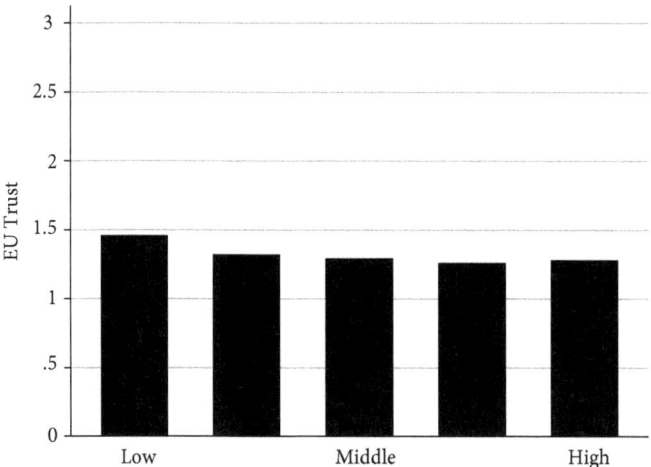

Figure 4.1 Mean level of EU trust by authoritarianism

Note: Each bar shows the mean level of EU Trust among respondents at each level of authoritarianism, with higher values indicating greater trust.

Source: EVS 2019.

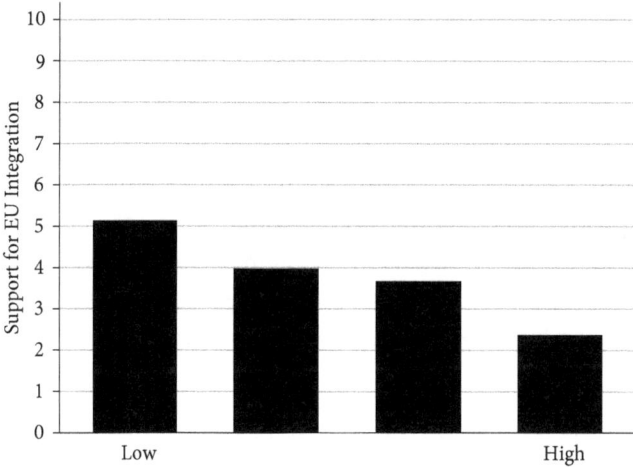

Figure 4.2 Mean support for EU integration by authoritarianism

Note: Each bar indicates the mean level of support for European integration (higher values indicate greater support) for respondents at each level of authoritarianism.

Source: German Longitudinal Election Study (Rattinger et al. 2014).

and the mean level of support for enlargement in the EVS data. The association is negative and relatively strong, with high authoritarians having a mean response more than 1 point lower than low authoritarians. In short, these descriptive patterns are in the expected direction, with high authoritarians being less favourable on average towards the EU.

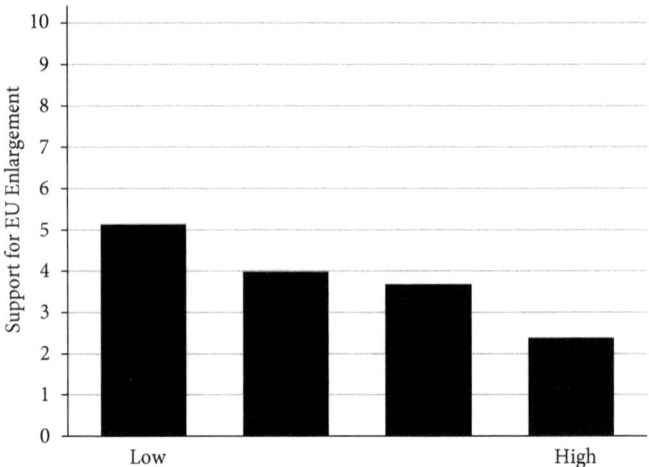

Figure 4.3 Mean support for EU enlargement by authoritarianism

Note: Each bar shows the mean level of support for further enlargement of the European Union (higher values indicate greater support) for respondents at each level of authoritarianism.

Source: EVS 2019.

The next question is whether these broad patterns hold in multivariate analyses of individual survey responses. The results of these analyses are presented in Tables 4.1 and 4.2. Table 4.1 reports the results from the analysis of the 2017 EVS data. Because respondents are nested within different member states, this analysis uses a multilevel regression design (Steenbergen and Jones 2002; Gelman and Hill 2007). *Authoritarianism* has a negative and significant coefficient, indicating that high authoritarians are less likely to trust the EU. This relationship holds even when measures of attitudes towards immigration, national pride, and hostility towards foreign religions are included.[1] The same pattern of results holds true in Table 4.2, where in each model higher scores on authoritarianism are associated with less support for European integration. These analyses include slightly fewer control variables due to the lack of consistent availability across national election surveys. Nonetheless, a measure of attitudes towards immigration is included in each, and *Authoritarianism* still has a negative and significant coefficient in each model. The coefficients for other control variables are inconsistent, though most are in the expected direction. In short, the results suggest a consistent negative relationship across different samples and different measurements of each variable between authoritarianism and support for the EU.

Does the same finding hold true for attitudes towards further EU enlargement? To examine that question, I use the 2017 wave of the European Values Survey. I

---

[1] Surprisingly, *National Pride* has a positive coefficient, indicating that those who are more proud in their nationality are more likely to trust the EU. While there are plausible reasons for this finding, it likely reflects that this variable does not measure exclusionary social identity well. However, the EVS does not include a measure of exclusive national identity.

Table 4.1 Authoritarianism and trust in the European Union

Variable	Coefficient	Standard Error
Authoritarianism	−.06*	.02
Immigration	−.20*	.02
Religious Hostility	−.29*	.03
National Pride	.11*	.02
Ideology	−.02*	.00
Economic Scale	.01*	.01
Religiosity	.06*	.01
Education	.02	.01
Income	.02*	.00
Manager	.07*	.02
Unskilled	−.07*	.02
Retired	.13*	.02
Unemployed	−.02	.04
Student	.25*	.04
Farmer	.04	.06
Gender	−.02	.02
Age	−.04*	.01
Locality	.03*	.01
Constant	2.3*	.07
N	9,654	
Chi Squared	791.3	

Note: Figures show unstandardized multilevel least-squares regression coefficients with standard errors in parentheses, * $p < .05$.

Source: EVS 2019.

include the same set of variables, with the exception that the dependent variable measures support for enlargement, which is measured on an eleven-point scale.[2] As in Table 4.1, the cell entries show the results of a multi-level model with a regression link to account for the fact that respondents are clustered within states (Steenbergen and Jones 2002; Gelman and Hill 2007). The results are presented in Table 4.3.

The results show that authoritarianism is associated with reduced support for enlargement. This finding is consistent with this chapter's argument while adding further nuance. High authoritarians are more likely to oppose expanding the powers of the EU and to oppose expanding the EU to include more member states. One interpretation is that high authoritarians fear increasing diversity (i.e. a loss of social cohesion) in addition to a loss of national control, which motivates opposition to enlargement as well as integration. An alternative interpretation that assumes less cognitive sophistication is that high authoritarians broadly oppose all expansions of the EU's power or reach because they view it as a threat

---

[2] This model does not include *National Pride*. Other analyses including it found it to have a coefficient close to 0 and far from statistical significance.

Table 4.2 Authoritarianism and support for European integration

Variable	Austria	Finland	Germany	Great Britain
Authoritarianism	−.64*	−.19*	−.39*	−.63*
	(.13)	(.04)	(.17)	(.05)
Immigration	−.68*	−.14*	−.39*	−.50*
	(.09)	(.02)	(.04)	(.02)
Ideology	−.15*	.06*	−.05	−.22*
	(.04)	(.02)	(.05)	(.02)
Economic Scale	.07	.09*	.03	−.14*
	(.11)	(.04)	(.04)	(.05)
Retrospective Economy	.59*	.19*	.24*	−.06
	(.08)	(.05)	(.11)	(.03)
Education	.15	.19*	.31*	.24*
	(.14)	(.05)	(.14)	(.04)
Retired	.40	−.06	.41	−.09
	(.23)	(.12)	(.30)	(.09)
Student	−.21	.45*	.04	.37
	(.38)	(.19)	(.38)	(.42)
Income	−.02	.04*	−.01	.02
	(.02)	(.01)	(.04)	(.01)
Gender	−.01	−.09	−.41*	−.25*
	(.15)	(.04)	(.19)	(.06)
Age	−.25*	.09*	−.07	−.10*
	(.07)	(.04)	(.10)	(.03)
Constant	5.5*	1.5*	7.0*	9.4*
	(.67)	(.32)	(.82)	(.25)
N	1963	675	762	10,047
Root MSE	2.4	1.0	2.5	2.6
R^2	0.23	0.28	0.23	0.32

Note: Figures show unstandardized least-squares regression coefficients with standard errors in parentheses, * $p < .05$.

to the normative social order within their own state. Either way, high authoritarians are more likely to oppose both European integration and EU enlargement.

Incorporating Social Identity

As described above, an extensive literature already shows that various measures of exclusive social identity have a negative relationship with EU support.[3] To what

---

[3] Carey 2002; Christin and Trechsel 2002; McLaren 2002; de Vreese and Boomgaarden 2005; Hooghe and Marks 2005; Luedtke 2005; Elgün and Tillman 2007; Azrout et al. 2011; Hobolt et al. 2011; de Vreese et al. 2012.

Table 4.3 Authoritarianism and support for EU enlargement

Variable	Coefficient	Standard Error
Authoritarianism	−.39*	.07
Immigration	−.71*	.06
Religious Hostility	−.60*	.11
Ideology	−.14*	.01
Economic Scale	−.06*	.02
Religiosity	.10*	.03
Education	−.02	.04
Income	.00	.01
Manager	.16*	.06
Unskilled	−.09	.08
Retired	.18*	.08
Student	.34*	.13
Unemployed	−.05	.13
Farmer	−.11	.20
Gender	.08	.05
Age	−.21*	.02
Constant	6.3*	.22
N	10,858	
Chi Squared	939.7	

Note: Figures show unstandardized multilevel regression coefficients and standard errors, * p < .05.

Source: EVS 2019.

extent does theorizing about and including a measure of authoritarianism advance our understanding beyond these findings? To contribute to the literature, this chapter should demonstrate that authoritarianism adds explanatory power to our understanding of EU support. To address that question, I use the 2017 EVS data to examine the link between authoritarianism, social identity, and EU support.

In the analysis that follows, I use several measures of exclusionary social identity. First, attitudes towards immigration are measured using a question asking respondents if they agree that natives should get priority over immigrants when jobs are scarce. Higher values indicate greater agreement with this sentiment. High authoritarians should favour more restrictive immigration practices (i.e. *Authoritarianism* should have a positive coefficient). Second, *National Pride* is scored 1 if the respondent indicates being 'very proud' of his/her nationality and 0 if he or she indicates some or no pride. Although this variable does not properly measure exclusionary national identity, high authoritarians should be more likely to express pride in their nationality, and those scoring high in national pride should oppose the loss of national sovereignty or changes to national culture.

I include a variable measuring levels of hostility towards members of other religions. The EVS presents respondents with a list of different groups of people and asks whether the respondent would prefer not to have such people as neighbours. Of this list, two are minority religious groups across Western Europe: Muslims and Jews. I score each mention of a preference not to have members of either group as neighbours as 0.5. Adding these two scores together produces the variable *Religious Hostility*, which has values of 0 (no hostility towards either group), 0.5 (hostility towards one of the two groups), or 1 (hostility towards both groups).[4] Notably, this variable includes members of one religion (Muslims) that might appear threatening to respondents given concerns over Islamic terrorism, but it also includes another (Jews) who are not associated with contemporary security threats in most European societies (though Jews are often blamed in nationalist conspiracy theories). High authoritarians should be more likely to express a preference not to have members of these groups as neighbours, and this in turn should be associated with greater opposition to the EU.

Table 4.4 presents the results of the analyses of the relationship between authoritarianism and each of these social identity variables in a multivariate model. In each model, *Authoritarianism* is significant and in the expected direction. High authoritarians are more likely to express pride in their nationality, more likely to oppose immigration, and more likely to express hostility towards members of foreign religions.[5] All of these findings are consistent with the argument that high authoritarians endorse more exclusive forms of social identity. This result is important given recent work highlighting the relationship between exclusive social identity and opposition to European integration.[6]

This finding suggests that the observed relationship between exclusive social identity and EU attitudes may be partially explained by authoritarianism. If social identity variables are at least partially endogenous to authoritarianism, then authoritarianism should have an indirect effect on EU attitudes running through those social identity variables. This possibility raises the questions of whether authoritarianism has a direct effect on EU attitudes independent of its effect on social identity, and whether the social identity variables have a significant, independent effect on EU attitudes once the effect of authoritarianism is modelled.

The appropriate way to model this relationship is to estimate a path analysis using the tools of structural equation modelling (SEM) because regression models cannot test for the presence of indirect effects. The path analysis allows the analyst to specify and test the effects of variables operating through multiple paths instead of assuming each explanatory variable to have an independent and simultaneous effect as in standard regression models. In particular, SEMs allow for the analyst to specify whether independent variables are exogenous (as in a standard regression model) or endogenous to other independent variables included in the model (Kline 2011). I expect that *Authoritarianism* is exogenous

---

[4] Including separate dummy variables measuring hostility towards each of these two religious groups generated the same substantive findings.

[5] In a previous analysis, Tillman (2013) found the same substantive results presented in this section when analysing the 2008–9 wave of the EVS, in addition to finding that high authoritarians are less likely to identify as European in any form—indicating rejection of an inclusive national/European identity.

[6] See note 3 for sources.

Table 4.4 Authoritarianism and exclusionary social identity

Variable	National Pride	Immigration	Religious Hostility
Authoritarianism	.36*	.71*	.05*
	(.06)	(.06)	(.01)
Ideology	.11*	.20*	.01*
	(.01)	(.01)	(.00)
Economic Scale	.09*	.03*	−.00
	(.02)	(.02)	(.00)
Religiosity	.12*	−.07*	−.01*
	(.02)	(.02)	(.00)
Education	−.17*	−.24*	−.01*
	(.03)	(.03)	(.00)
Income	−.00	−.05*	−.00*
	(.01)	(.01)	(.00)
Manager	−.12*	−.30*	−.01*
	(.05)	(.05)	(.01)
Unskilled	−.06	.19*	.03*
	(.06)	(.07)	(.01)
Retired	.06	.13	−.02*
	(.07)	(.07)	(.01)
Student	−.20	−.36*	−.02
	(.12)	(.12)	(.01)
Unemployed	.05	.12	−.04*
	(.11)	(.11)	(.01)
Farmer	−.30	.15	.02
	(.17)	(.18)	(.02)
Gender	.00	.08	.02*
	(.04)	(.05)	(.00)
Age	.06*	.05*	.01*
	(.02)	(.02)	(.00)
Constant	−.87*	−.38	.12*
	.25	(.29)	(.02)
N	10,630	11,261	11,365
Chi Squared	507.3*	1101.6*	650.4*

Note: Figures show unstandardized multilevel logistic regression coefficients for National Pride and Immigration, and unstandardized multilevel regression coefficients for Religious Hostility with standard errors in parentheses, * $p < .05$.

(along with the control variables) and to exert a direct effect upon the dependent variable and the four social identity variables.[7] I also expect *Authoritarianism* to

---

[7] I tested for the possibility that *Authoritarianism* is not exogenous by specifying alternative path analyses in which the social identity variables and measures of religion, religiosity, and age predicted *Authoritarianism*. While these variables had significant effects in some cases, the underlying relationship between authoritarianism, social identity, and EU support was unaffected. I present the model that reflects the theorized relationship.

have an indirect effect through the social identity variables, meaning that the effect of the social identity variables on EU attitudes is endogenous to authoritarianism. These indirect effects represent the effect of *Authoritarianism* running through each of the social identity variables, and they are independent of the direct effect estimated in the model.

I use the 2017 EVS data to estimate this relationship. *EU Trust* is the dependent variable. *Immigration*, *National Pride*, and *Religious Hostility* are endogenous variables, while *Authoritarianism* and the other control variables shown in Table 4.5 are exogenous. The results are presented in Table 4.5. The coefficients in Table 4.5 show that *Authoritarianism* has a significant effect in the expected direction on each endogenous variable: high authoritarians are more likely to favour natives over immigrants, to express hostility towards members of foreign religions, and to express pride in their nation. The endogenous variables also have a significant effect in the expected direction on *EU Trust*. Even with these endogenous relationships included in the model, the direct relationship between *Authoritarianism* and *EU Trust* is significant. Figure 4.4 shows a simplified graphical display of the relationship between the key variables. The standardized

Table 4.5 Direct and indirect effects of authoritarianism on EU attitudes

Variable	Immigration	Religious Hostility	National Pride	EU Trust
Immigration	–	–	–	−.21*
				(.01)
Religious Hostility	–	–	–	−.31*
				(.03)
National Pride	–	–	–	.10*
				(.01)
Authoritarianism	.18*	.05*	.09*	−.04*
	(.01)	(.01)	(.01)	(.02)
Ideology	.04*	.01*	.03*	−.02*
	(.00)	(.00)	(.00)	(.00)
Education	−.08*	−.02*	−.04*	.05*
	(.01)	(.00)	(.01)	(.01)
Income	−.02*	−.00*	.00	.01*
	(.00)	(.00)	(.00)	(.00)
Gender	.01	.02*	−.03*	−.03*
	(.01)	(.00)	(.01)	(.01)
Age	−.00	.00*	.02*	−.03*
	(.00)	(.00)	(.00)	(.00)
Constant	.55*	.08*	.37*	2.5*
	(.02)	(.01)	(.02)	(.04)
N	14,153			
Chi Squared	691.8*			

Note: Figures show unstandardized structural equational model regression coefficients with standard errors in parentheses, * p < .05.

coefficient next to each solid line represents a direct effect between those two variables in the indicated direction. By following the paths going through the social identity variables, one can observe the indirect effects of *Authoritarianism* on *EU Trust*. These indirect effects are the product of the direct effect of *Authoritarianism* on the social identity variable and that social identity variable's direct effect on *EU Trust*. For example, the indirect effect of *Authoritarianism* on *EU Trust* running through *Immigration* is –.021 (0.23 * –0.093). Using the results of the model presented in Table 4.5, the total effect of *Authoritarianism* on *EU Trust* measured in standardized coefficients is –.042 (–.082 in unstandardized coefficients), which represents the direct effect and the product of the three indirect effects.

These results demonstrate several key points. First, they show that the relationship between authoritarianism and EU attitudes is robust to the inclusion of measures of social identity. Second, part of the observed relationship between exclusionary social identity and EU attitudes is endogenous to authoritarianism. Thus, future scholars should give more attention to the role of dispositional factors such as authoritarianism when considering the relationship between exclusionary social attitudes and political behaviour. Finally, they support the interpretation that the negative relationship between authoritarianism and EU support derives from the perceived threat that the EU poses to the normative social order. Because the effect of authoritarianism partially operates through exclusionary social identity variables, it suggests that high authoritarians oppose the EU because they wish to preserve the cohesion of their national societies from demographic change. The next section tests this argument further.

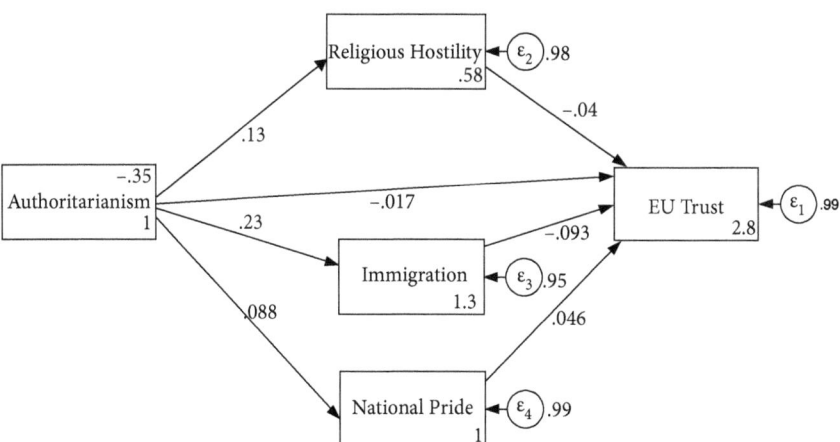

Figure 4.4 Path analysis of authoritarianism, social identity, and EU support

Note: The chart shows a path analysis with standardized coefficients. For ease of presentation and interpretation, no control variables are included in the model. All coefficients are significant at the 0.05 level.

Source: EVS 2019.

Authoritarianism and Perceived Threat from European Integration

The previous section presents evidence that authoritarianism is negatively associated with support for European integration. The argument is based on the idea that the EU poses a threat to the social cohesion and order—what Stenner (2005) terms the 'normative order'. High authoritarians are more sensitive to such threats, so they respond with greater hostility towards the sources of these threats. Because most elite arguments against the EU emphasize the threat that it poses to the normative order, high authoritarians are more likely to oppose the EU. So far, high authoritarians' perception of threat from the EU has been assumed rather than measured. While this assumption seems reasonable given the expanding powers of the EU and the increased elite debate focusing on this possible threat, it bears examining whether high authoritarians actually perceive more threat from the EU than low authoritarians. This section presents an analysis of this question.

The role of threat is central to contemporary theorizing about authoritarianism. While authoritarianism represents a general orientation towards social cohesion, it translates into specific authoritarian attitudes when activated by a perceived threat against the normative social order (Feldman 2003; Stenner 2005). When an object is not threatening, high authoritarians are less likely to differ from low authoritarians in their attitudes towards it. This describes most the situation concerning EU attitudes in the 1990s. When there is a perceived threat, high authoritarians will respond differently to low authoritarians. Thus, the effect of authoritarianism on political attitudes and behaviour is situational.

Studies of authoritarianism have often examined the effect of two different types of threat. The first can be termed a 'threat to the normative order'. Stenner (2005) defines the normative order as a

> system of oneness and sameness that makes 'us' an 'us'; some demarcation of people, authorities, institutions, values, and norms that…defines who 'we' are and what 'we' believe in.   (Stenner 2005: 17)

A normative threat is one that challenges the 'common authority and shared values' (Stenner 2005: 17) that make this social order possible. A normative threat is primarily concerned with shared values or a way of life, and it could emanate from internal dissidents or deviants, or the infiltration of foreign groups or value systems. Defending against that normative threat requires taking steps to preserve the 'common authority and shared values' that link a social group together. It is important to note that a normative threat only exists to the extent that one perceives a 'system of oneness and sameness' that is worth defending or preserving.

The second type of threat is a threat to one's safety, which we might term an existential threat. Examples of such threats might be those arising as a result of terrorism or crime, which could threaten an individual with death, injury, or the loss of material resources. An important distinction between such threats to safety and threats to the normative order is that everyone (presumably) will want to protect against threats to safety, while only high authoritarians fear threats to the normative order.

The type of threat should determine whether authoritarianism conditions the response. Threats to the normative order generate divergent responses by high authoritarians and low authoritarians. While everybody would presumably perceive the existence of the *challenge* to the normative order posed by these actors or groups, only high authoritarians would perceive them as a *threat* to society that must be resisted. By contrast, low authoritarians would see these internal 'troublemakers' or outsiders as unthreatening, or possibly even desirable insofar as they expand the boundaries for individual autonomy within society. Thus, high authoritarians should respond to threats to the normative order with hostility, while low authoritarians should not. By contrast, authoritarianism should not condition responses to threats to safety. Such threats can lead to a convergence of attitudes between low and high authoritarians, because low authoritarians will embrace protective and punitive attitudes towards the source of such threats. For example, both low and high authoritarians who were worried about a possible terrorist attack supported intrusive and punitive government measures designed to prevent terrorism (Hetherington and Suhay 2011). Because high authoritarians would already be likely to support protective measures against suspected terrorists of Middle Eastern origin (in the case of the United States in the years following the 11 September 2001 terror attacks), the increase in support for such measures came from the changing responses of low authoritarians—who only adopted such attitudes when they felt threatened by the possibility of terrorism. Thus, the relationship between authoritarianism, threat, and attitudes depends on the nature of the threat.[8]

How will European integration translate into perceptions of threat? Revisiting the motto of the EU—'United in Diversity'—highlights two major effects. The first is a transfer of political authority (sovereignty) from the nation state to the European level ('united'). The second effect is the opening of social and political borders to increased intra-EU migration ('diversity'). Thus, high authoritarians should find this transfer of political authority and increased diversity threatening. By contrast, low authoritarians may view those same features of European integration favourably insofar as they expand individual autonomy, but at least they should not find them threatening in the same way. Drawing on this

---

[8] Another possibility, considering in earlier work such as that of Altemeyer (1981, 1996), is that threat causes authoritarianism. Newer theorizing dismisses this possibility, because authoritarianism is viewed as a deeper predisposition that is not caused by more situational factors such as threat. As such, the effect of threat is more likely to activate the authoritarian predisposition and lead to the expression of authoritarian attitudes.

discussion, I expect to find evidence that high authoritarians perceive more threat from European integration than do low authoritarians.

The analysis uses data from a series of survey questions included in the May 2014 wave of the German Longitudinal Election Study (GLES). This wave of the GLES contains a special battery of questions about potential threats from the EU. Specifically, respondents are asked to what extent they are worried about the following potential consequences of European integration:

- There will be an increase in migrants coming to Germany.
- Germany will be forced to change its laws by the EU.
- Germany will be forced to pay more money to support other EU member states.
- Germany will lose jobs to other EU member states.

For each question, respondents could place themselves on a four-point scale with the following values: 0 (not at all worried), 1 (a little worried), 2 (somewhat worried), and 3 (very worried).

These questions measure different types of threats to Germany society and politics. The first asks about a potential threat to the national community from the entry of more migrants from other European countries. Because free movement is a core principle of the modern EU, this potential threat is credible. There should be a clear distinction between high authoritarians, who are likely to find this possibility threatening, and low authoritarians, who should not find this scenario threatening. Thus, high authoritarians should indicate greater levels of worry about increased migration than low authoritarians.

The second question asks about a potential normative threat emanating from the reordering of legitimate authority. The power to decide on Germany's laws would be removed from German state leaders (representatives of the national community) to external political entities. However, this question does not address the substance of any legal changes. Thus, respondents are indicating their level of worry that Germany could be forced to transfer sovereign authority to the EU. High authoritarians should be more likely to worry about the transfer of authority from the legitimate national authority to one in which decisions will be shared with other member states.

The third item poses a different type of threat. In this case, there is no direct threat to social cohesion or its traditions. Rather, the threat is to the ability of the in-group to use its resources for its own benefit. This prospect should appear more threatening to high authoritarians, who display higher levels of in-group preference (Stenner 2005) and will thus be unlikely to endorse the idea of German money being redirected to members of out-groups. Low authoritarians should be less likely to perceive this possibility as threatening.

The final item measures a direct economic threat to German workers. In this case, the prospect of job losses poses a material threat. However, this question poses no normative threat to members of the in-group because there is no challenge to the 'common authority and shared values' of Germany (Stenner 2005: 17). Rather, job losses due to European integration constitute a material threat to all German workers, which should affect high authoritarians and low authoritarians equally. For this reason, high authoritarians should not be more likely to worry about the threat of job losses. Instead, such concerns should reflect utilitarian judgments based on the respondent's economic circumstances and human capital (Gabel 1998).

In short, the questions described here consider two different types of threat from European integration that should distinguish high and low authoritarians. The first type described in the first two questions is a threat to the normative order—the 'oneness' of society. The second type described in the latter two questions is a group economic threat. While this type of threat does not concern the normative order, the first question addresses the diversion of the group's collective resources towards outsiders who may not share the collective values of the group. However, the second question examines a more generalized material threat to workers under economic integration. Thus, high authoritarians should be more likely to worry about the threats described in the first three questions (Migrants, Laws, and Pay Money) but not in the final question (Jobs).

The analysis starts by comparing the mean responses to each question among high authoritarians (those scoring above 0 on *Authoritarianism*) and low authoritarians (those scoring below 0), respectively. The results are given in Figure 4.5.

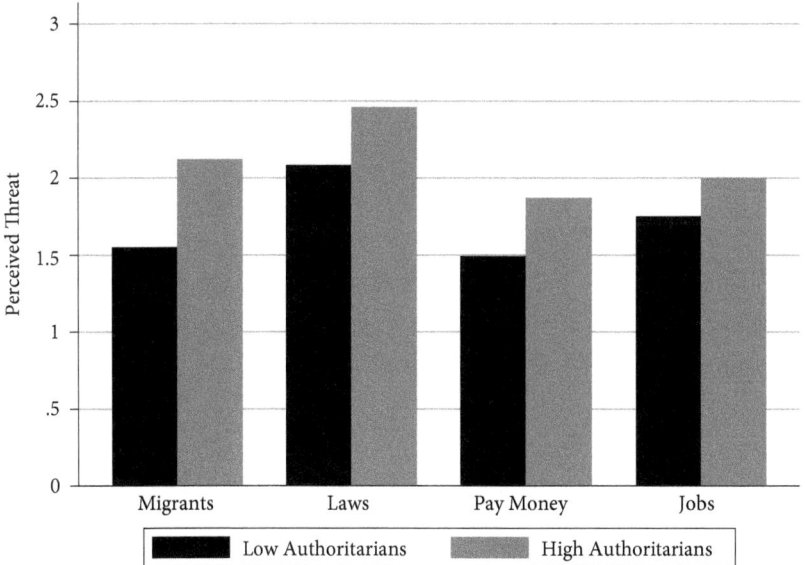

Figure 4.5 Mean perceived EU threat by authoritarianism, Germany 2014

Note: Each bar shows the mean perceived threat (rescaled to 0–3 with higher values indicating greater threat) among low authoritarians and high authoritarians, respectively.

Source: German Longitudinal Election Study T24 (Rattinger et al. 2014).

Table 4.6 Authoritarianism and perceived threat from European
integration, Germany

Variable	Migrants	Laws	Pay Money	Jobs
Authoritarianism	.10*	.11*	.09	−.01
	(.05)	(.05)	(.06)	(.06)
Ideology	.03*	−.02	.00	.00
	(.01)	(.01)	(.01)	(.02)
Immigration	.22*	.16*	.14*	.10*
	(.01)	(.01)	(.01)	(.01)
Tax-Spend	−.05*	−.05*	.00	−.02
	(.01)	(.01)	(.01)	(.02)
National Economy	−.06	−.09*	−.18*	−.11*
	(.03)	(.03)	(.04)	(.04)
Education	−.08*	−.06	−.19*	−.13*
	(.04)	(.04)	(.05)	(.05)
Income	.00	.01	−.01	.00
	(.01)	(.01)	(.01)	(.02)
Religiosity	−.00	−.00	.02	.10*
	(.03)	(.03)	(.04)	(.04)
Student	−.07	−.00	−.17	−.01
	(.11)	(.11)	(.13)	(.14)
Unemployed	.15	−.02	.04	−.16
	(.16)	(.15)	(.18)	(.20)
Retired	.01	.06	.02	−.17
	(.10)	(.10)	(.12)	(.12)
Age	−.02	−.01	−.02	.06
	(.03)	(.03)	(.03)	(.03)
Gender	.06	.03	.03	−.10
	(.05)	(.05)	(.06)	(.07)
Constant	.72*	1.9*	1.7*	1.6*
	(.22)	(.21)	(.26)	(.27)
N	794	796	789	786
Root MSE	.73	.72	.87	.91
Adjusted R^2	0.49	0.34	0.26	0.13

Note: Cell entries show unstandardized least-squares regression coefficients with standard errors in parentheses, * $p < .05$.

The descriptive results suggest that high authoritarians worry more about the threat posed by European integration to the normative order. The gap between high and low authoritarians is largest for the question about more migrants coming to Germany: high authoritarians gave a mean response of 2.12 while low authoritarians averaged a response of 1.54, a gap of 0.58 points on a four-point scale. The gap is somewhat smaller for the question about changing laws (0.38

points) and about being forced to pay money (0.39 points). However, there is less difference between high authoritarians and low authoritarians in responses to the question concerning the loss of jobs: high authoritarians' mean response of 2.0 is 0.25 points higher than low authoritarians' mean response of 1.75.[9]

A better test of these patterns requires multivariate regression models in which each perceived threat is the dependent variable and a number of standard control variables are included alongside authoritarianism on the right-hand side of the model. The control variables include self-reported measures of left–right ideology, preferences on economic policy and immigration, and evaluations of the national economy. A set of variables measuring human capital (Gabel 1998) includes occupational indicators, income, and education. A final set of variables measure gender and age.

The results of the analyses appear in Table 4.6. The variable for authoritarianism is positive and statistically significant in the first two models, indicating that high authoritarians worry more about threats to the normative order emanating from European integration. However, the coefficients are not significant in the latter two models, suggesting that high authoritarians do not worry more than low authoritarians about threats to group economic interests. In particular, the fourth model has limited explanatory power, suggesting that fears about job loss reflect factors other than concern about protecting the normative social and political order. The lack of a significant coefficient in the third model (Pay Money) is surprising, though it would be reasonable to assume that utilitarian factors matter relatively more for this question than the first two questions. Overall, these findings are consistent with the claim that high authoritarians are more likely to oppose the EU because they view it as a threat to national community and sovereignty.

Conclusion

This chapter has examined the relationship between authoritarianism and attitudes towards the European Union. It has developed and tested the argument that high authoritarians are more likely to oppose European integration and EU enlargement given the threat to national cohesion and sovereignty. Evidence from the European Values Survey and several national election studies is consistent with this argument. The chapter tests and finds evidence for two further predictions. First, this relationship between authoritarianism and EU attitudes partially accounts for previous findings linking exclusive social identity and opposition to the EU (e.g. Carey 2002; McLaren 2002). Second, high authoritarians are more likely to perceive threats from European integration to national community and sovereignty, though authoritarianism has less bearing on perceptions of economic threat.

[9] A t-test finds that all of these differences are significant at the 0.05 level, two-tailed.

These findings are consistent with the broader argument that the EU threatens high authoritarians' views of the normative order.

The results of this chapter provide an important advance in our understanding of EU support. The findings provide strong and consistent support that authoritarianism shapes EU support in contemporary Western Europe. In doing so, these findings provide an account for the existing literature linking exclusionary social identity attitudes and Euroscepticism.[10] While there is a clear relationship between exclusionary social identity and opposition to the EU, this chapter shows that at least part of this relationship is endogenous to authoritarianism. High authoritarians are more likely to express exclusionary attitudes related to national identity, immigration, and religious diversity—and, in turn, to oppose European integration. This finding provides an advance to our understanding of the factors driving opposition to the EU. This chapter also improves our understanding of the motivations driving Euroscepticism. The results indicate that high authoritarians are more likely to oppose the EU because they want to preserve the cohesion of national society, and they see the EU as a threat to that goal. High authoritarians are more likely to worry that European integration will weaken their national society's ability to preserve its culture and politics.

This chapter's findings can also provide insight into what factors could affect EU support. Maintaining social cohesion is a core concern of high authoritarians and not merely a distraction from the economic benefits of European integration. Part of the worldview division between high and low authoritarians concerns the desire for a more cohesive society versus one that is more atomized. Low authoritarian advocates of European integration may not recognize that arguments for the EU emphasizing educational, employment, or travel opportunities may be threatening rather than appealing to high authoritarians. In addition, arguments proclaiming the economic gains from European integration are unlikely to persuade high authoritarians when the counter-arguments emphasize preserving control over national politics and culture. These findings raise the question of what type of pro-EU arguments could be persuasive to high authoritarians, given the current nature of the EU.

This chapter demonstrates that authoritarianism structures contemporary EU attitudes. However, this book's argument is that Western Europe has experienced a worldview evolution, in which authoritarianism has become an important determinant of political attitudes and behaviour. In order to demonstrate that point, it is necessary to show that the relationship between authoritarianism and EU attitudes has changed in the past several decades. The next chapter examines that claim, tracking the evolving effect of authoritarianism on EU attitudes from 1990 to the present era.

---

[10] See note 3 for sources.

5

The Evolving Relationship between Authoritarianism and EU Attitudes

Introduction

Since the ratification of the Maastricht Treaty in 1992, European integration has grown increasingly contentious. Public support for EU membership has dropped from roughly 65 per cent in the early 1990s to about or below 50 per cent in recent years. While some of this decline is the result of enlargement to include more Eurosceptical publics, the issue of EU membership and of future European integration has become more contentious in even the original six member states. Evidence of this growing contention can be seen in the failure of referendums on the constitution in France and the Netherlands (Hobolt 2009), the British membership referendum (Clarke et al. 2017), and the rise of Eurosceptical parties. This growing contention over European integration has practical consequences. National elites face greater pressure to put European treaties up to referendums, in which electorates are increasingly likely to reject further integration (Hobolt 2009), and European issues are becoming increasingly important in the national electoral politics of a growing number of member states (Tillman 2004; de Vries 2007), contributing to the electoral strength of radical right parties. In short, mass opposition to the European Union (EU) has risen, resulting in a shift by which public opinion increasingly acts as a 'constraining dissensus' to further European integration rather than providing a 'permissive consensus' in support of further integration (Lindberg and Scheingold 1970; Hooghe and Marks 2009.

The previous chapter shows that authoritarianism structures attitudes towards the EU. This finding builds on explanations rooted in social identity, which argue that those with exclusionary attitudes towards national identity or religion are less supportive of the EU (McLaren 2002; de Vreese and Boomgaarden 2005; Elgün and Tillman 2007; Azrout et al. 2011; Hobolt et al. 2011; de Vreese et al. 2012). This book's explanation builds on those previous results by developing an explanation that accounts for those findings while using child-rearing measures of authoritarianism that are less likely to be affected by political attitudes. In the current era, an authoritarian worldview motivated by social conformity and security results in less support for the EU.

These findings seem to challenge earlier research showing the importance of utilitarian attitudes in structuring EU attitudes (e.g. Gabel 1998). Did those

Authoritarianism and the Evolution of West European Electoral Politics. Erik R. Tillman, Oxford University Press.
© Erik R. Tillman 2021. DOI: 10.1093/oso/9780192896223.003.0005

earlier studies studying EU attitudes in the 1990s or early 2000s simply get it wrong? No. Instead, this chapter suggests that the structure of EU attitudes has evolved since the 1990s as the political context and the structure of elite conflict over European integration have changed. The negative relationship between authoritarianism and EU support is a twenty-first-century phenomenon, consistent with this book's argument of an ongoing worldview evolution in West European politics.

As elite messages over Europe have become more divided, with negative messages emphasizing the threat to national cohesion and sovereignty, mass attitudes towards the EU have shifted. High authoritarians have been drawn to those new anti-EU messages, while low authoritarians have rejected them. As a result, authoritarianism has developed into an important factor structuring EU attitudes in recent years. However, the development of this relationship at the mass level varies with elite conflict. Some West European countries have experienced higher levels of elite conflict over Europe than others. The increase in elite conflict has been the result of the emergence (or amplification) of anti-EU elite messages, primarily by populist right-wing political parties and movements. Thus, elite debate has expanded since the 1990s from a one-sided (positive) message flow to one in which there is increasingly a two-sided message flow (Zaller 1992), which is to say an elite debate between proponents and opponents of the EU. In those states where elite conflict emerged earlier, the negative relationship between authoritarianism and EU support emerged sooner.

This chapter elaborates and tests these claims. It builds on the previous chapters' arguments to explain why the nature of EU attitudes has evolved since the 1990s to the pattern seen in Chapter 4. Analysis of data from the European Values Survey (EVS) (EVS 2011a, 2011b, 2016, 2019) between 1990 and 2017 demonstrates this evolution in EU attitudes. Finally, the analysis shows that cross-national differences in the level of elite conflict over Europe have affected the pace and degree of this evolution in EU attitudes.

The Evolution of EU Attitudes

Authoritarianism structures EU attitudes in the present era, as shown in Chapter 4. This alignment of attitudes is the result of the major changes to the EU in recent decades, along with increasingly contentious elite debate about European integration. The EU has expanded its institutional powers since the early 1990s, leading to a greater loss of national sovereignty, and it has enlarged to include thirteen new members states representing a wider range of societies and cultures. These dual transformations created a favourable environment for political elites to frame anti-EU arguments as a defence of national sovereignty and community. These arguments appeal to high authoritarians, drawing them towards anti-EU attitudes. However, pro-EU arguments emphasizing greater individual autonomy and diversity appeal to low authoritarians, drawing them towards pro-EU positions. The result is that EU attitudes today are structured by authoritarianism.

What has changed about the EU to trigger such a shift in attitudes? Until the ratification debates over the Treaty of Maastricht in 1992–3, European integration was not polarizing at the mass level (Eichenberg and Dalton 1993). In its early years, the EU stimulated little attention in mass politics. Elite messages about European integration tended to emphasize its contributions to continuing peace and prosperity. Importantly, mainstream political elites largely supported European integration, and there were relatively few critical voices in elite debate. During the pre-Maastricht era, the institutional powers of the EC were relatively limited and less visible to European citizens. Concurrently, the membership of the EC was smaller and relatively more homogeneous. While the accession of three Mediterranean countries (Greece, Portugal, and Spain) in the 1980s changed this reality somewhat, there was less cause for concern given the limited development of citizenship and labour rights.

The ratification of the Treaty on European Union (the Maastricht Treaty) marked a turning point in the history of European integration. The dual agendas to expand the EU's institutional powers and enlarge EU membership generated new threats to national sovereignty and cohesion. The increasing use of European symbols such as the flag and anthem, and in particular the efforts to establish the common currency, increased the visibility of the EU among European publics. Elite debate reflected this evolution in the nature of the EU. Prior to Maastricht, there was typically little elite debate in mass or electoral arenas over European integration. European integration was largely an elite affair, conducted by national and European leaders. Elite messages tended to reinforce the positive character of European integration, creating a 'one-sided' message flow (Zaller 1992) in which European publics received limited and pro-EU messages from elite sources. This was the context in which the permissive consensus developed (Lindberg and Scheingold 1970). The permissive consensus described the era of public opinion (lasting from the early years of European integration until around the time of Maastricht) that tended to support European integration but weakly so, as most Europeans paid little attention to European integration in response to the low level of attention and disagreement coming from national political elites and media.

The ratification of the Treaty of Maastricht created the first serious public debates over European integration in most member states. Elite and media opposition to the provisions of the treaty emerged. In this context, referenda to ratify the treaty in France and Denmark became surprisingly contentious. The treaty was ratified only narrowly in France, while Danish voters initially rejected it before approving it in a second referendum after a series of Danish opt-out clauses were negotiated. These Maastricht referenda signalled the beginning of a new era in which European elites and publics became increasingly divided over further European integration while the issue became increasingly salient (Hobolt 2009). The increase in the number of anti-EU elite messages has created a situation approaching a 'two-sided' message flow in many EU states (Zaller 1992).

The emergence of increased elite and mass contention over European integration has had several notable effects beyond the increased polarization in public opinion. First, voters have more frequently rejected European integration in EU-related referenda (Hobolt 2009). Irish voters initially rejected the Treaty of Nice in 2002, and the proposed Constitutional Treaty was abandoned after Dutch and French voters rejected it in 2004. A second phenomenon has been the apparent emergence of EU issue voting—Europeans basing their voting decisions in national elections on EU-related questions (Tillman 2004; de Vries 2007). The emergence of EU issue voting has depended on the nature of party conflict over European integration and salient events such as accession negotiations or major treaties.

Why have these events led to the polarization of mass opinion on the EU? The increasing intrusion of the EU into matters of national sovereignty and its increasing social diversity would generate a greater perception of threat among high authoritarians. High authoritarians see the supranational powers of the EU as undermining the proper and traditional role of the sovereign nation state. European integration increasingly allows for governance either through the supranational Commission or through decisions made collectively in the Council or the European Parliament. High authoritarians would tend to reject European federal or supranational governance due to its potential to undermine the established political arrangement within their country. Additionally, the growing diversity of the EU threatens social cohesion by allowing for the free movement of labour from other member states. The ongoing enlargement of the EU magnifies this threat. As a result of the enlargements between 2004 and 2013, the EU is now significantly larger and more diverse than it was in 2000.

The deepening and widening of the EU creates a greater perception of threat for high authoritarians. Increasing media and elite debate over European integration generates more awareness of the potential threat to national sovereignty and cohesion. This increased debate over the EU makes threat-related perceptions of the EU more accessible and salient to voters (Zaller 1992). This shift in debate also opens space for issue entrepreneurs who seek to gain electoral support by generating conflict on a pro-/anti-European dimension (de Vries and Hobolt 2012). As a result, high authoritarians should have become increasingly opposed to the EU between 1990 and 2017.

Low authoritarians will not display the same pattern of responses. In fact, it is possible that they will display the opposite response. Elite messages emphasizing the increased potential for supranational governance and an integrated, multicultural Europe may actually generate increased support. Because low authoritarians prioritize individual autonomy over social cohesion, European integration is more likely to pose an opportunity than a threat. By contrast, elite criticisms of the EU, which emphasize threat to the normative order, do not resonate with low authoritarians. For example, messages claiming that European integration reduces the ability of member states to control migration would appeal to high authoritarians, but low authoritarians would likely view such messages as xeno-phobic or restrictive of individual autonomy.

This shift in EU attitudes is part of the broader worldview evolution occurring in Western Europe described in Chapter 2. The increased salience of debates over national protection and immigration, and their linkage to the issue of European integration, is at the heart of this shift. In other words, European integration is not the primary issue driving this worldview evolution. For most Europeans, the EU is too remote and too complex to function as the easy issue (Carmines and Stimson 1989) that could trigger a realignment of attitudes and party loyalties. However, the elite framing of the European issue in recent decades fits comfortably into this evolving worldview alignment, and it generates increasingly strong mass opinions as elites connect it to core political values (Pollock et al. 1993). Thus, EU attitudes are shifting to reflect the new worldview conflict, with high authoritarians becoming more anti-EU and low authoritarians staying pro-EU or even becoming more pro-EU.

This discussion suggests two main implications about the evolution of EU attitudes. First, the years following the ratification of the Treaty of Maastricht have seen a notable shift in the structure of EU attitudes. In the early 1990s, authoritarianism should have had no relationship to EU attitudes. This situation changed over the subsequent two decades as high authoritarians became increasingly negative toward the EU—motivated by concerns emphasized by political elites of a threat to national cohesion and sovereignty. Although this process has occurred at different rates across member states in Western Europe, the direction of change in attitudes has been the same: high authoritarians have become increasingly anti-EU. The result is that EU public opinion at present looks very different than it did in 1990. High authoritarians are likely to oppose further European integration. Low authoritarians are more likely to support the EU.

The rate at which EU attitudes evolved depends in part on the extent of elite conflict over the EU within each member state. The development of elite conflict over Europe varies cross-nationally, depending on such factors as the emergence of a viable populist radical right (PRR) party or the strategies taken by rival mainstream parties to counter the radical right. In general, the emergence of a PRR party will lead to greater elite conflict, while mainstream parties may effectively keep conflict suppressed in the absence of such a challenger party. In those states with more elite conflict, the evolution in EU attitudes should occur more quickly. In other words, high authoritarians should be more likely to oppose the EU and low authoritarians to support the EU at an earlier point in time where conflict is higher. This evolution in EU attitudes should be more gradual in member states with less elite conflict over European integration. This discussion leads to two hypotheses.

H1:   Attitudes diverge between high and low authoritarians in the post-Maastricht era. There should be no relationship between authoritarianism and EU attitudes in the 1990s, but a negative and significant relationship should emerge in the twenty-first century.

H2:   There is a positive relationship between the level of elite conflict over European integration and the strength of the relationship between authoritarianism and EU attitudes. The relationship should be stronger in states with high levels of elite conflict.

The first hypothesis predicts a divergence between the attitudes of high and low authoritarians since 1990. In other words, there should be no significant difference between high and low authoritarians' EU attitudes in 1990. By 2008, high authoritarians should be significantly less supportive of the EU than low authoritarians. The second hypothesis predicts cross-national differences depending on the degree of elite conflict over Europe. In short, the gap emerges between high and low authoritarians' attitudes in the context of increased elite conflict. Cross-national differences in the timing and magnitude of elite conflict should produce observable differences in the pace of the evolution of EU attitudes. The gap between high and low authoritarians will emerge sooner where elite conflict is high but not where it is low.

Analysis

This section presents a test of the two hypotheses using data from the 1990, 1999, 2008, and 2017 waves of the EVS (EVS 2011a, 2011b, 2016, 2019).[1] These data contain appropriate questions to measure the key concepts of interest, and the time coverage of these surveys allows me to examine the relationship between authoritarianism and EU attitudes, as the worldview evolution should have been occurring. Few surveys contain all of these necessary features, so the EVS data are appropriate for this task.[2]

---

[1]   One obvious weakness of this survey series is that data are only available in waves collected every nine years, making it a somewhat blunt tool to measure change over time. However, the EVS is the only survey with the adequate range of questions going back to the early 1990s. A finding that attitudes have diverged since then will be consistent with this book's argument, though it would be weaker than if more survey waves were available in shorter frequencies.

[2]   Due to differences in survey coverage across each wave, the analysis includes only those respondents in states appearing in each survey wave. Those states are Austria, Denmark, Finland, France, Germany, Italy, the Netherlands, Sweden, and the United Kingdom.

Data and Measures

Attitudes towards the EU are measured using a question common to all four survey waves: 'How much confidence do you have in [the European Union]: a great deal, quite a lot, not very much, or none at all?' Answers to this question are reordered so that higher values indicate greater confidence. While this question does not perfectly measure EU support, it does correlate positively with other measures of EU attitudes that are available in the 2008 EVS survey in the range of 0.2 to 0.3. In other words, those who have higher confidence in the EU are moderately more likely to support initiatives to expand the powers of the EU or to enlarge it.

Authoritarianism is measured using a variant of the child-rearing items available in the EVS. The EVS includes a question asking respondents to choose up to five from a list of eleven characteristics that should be encouraged in children. Three responses indicate authoritarian traits: good manners, obedience, and religious faith. Three responses reflect non- or low authoritarian traits: independence, imagination, and 'tolerance and respect for other people'. Each authoritarian response is scored as 1, and each non-authoritarian response is scored as −1. The five remaining responses, which do not directly measure authoritarian or non-authoritarian values (hard work, feeling of responsibility, thrift, determination, and unselfishness), are scored 0. A respondent could thus score from 3 (indicating three authoritarian responses and no non-authoritarian responses) to −3 (vice versa). This variable is rescaled to run from −1 to 1 and is labelled *Authoritarianism*.

This measure of authoritarianism is preferable to others based on socio-political attitudes or values. Though these measures of authoritarianism correlate in the expected fashion with values-based measures, using the latter introduces several complications. First, values-based measures are more likely to measure *activated* authoritarian attitudes rather than the predisposition (Stenner 2005). As such, analyses using these measures will identify a strong relationship between authoritarianism and the dependent variable of interest, but it will only identify those high authoritarians whose predispositions have been activated as well as those (less common) low authoritarians who happen to hold exclusionary social attitudes. Given this book's argument about the evolution of the relationship between authoritarianism and EU attitudes, measures of authoritarian attitudes would be inappropriate here. Moreover, such values-based measures introduce multiple dimensions of attitudes and measurement complexity. For example, the Human Values Inventory includes several dimensions—Traditionalism, Conformity, Security, Self-Direction, Stimulation, and Universalism—which may correlate strongly with high or low authoritarianism (Schwartz and Bilsky 1987; Schwartz 1992, 1994). Researchers' decisions to measure authoritarianism by including some measures of these dimensions but not others could influence the results without much theoretical clarity (e.g. Norris and Inglehart 2019). In short, measuring authoritarian predispositions directly with simple measures is preferable in most regards.

The analysis includes a range of control variables that have been shown to influence EU attitudes in previous studies. Several variables measure ideological and attitudinal factors that may influence EU trust. *Ideology* measures the respondent's self-placement on a standard left–right ideological scale where higher values indicate a more right-wing position. *Economic Scale* measures the mean response to a series of questions about economic policy, with higher numbers indicating more right-wing (pro-market) positions. *Immigration* reflects respondents' agreement with the claim that citizens should receive preference for jobs over immigrants. Because of differences in measurement between survey waves, it is coded as a binary variable reflecting agreement (1) or disagreement (0) that citizens should be preferred. This variable should have a negative coefficient. *Religious Hostility* is coded based on two questions asking respondents whether they would not want to have Muslims or Jews, respectively, as neighbours. Higher values indicate a preference not to have one or both groups as neighbours. This variable should have a negative coefficient.

Several variables measure the respondent's ability to benefit from European integration in terms of occupational standing, education, and income. Those who are better positioned to benefit from European integration should be more likely to support it (Gabel 1998). *Manager* is coded 1 for respondents in professional or managerial positions, and 0 otherwise. This variable should have a positive effect. *Unskilled* is coded 1 for those who work in manual labour positions and 0 otherwise. This variable should have a negative relationship with EU support. *Retired, Unemployed*, and *Student* each are coded 1 if the respondent is a member of that respective group and 0 otherwise. Retirees and the unemployed may be less likely to support the EU while students may be more supportive. *Education* is measured on a four-point scale, with 1 indicating primary education and 4 indicating post-secondary educational attainment.[3] *Income* is measured on a fifteen-point country-specific scale, with 15 indicating the highest income bracket and 1 the lowest. Higher income and educational attainment should correlate with increased EU trust. *Religiosity* measures the self-reported frequency of religious attendance. Being embedded in mainstream social institutions, frequent churchgoers may be more likely to trust the EU (e.g. Nelsen et al. 2002), and the less religious are more likely to support PRR parties (Arzheimer and Carter 2009).

Finally, the analysis includes several demographic variables. *Gender* is coded 1 for female respondents and 0 for male respondents. *Age* is measured in six bands, with 1 indicating those under age 24 and 6 indicating those 65 and older. *Locality*

---

[3] In the 1990 survey, respondents are asked to indicate the age at which they finished full-time education. I recode these answers to reflect equivalent values (1 = under 14 years, 4 = over 18 years).

shows the size of the town or city in which the respondent lives on an eight-point scale, with higher values indicating a larger community. The expected effects of these variables on support for the EU are less clear, but each merits control in this study.

Has the Relationship between Authoritarianism and EU Attitudes Evolved?

The analysis starts with a simple comparison of mean levels of EU Trust by authoritarianism in 1990 and 2017. If hypothesis H1 is correct, there should be a negative relationship among respondents in 2017, with high authoritarians exhibiting lower levels of trust on average than low authoritarians. By contrast, no such pattern should appear in 1990. These comparisons are shown in Figure 5.1. The descriptive results are consistent with expectations. The mean levels of EU Trust drop as authoritarianism increases among respondents in 2017, suggesting a negative relationship. In 1990, the results imply a positive relationship with high authoritarians being *more* likely to trust the EU. Hypothesis H1 did not predict the nature of the relationship in 1990 other than to predict that it would not be negative. Thus, this finding is consistent with expectations.

The patterns observed in Figure 5.1 are suggestive of an evolving relationship between authoritarianism and EU trust, but a multivariate regression analysis will provide a better test of H1. The analysis uses a multilevel regression approach due

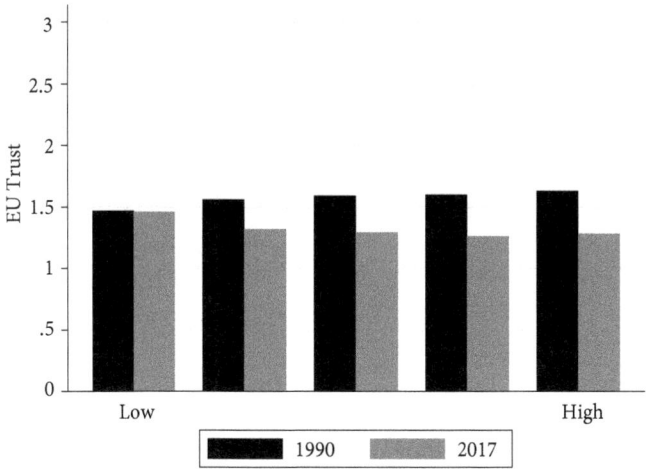

Figure 5.1 Authoritarianism and EU trust, 1990 and 2017

Note: Each column shows the mean value of EU Trust for respondents at each respective level of authoritarianism in the 1990 and 2017 wave of the European Values Survey.

Sources: EVS 2011a, 2019.

Table 5.1 Authoritarianism and EU attitudes by survey wave

Variable	Coefficient	Standard Error
Authoritarianism	.13*	.02
1999 Wave	−.23*	.01
2008 Wave	−.26*	.01
2017 Wave	−.21*	.02
Authoritarianism X 1999	−.02	.03
Authoritarianism X 2008	−.18*	.03
Authoritarianism X 2017	−.29*	.03
Immigration	−.15*	.01
Religious Hostility	−.18*	.02
Ideology	−.00	.00
Economic Scale	.03*	.00
Religiosity	.05*	.00
Education	.03*	.01
Income	.01*	.00
Manager	.07*	.01
Unskilled	−.05*	.01
Retired	.10*	.01
Unemployed	−.02	.02
Student	.16*	.02
Farmer	−.03	.03
Gender	.01	.01
Age	−.02*	.00
Locality	.01*	.00
Constant	2.2*	.06
N	34,323	
Chi Squared	1929.5	

Note: Figures show unstandardized multilevel regression coefficients and standard errors, * $p < .05$.

to the fact that respondents are nested within countries and survey waves (Jones and Steenbergen 2002; Gelman and Hill 2007). To examine the changing effect of authoritarianism on EU trust, the analysis includes interaction terms between authoritarianism and each wave of the survey. The component variables of the interaction terms (minus the 1990 survey wave, which serves as the reference category) also appear in the model in order to generate unbiased results (Brambor et al. 2006). The results of this analysis are shown in Table 5.1. Interpreting coefficients in a model with interaction terms is complicated. For example, the coefficient for Authoritarianism shows its effect on EU Trust in 1990 (the reference year), and the coefficient for each interaction term shows the relative effect of *Authoritarianism* in that subsequent survey wave. Therefore, it is more useful to estimate the marginal effects of Authoritarianism on EU Trust in each survey wave using the results from this regression (Brambor et al. 2006). I do so using the 'margins' command in Stata, which estimates the marginal effect of

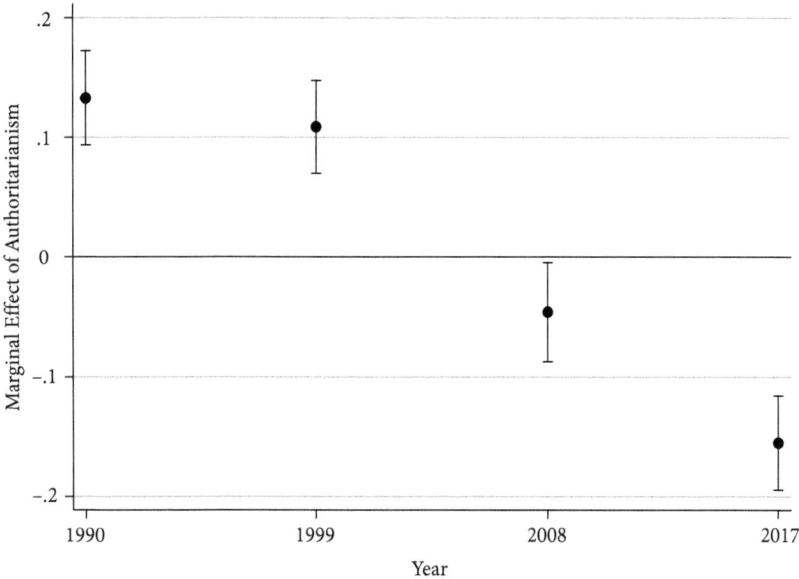

Figure 5.2 Marginal effect of authoritarianism by survey year

Note: Each dot represents the marginal effect of authoritarianism on EU Trust with other control variables held constant. The bars represent the 95 per cent confidence intervals.

Sources: EVS 2011a, 2011b, 2016, 2019.

authoritarianism for each survey wave with all other variables held constant at mean or median values. These estimates are shown graphically in Figure 5.2, which shows the estimate of the marginal effect surrounded by the 95 per cent confidence intervals for each year.

The estimates in Figure 5.2 are consistent with hypothesis H1. The relationship between *Authoritarianism* and *EU Trust* evolves dramatically during the four survey waves—and in particular between 1999 and 2008, during which time the common currency entered circulation and the EU enlarged to include ten new post-communist member states. In fact, the results show no significant change in the relationship between 1990 and 1999, suggesting that the growing (but still limited) elite conflict over European integration had not yet affected the attitudes of high authoritarians. By 2008, *Authoritarianism* has a negative and significant marginal effect on EU Trust (as indicated by the upper bound of the confidence interval being below the line indicating 0 marginal effect). The marginal effect becomes significantly more negative in 2017 (as indicated by the fact that the confidence intervals of the marginal effects in 2008 and 2017 do not overlap), showing that the evolution of EU attitudes continued to gain strength. In short, the effect of *Authoritarianism* on EU Trust shifted dramatically between 1999 and 2017 to generate the negative relationship observed today. This finding is consistent with hypothesis H1 and with this book's argument of a worldview evo-lution in West European politics.

To put these findings in context, it is worthwhile to ask how the relationships between other independent variables and EU trust have evolved during the same time period. Have other measures of exclusionary social identity (Carey 2002; McLaren 2002) also become more important, which might suggest that the structure of EU attitudes has shifted from an economic to cultural orientation? Or have variables reflecting human capital (Gabel 1998), such as education or occupational status, also become more important? To examine this question, I estimate another regression model including each of the independent variables shown in Table 5.1. Here, each independent variable appears alone and in interaction with the survey wave variable. The coefficient of the variable thus shows its effect in the 1990 survey wave, while the coefficient of the interaction term shows the change in its effect over the subsequent three waves (Althaus 2003). For the ease of presentation, the survey wave variable is treated as continuous in this analysis, so that only one interaction between each variable and the survey wave appears. The results are shown in Table 5.2.

The results show that the effects of authoritarianism and exclusionary social identity grow stronger over time. The negative coefficients of *Immigration* and *Religious Hostility* become stronger in each subsequent wave. These results are consistent with the view that EU attitudes increasingly reflect orientations towards society and culture today with those who prefer to preserve social cohesion and sameness increasingly opposing the EU while those who favour autonomy and diversity increasingly support the EU. By contrast, the patterns are less evident for occupational and human capital variables. The effects of *Education* and *Income* show no major changes over subsequent waves, while the effects of occupational variables are inconsistent. In addition, the effects of *Ideology* and *Economic Scale* appear to grow weaker over the subsequent waves. In short, this analysis suggests that differing worldviews have become more central to EU atti-tudes while economic interests or general political orientations have not.

Elite Conflict and the Evolution of EU Attitudes

The analysis thus far shows that authoritarianism and EU trust have an increasingly negative relationship since the 1990s, as part of a broader pattern in which exclusionary social attitudes correlate negatively with EU support. This chapter argues that this evolution of attitudes is partially due to increased elite conflict over the EU that has emerged in the 1990s and early twenty-first century. However, the timing and intensity of elite conflict varies cross-nationally. If this chapter's argument is correct, differences in elite conflict should influence the evolution of EU attitudes. The negative relationship between authoritarianism

Table 5.2 Change in effects of variables over time

Variable	Coefficient	Coefficient X Wave
Authoritarianism	.10*	−.07*
	(.02)	(.01)
Immigration	−.03*	−.07*
	(.02)	(.01)
Religious Hostility	−.07*	−.07*
	(.03)	(.02)
Ideology	.02*	−.01*
	(.00)	(.00)
Economic Scale	.04*	−.01*
	(.01)	(.00)
Religiosity	.06*	−.00
	(.01)	(.00)
Education	.04*	.00
	(.01)	(.01)
Income	.01	.00
	(.00)	(.00)
Manager	−.04	.05*
	(.02)	(.01)
Unskilled	−.04	.01
	(.02)	(.01)
Retired	.06*	.03*
	(.03)	(.01)
Unemployed	−.06	.02
	(.04)	(.02)
Student	.03	.09*
	(.04)	(.02)
Farmer	−.15*	.07*
	(.05)	(.03)
Gender	.06*	−.03*
	(.02)	(.01)
Age	−.01	−.01*
	(.01)	(.00)
Locality	.01	−.00
	(.00)	(.00)
Constant	1.9*	
	(.07)	
N	34,305	
Chi Squared	1906.2*	

Note: Figures show multilevel regression coefficients with standard errors in parentheses, * p < .05.

and EU trust should emerge sooner in those member states with higher levels of elite conflict.

One empirical challenge for this analysis is measuring elite conflict over the EU. The Chapel Hill Expert Survey (CHES) has conducted elite surveys of political scientists and other experts on each EU member state, in which it asks experts to place each national political party on a scale of European integration (from being opposed to supportive) and on a general left–right ideological scale (along with other scales). These surveys have been conducted in 1999, 2002, and every four years afterwards. Using the compiled scores for each national party system in the surveys between 1999 and 2014, it is possible to calculate measures of party conflict for each party system. Because different experts rate each country's party system, direct cross-national comparisons of party conflict are not possible. However, it is possible to use each country's expert ratings of the level of conflict over European integration compared to the level of general ideological conflict (on the standard left–right scale) to examine whether EU party conflict is relatively high or low in that country compared to overall ideological conflict. Because left–right conflict is generally more established in West European party systems, the level of conflict over the EU in relation to left–right conflict provides a reasonable measure of whether EU conflict is high or low in each country (see de Vries 2007). To do this, I divide the standard deviation of the general left–right ideological measure for that country by the standard deviation of the European integration measure to produce a ratio of ideological conflict to EU conflict.[4] Table 5.3 shows these results.

Table 5.3 shows that the ratio is greater than 1 in every case, indicating that left–right ideological conflict remains greater than EU conflict. However, a divide

Table 5.3 Party conflict on European integration and ideology

Country	Ideology	European Integration	Ratio
Austria	2.29	1.92	1.19
Denmark	2.52	2.16	1.17
Finland	1.70	1.60	1.06
France	2.73	2.01	1.36
Germany	2.47	1.61	1.53
Italy	2.17	1.55	1.40
Netherlands	2.39	1.66	1.44
Sweden	2.23	1.93	1.16
United Kingdom	2.20	1.91	1.15

Note: The figures in the first two columns give the standard deviation of the expert ratings of the party positions for that country on left–right ideology and European integration, based on the Chapel Hill Expert Survey (CHES) 1999–2014. The final column shows the ratio of those two standard deviations.

---

[4] The EU and ideology measures are on seven-point and eleven-point scales, respectively. Rescaling the EU support variable produces a comparable measure and a more intuitive ratio, though the relative values of the ratio are identical whether or not the EU measure is rescaled.

emerges between those states in which the ratio is below 1.2 (indicating relatively higher levels of elite conflict over Europe) and those where the ratio is greater than 1.3 (indicating relatively lower levels of elite conflict over Europe). The former group of countries—Austria, Denmark, Finland, Sweden, and the United Kingdom—is classified as high-conflict, while the latter group of France, Germany, Italy, and the Netherlands is classified as low-conflict. An indicator variable for each group of states is included in the following analysis, allowing for a comparison of the evolution of the relationship between authoritarianism and EU trust in each group of states.

Table 5.4 Authoritarianism and EU trust by time and party conflict

Variable	Coefficient	Standard Error
Authoritarianism	.09*	.02
1999 Wave	−.17*	.02
2008 Wave	−.23*	.02
2017 Wave	−.26*	.02
Authoritarianism X 1999	.03	.03
Authoritarianism X 2008	−.08*	.04
Authoritarianism X 2017	−.22*	.03
Conflict	−.17*	.07
Authoritarianism X Conflict	.16*	.05
Conflict X 1999	−.18*	.03
Conflict X 2008	−.14*	.03
Conflict X 2017	.09*	.03
Auth X Conflict X 1999	−.25*	.06
Auth X Conflict X 2008	−.32*	.06
Auth X Conflict X 2017	−.16*	.06
Immigration	−.15*	.01
Religious Hostility	−.18*	.02
Ideology	−.00	.00
Economic Scale	.03*	.00
Religiosity	.05*	.00
Education	.03*	.01
Income	.01*	.00
Manager	.07*	.01
Unskilled	−.04*	.01
Retired	.10*	.01
Unemployed	−.02	.02
Student	.17*	.02
Farmer	−.03	.03
Gender	.01	.01
Age	−.02*	.00
Locality	.01*	.00
Constant	2.3*	.06
N	34,323	
Chi Squared	2114.4	

Note: Figures show multilevel regression coefficients with standard errors, * p < .05.

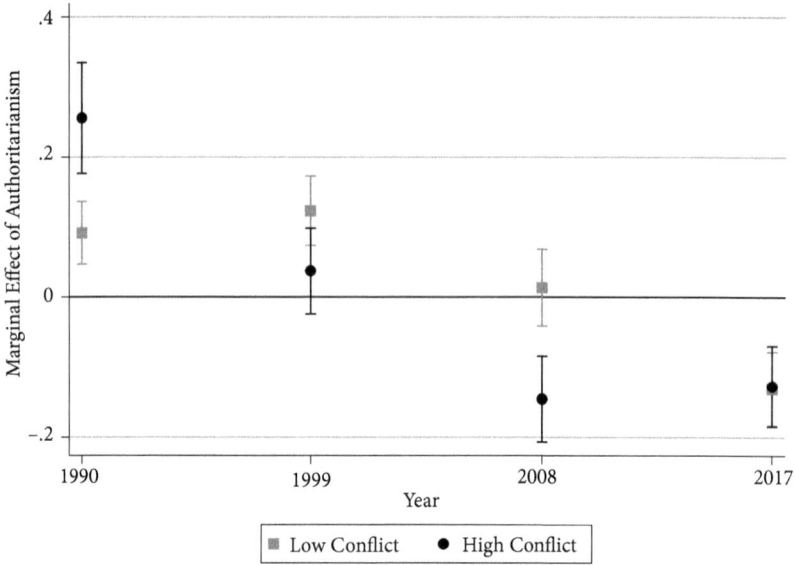

Figure 5.3 Marginal effect of authoritarianism by survey year and party conflict

Note: Each plot shows the marginal effect of authoritarianism on the probability of voting for a PRR party for voters living in high conflict or low conflict systems, respectively. The bars show the 95 per cent confidence intervals.

Sources: EVS 2011a, 2011b, 2016, 2019 and Chapel Hill Expert Survey 1999–2014.

The analysis presented in Table 5.4 includes a triple interaction between *Authoritarianism*, *Wave*, and *Conflict*. In addition, each constituent term, the two-way interactions between them, and the standard control variables are included in the analysis. Due to the complexity of interpreting triple interactions, I present the results graphically. Figure 5.3 shows the marginal effect of Authoritarianism on EU Trust for each survey wave (shown along the x-axis) and for respondents in the high-conflict states and low-conflict states, respectively.

The results are consistent with the prediction of hypothesis H2. In the high-conflict states, the relationship between Authoritarianism and EU Trust changes more quickly, becoming negative and significant in 2008 and remaining so in 2017. By contrast, the change in the marginal effect is more gradual in the low-conflict states. In 2008, the marginal effect of *Authoritarianism* on *EU Trust* is indistinguishable from 0. This difference in 2008 between the high-conflict and low-conflict states is statistically significant, as seen by the lack of overlap between each estimate's confidence intervals. By 2017, this gap has disappeared as the relationship strengthens in the low-conflict states. In both groups of states, the marginal effect of *Authoritarianism* on *EU Trust* is negative and significant, and the coefficients are statistically indistinguishable from each other. The results of this analysis suggest that the first decade of the twenty-first century (i.e. the period between the 1999 and 2008 survey waves) was an important period in which the increased politicization of Europe in the high-conflict states led to a major shift in the structure of EU attitudes. Meanwhile, this shift does not occur in the low-conflict states during that time period. In the following decade (i.e. between the 2008 and 2017 survey waves), this evolution of EU attitudes occurs in the low-conflict states, which likely results from the emergence or intensification of elite conflict in those states. The result is that the structure of EU attitudes has converged in the high-conflict and low-conflict states by 2017, consistent with this book's argument of a worldview evolution in West European politics.

Conclusion

The shift from the permissive consensus to a 'constraining dissensus' has created a challenge for European policymakers (Hooghe and Marks 2009), in that popular legitimation is increasingly necessary for European integration even as popular support declines. As more European decisions are put to national referenda (Hobolt 2009) and voting on European issues becomes more common in national elections (Tillman 2004; de Vries 2007), there are more opportunities for Eurosceptical publics to block the integration process. Thus, understanding the causes behind this decline in support is an important task.

This and the preceding chapter have developed and tested two claims deriving from this book's thesis of a worldview evolution in West European politics. Specifically, the shifting nature of European integration and of elite conflict has led to an evolution in EU attitudes. As European leaders have pursued a series of major and visible initiatives—the common currency, the eastern enlargement, the proposed Constitution—elite conflict has increasingly portrayed the EU in terms of promise to enhance individual autonomy and promote diversity while undermining national sovereignty and community. The result has been a shift in the structure of attitudes. High authoritarians, who value the preservation of national community and are more likely to view threats to the normative order with hostility, have become increasingly opposed to the EU as a result. As Eurosceptical elites have generated increasing debate over the EU on these terms, this shift in attitudes has occurred. Whereas EU attitudes in the 1990s were influenced by utilitarian variables (Gabel 1998) and bore no relationship to authoritarianism, they are now structured by authoritarianism.

This chapter has tested this argument using data from the European Values Survey collected between 1990 and 2017. In addition to supporting this main claim, the analysis further shows that increasing elite conflict fuels this worldview division on European integration. Because the pre-Maastricht permissive consensus was largely positive, the increase in elite conflict has come as a result of more Eurosceptical voices entering the public arena—mostly in the form of PRR parties. Those polities experiencing higher levels of elite conflict feature more anti-EU messages, while those member states with low levels of conflict still retain broad elite support. The effect of authoritarianism on EU trust emerged initially by 2008 only in those high-conflict states, whereas this same evolution of EU attitudes did not become apparent in the low-conflict countries until 2017—after the European financial crisis and migrant crisis. This finding is consistent with an elite-driven model of public opinion (e.g. Carmines and Stimson 1989; Zaller 1992; Hetherington and Weiler 2009) in which elite messages define the debate and help to shape mass attitudes and loyalties.

What do these results add to our understanding of EU attitudes? The results point to an increasing polarization of authoritarians and non-authoritarians on EU attitudes. This finding should challenge how we think about the sources of EU attitudes, as they may be rooted more in psychology than previous studies have considered. Moreover, these results can fill in our understanding of the increasing public 'dissensus' over Europe by shedding light on who is likely to support further European integration and who will not. If this analysis is correct and high authoritarians are turning against the EU due to concerns about the protection of national community, then elite messages emphasizing the promotion of individual autonomy or diversity will not be persuasive. While such pro-EU messages will resonate with the transnationals who form the core of EU support (Kuhn 2015), persuading high authoritarians to support the EU would require a rather different message. In a similar vein, it is unlikely that messages emphasizing the economic benefits of European integration—or warning of the economic costs of reversing integration—would persuade high authoritarians, as the Remain campaign in the British EU referendum may have discovered (Clarke et al. 2017). In short, this book's findings should improve our understanding of EU attitudes and what might influence them in the future.

The analysis in this chapter suffers from some limitations. The most obvious of these weaknesses is that there are only four waves in the EVS, providing a blunt measure of change over time. Future work could build on this by examining national election studies series, which have more frequent survey waves. Additionally, the dependent variable measures trust in the EU rather than support for integration, while perceived threat from the EU could not be measured directly given the available data. The dependent variable is less likely to pose a problem, as trust is likely to correlate with support. Future work might also measure perceived threat directly in order to examine whether and how it shapes EU attitudes.

6

Authoritarianism and Support for Populist Radical Right Parties

The Rise of the Radical Right?

Recent years have seen populist radical right (PRR) parties make electoral breakthroughs in a number of West European states. In states ranging from Austria, Denmark, Finland, France, Germany, the Netherlands, and Sweden, PRR parties have become the second or third largest parties with vote shares of greater than 10 per cent. In Austria, Denmark, and the Netherlands, these parties have joined or supported governing coalitions, moving closer to the political mainstream in the process. In Switzerland, the Swiss People's Party (SVP) has been the largest in recent elections, gaining a leading position in the cabinet by virtue of the 'magic formula' used to determine the government. Marine Le Pen, the leader of the National Front in France, reached the run-off of the 2017 presidential election and finished with over 33 per cent of the vote. In short, PRR parties have become increasingly important fixtures in West European party systems, making it important to understand their sources of electoral support.

Prior research has focused on the contextual determinants of PRR party support or on the attitudes of PRR voters. Early studies examined whether unemployment or immigration levels affected PRR party support, finding mixed results (e.g. Knigge 1998; Lubbers et al. 2002; Golder 2003; Jesuit et al. 2009). Other studies emphasized the effect of political opportunity structure, such as the electoral system and strategic behaviour of rival parties (e.g. Golder 2003; Norris 2005; Arzheimer 2009). Research on individuals who support PRR parties has focused on their attitudes and identities, with many recent studies identifying the importance of cultural threats such as immigration (e.g. Givens 2005; Ivarsflaten 2005, 2007; Lucassen and Lubbers 2012). To date, relatively few recent studies have examined the dispositional traits of PRR voters.

This chapter is the first of three that examines the relationship between authoritarianism and PRR party support. A few recent studies have examined this potential relationship, finding mixed results (e.g. Zandonella and Zeglovits 2013; Dunn 2015; Vasilopoulos and Lachat 2018). These mixed findings are puzzling given the intuitiveness of the argument linking authoritarianism to PRR party support, so the question merits further investigation. Several traits associated with authoritarianism—strong in-group attachment and hostility towards

Authoritarianism and the Evolution of West European Electoral Politics. Erik R. Tillman, Oxford University Press.
© Erik R. Tillman 2021. DOI: 10.1093/oso/9780192896223.003.0006

out-groups, conventionalism, and need for security (Adorno et al. 1950; Altemeyer 1981, 1996; Feldman and Stenner 1997; Stenner 2005; Hetherington and Weiler 2009)—predict greater PRR support. However, other traits associated with authoritarianism—such as greater attachment to tradition and an aversion to change—may make one less likely to support PRR parties, which are often portrayed as 'anti-establishment' or 'extreme'. Thus, there may be reasons to expect no relationship between authoritarianism and PRR party support. Nonetheless, the intuitiveness of this argument suggests a relationship, which I investigate by analysing the effect of authoritarianism on PRR party support in recent West European national election surveys.

The analysis generates two main findings. First, analysis of data from the 2013–17 period shows that authoritarianism correlates positively with PRR party support in a range of West European national elections. High authoritarians are more likely to vote for PRR parties. Second, there is limited evidence that the relationship between authoritarianism and PRR party support may be stronger among those who are less attached to the political establishment—particularly in Germany, where the Alternative for Germany (AfD) was a new party. Taken together, these findings suggest that PRR parties appeal to high authoritarians' desire for maintaining social cohesion but must overcome their aversion to change and attachment to tradition, which occurs as PRR parties become normalized. Finally, this relationship between authoritarianism and PRR party support is stronger among those holding anti-immigration attitudes, consistent with arguments that perceived threat to the normative order drive authoritarian responses. However, self-reported economic anxieties have no effect on PRR party support.

This chapter's findings contribute to this book's argument of a worldview evolution in West European electoral politics. The identification of a relationship between authoritarianism and PRR party support highlights the growing role of worldview on voting behaviour. High authoritarians support PRR parties because their messages resonate with the authoritarian worldview focused on the preservation of social cohesion, rather than because PRR parties appeal to group interests such as class. The finding of a positive interaction between authoritarianism and anti-immigration attitudes, but not between authoritarianism and economic anxiety, further supports the argument that perceptions of threat to the normative order drive this relationship. These findings have important consequences for how we understand PRR party support and for how rival parties might contest them electorally.

Authoritarianism and Support for the Radical Right

Why would high authoritarians be more likely to vote for populist radical right parties? The arguments and evidence presented in Chapters 2 and 3 demonstrate that high authoritarians are motivated by a need to preserve the social order and are willing to subordinate individual autonomy to this end. Demographic, cultural, and values changes pose threats to the normative order, which generate an authoritarian reaction. Under these conditions, high authoritarians are more likely to support policies or leaders focused on protecting society against these threats. PRR parties appeal to these dispositional needs of high authoritarians.

Populist radical right parties generally share a core ideology based around nativism, populism, and authoritarianism (Mudde 2007). These three dimensions form the main basis of their appeal to high authoritarian voters. Although PRR parties campaign on other issues, these are less consistent across parties and even over time within parties. On issues such as economic policy, PRR party positions are often vague, inconsistent, or varying across parties (de Lange 2007; Eger and Valdez 2015). As a result, voters are more likely to support PRR parties because of their messages on core issues such as immigration or values rather than on secondary issues such as the economy (Ivarsflaten 2005, 2007).

Nativism

The first dimension of PRR party ideology is nativism. Mudde (2007: 19) defines nativism as:

> An ideology, which holds that states should be inhabited exclusively by members of the native group ("the nation") and that nonnative elements (persons and ideas) are fundamentally threatening to the homogeneous nation-state.

Though nativism can be rooted in various concepts of ethnicity or religion, it will always have a cultural component at its core (Mudde 2007: 19; see also Higham 1955). In the West European context, nativism primarily concerns immigration and values change. By rejecting immigration and multiculturalism, PRR parties emphasize preserving social cohesion and cultural traditions of the dominant nationality. Consider the following representative quotes from the party programme of the Danish People's Party (DF):

> [Denmark] is founded on the Danish cultural heritage and, therefore, Danish culture must be preserved and strengthened. This culture consists of the sum of the Danish people's history, experience, beliefs, language, and customs. Preservation and further development of this culture is crucial to the country's survival . . . . Denmark is not an immigrant-country and never has been. Thus we will not accept transformation to a multiethnic society. Denmark belongs to the Danes, and its citizens must be able to live in a secure community founded on the rule of law, which develops along the lines of Danish culture.[1]

---

[1] Quoted from the 'The Party Program of the Danish People's Party', https://danskfolkeparti.dk/politik/in-another-languages-politics/1757-2/ (accessed 30 October 2018).

In this quoted passage, DF promise to defend against two linked threats to Denmark. The first is the threat to the 'Danish cultural heritage', which consists of the shared history, language, and customs of the Danish people. The second is the threat to the Danish people posed by immigration and ethnic transformation. These two threats are linked insofar as only a secure Danish community could preserve Danish culture. Immigration would threaten the survival of a cohesive Danish nation, so it must be restricted. The DF programme states further that immigration is acceptable within limits and given that foreign nationals will be absorbed into Danish society, which implies a process of assimilation. In other words, nativism in the West European context implies a defence of the national culture and community from the threats posed by multiculturalism and demographic change.

West European PRR parties often extend their emphasis on nativism to economic policy. Although it is often hard to characterize the economic ideology of PRR parties, many embrace welfare chauvinism, which combines a defence of the welfare state with an emphasis on reserving it for members of the national community (Eger and Valdez 2015). In this context, immigration poses a threat to the welfare state by placing burdens on public services, reducing their availability for members of the national community. This concern with ensuring that public services exist for the benefit of members of the national community fits with the broader nativist ideology.

Through their promises to protect the national community from threats posed by immigration and cultural change, PRR parties appeal to high authoritarians. By contrast, low authoritarians are less likely to view cultural or demographic change as a threat to their conception of the ideal society, and they may welcome it for the greater opportunities for individual autonomy that it brings. Low authoritarians are also less likely to support welfare chauvinism, as a broader concern for individual autonomy would lead to a preference for universalism.

Authoritarianism

At first glance, characterizing PRR parties as authoritarian would create a circular argument, but this argument hinges on differences in the meaning of the term in each context. As used by Mudde (2007) to define PRR party ideology, authoritarianism describes an emphasis on the maintenance of traditional values, strong law-and-order policies to deter and punish crime, and on the acceptance of a hierarchical society. These policies are typically motivated by a concern with preventing crime and social disorder, which PRR parties often link to immigration and value change. As such, PRR parties often propose increased spending on policing, tougher sentencing for criminals, the promotion of traditional national values in schools and society, and the preservation of traditional social arrangements such as marriage. Linking nativism and authoritarianism, PRR parties often propose making it easier for the government to deport immigrants convicted of serious crimes.

High authoritarians are more likely to be concerned with maintaining social order. They should be uniquely supportive of policies to maintain the normative order—such as preserving traditional national or religious values—particularly when these policies are linked to the preservation of social cohesion. Tough law-and-order policies should also appeal to high authoritarians generally, though low authoritarians may also support these policies when there is a threat to public safety (Hetherington and Suhay 2011). Thus, the authoritarian nature of PRR party ideology should appeal to the worldviews of high authoritarian voters.

Populism

Populism is an ideological style that divides society into a good, homogeneous people and a corrupt elite, and it views politics as a struggle between these two groups (Mudde 2007; Müller 2016). Populist parties claim that there is a 'general will' among the citizenry, which they can understand and translate into policy because of their connection with the ordinary people. Underlying this claim is a belief that the citizenry is largely homogeneous—sharing common values and interests, which are only corrupted by political elites and outsiders.

PRR parties adopt populist rhetoric, and they tend to advocate political reforms consistent with this ideology. Commonly, PRR parties support expanding direct democracy (e.g. the use of referenda) and weakening bureaucratic or technocratic restraints upon the exercise of power by elected governments. PRR parties also link their populism to the dominant national community and its shared values, ignoring minority groups or views. However, part of the populist appeal of PRR parties includes positioning themselves as political outsiders contrasted against a corrupt and out-of-touch 'establishment'. As such, they position themselves as agents of change against the traditional parties that have dominated government in their respective countries, but their change often involves trying to recreate earlier policies or social realities. However, they claim to be political outsiders only because the political establishment has lost touch with the will of the ordinary people. Thus, populists of the radical right describe themselves as agents of change wanting to restore politics to the will of the majority.

High authoritarians are likely to be attracted to the populism of PRR parties. Populist messages about the 'general will' or shared national values should resonate with high authoritarians' concern for maintaining social cohesion. High authoritarians, who display more tendencies towards 'black-and-white' thinking (Oesterreich 2005; Hetherington and Weiler 2009), may also be drawn to PRR parties' tendency towards binary rhetoric that divides politics into a good people and corrupt elites. By contrast, low authoritarians tend to emphasize diversity and autonomy, and they may be more likely to embrace complexity in political thought. All of these factors will make low authoritarians less likely to vote for PRR parties.

Explaining Support

Why would high authoritarians be more likely to support PRR parties? Recent scholarship has found a link between personality and party support. Though the particular concepts and measures vary across studies, individuals with 'open' personalities are more likely to adopt liberal cultural positions and support left-wing parties, while those with 'closed' personalities are more likely to adopt conservative cultural attitudes and support right-wing parties.[2] High authoritarianism is one indicator or facet of a 'closed' personality style while low authoritarianism would fit into the 'open' personality style. Importantly, the link between personality and socio-cultural attitudes is direct, while the link to economic attitudes is often mediated by the structure of political competition in each country (Malka et al. 2014). As a result, dispositional factors such as authoritarianism should lead individuals to support a party because of its positions on socio-cultural issues rather than on economic issues (Johnston et al. 2017).

Prior research has generated findings consistent with this study's argument using different measures. Attitudes towards cultural issues such as immigration and ethnic threat predict PRR party support better than economic attitudes (e.g. Ivarsflaten 2005, 2007; Lucassen and Lubbers 2012). High authoritarians are less likely to support immigration and are more likely to view it as a threat to social cohesion. In addition, PRR party supporters score lower in personality traits including openness to experience and agreeableness (Bakker et al. 2016a; Bakker et al. 2016b). These personality traits correlate negatively with authoritarianism (Sibley and Duckitt 2008; Hirsh et al. 2010). Prior research provides evidence consistent with the argument that authoritarianism increases support for PRR parties.

Nonetheless, recent studies testing the link between authoritarianism and PRR party support have generated mixed results (e.g. Zandonella and Zeglovits 2013; Dunn 2015; Vasilopoulos and Lachat 2018). These mixed findings prompt further examination of the possible relationship between authoritarianism and PRR party support. Although the conceptual link seems strong, there may also be reasons to expect that high authoritarians would be less likely to support PRR parties. As described above, high authoritarians should be more likely to support PRR parties because of their commitment to protect the normative social order against threats emanating from demographic and values changes. But could that same attachment

---

[2] See e.g. Barbaranelli et al. 2006; Schoen and Schumann 2007; Hetherington and Weiler 2009; Mondak 2010; Malka et al. 2014; Bakker et al. 2016a; Johnston et al. 2017.

to tradition and the established social order also reduce high authoritarians' tendency to vote for PRR parties?

There may be two reasons to expect high authoritarians not to support PRR parties. First, high authoritarians are more likely to identify with traditional sources of authority. Although PRR parties often portray themselves as defenders of traditional values that mainstream parties have abandoned, they also often position themselves (and are widely portrayed by rival mainstream parties and the media) as 'outsiders' or 'anti-establishment'. As parties with little or no history of participation in governance and lacking a historical core of supporters, they must rely on voters abandoning mainstream parties. Because high authoritarians are more sensitive to maintaining established social norms and traditions (Oyamot et al. 2012), they may be less likely to abandon an established party for a PRR party.

A second, and related, reason concerns high authoritarians' higher needs for order and aversion to change. Many voters develop habits of supporting a particular party early in adult life, which may be rooted in affiliations such as class or religious identity. This tendency should be even greater among high authoritarians, who should demonstrate more loyalty towards a preferred party (or habitualness in voting behaviour) and less tendency to switch parties. Individuals scoring low in Openness personality traits—which correlates negatively with authoritarianism (Stenner 2005)—are less likely to switch party loyalties when dissatisfied with their current party (Bakker et al. 2016b). In addition, high authoritarians are less likely to search for new information under conditions of threat (Lavine et al. 2005), which may reduce their likelihood of investigating new parties. Low authoritarians, who display more openness to change and novelty, should be more likely to switch party support.

Taken together, these arguments offer reasons why high authoritarians may be less likely to support PRR parties. High authoritarians are likely to support PRR party messages on immigration, crime, and the preservation of national identity, but they may be less likely to start supporting a new political party that identifies as political outsiders or anti-establishment. Unfortunately, the measurement of authoritarianism makes it difficult to disentangle these different mechanisms. However, one can compare the behaviour of different subgroups of high authoritarians. Younger voters and those expressing less support for the political system are less likely to have a strong attachment to an established party. Such voters should be more likely to support a PRR party. By contrast, older voters and those who express more attachment to the political system are more likely to support an established party and should be less likely to vote for a PRR party.

This discussion suggests a series of hypotheses. The first, and most straightforward, hypothesis is that high authoritarians are more likely to vote for PRR parties than low authoritarians. This hypothesis derives from the logic that high authoritarians will support PRR parties because they propose policies that address the threats to the social order caused by values change and demographic change. The second set of hypotheses proposes that the relationship between authoritarianism and PRR party support should be stronger among those who indicate less trust in or support for the political system. The relationship between authoritarianism, age, and PRR party support is the subject of Chapter 8.

Analysis

I analyse national election study data from Austria, Britain, Finland, Germany, and Switzerland, and cross-national survey data from the 2017 wave of the European Values Study (EVS 2019). The national studies are the 2013 Austrian Election Study (AES) (Kritzinger et al. 2014), the British Election Study panel survey (BES) Wave 6 (collected after the 2015 general election) (Fieldhouse et al. 2019), the 2015 Finnish National Election Study (2018), the German Longitudinal Election Study (GLES) wave conducted in May 2014 (Rattinger et al. 2014),[3] and the 2015 Swiss Election Study (Lutz and Pekari 2015). These election studies are appropriate as they fulfil two necessary conditions. First, there is a viable PRR party in each country participating in that election. These parties are the Freedom Party of Austria (FPÖ), the UK Independence Party (UKIP) in Great Britain, the Finns Party (PS) in Finland, the Alternative for Germany (AfD) in Germany, and the Swiss People's Party (SVP) in Switzerland. Second, each survey includes necessary measures of authoritarianism in the questionnaire, along with other necessary control variables. The analysis proceeds in three sections. After describing the data and variables, I present basic descriptive statistics designed to show the broad relationship between authoritarianism and party support in each country. The second stage presents multivariate logistic regression analyses in which the relationship between authoritarianism and PRR party support is tested in the presence of control variables. Finally, the third section examines whether economic anxieties or immigration attitudes moderate the results from the second section.

Data and Variables

Drawing upon the available measures in each national survey, I use several scales to measure authoritarianism. In recent years, the preferred approach among political scientists to measuring authoritarianism uses questions concerning child-rearing values (e.g. Feldman and Stenner 1997; Stenner 2005; Hetherington

---

[3] Although the GLES study was not conducted during the 2013 parliamentary election campaign, it included questions measuring authoritarianism that were necessary for this analysis.

and Weiler 2009; Tillman 2013; Dunn 2015). Prior research has shown that the child-rearing values questions generate valid and reliable measures of authoritarianism across different national contexts (Stenner 2005; Hetherington and Weiler 2009). In addition, child-rearing values are more likely to be causally distinct from political behaviour than questions based on attitudinal measures such as the Right-Wing Authoritarianism (RWA) scale (Altemeyer 1981, 1996), as they measure a basic orientation to how children should be socialized rather than attitudes towards contemporary social or political objects. These questions capture respondents' fundamental orientation towards the trade-off between individual autonomy and social conformity—a core aspect of authoritarianism (Feldman 2003).

These child-rearing questions are available in the German and Swiss surveys, and a slightly different version appears in the EVS. In the German and Swiss surveys, the questions ask respondents to choose between paired items indicating preferences for which values should be instilled in children. The German survey contains three such items while the Swiss survey contains four. Responses to these questions are averaged to generate a scale ranging from −1 (low authoritarian) to 1 (high authoritarian). In the EVS, respondents are asked to select up to five desirable traits in children from a list of eleven. Three responses indicate authoritarian traits (good manners, obedience, and religious faith), while three responses reflect non- or low-authoritarian traits (independence, imagination, and 'tolerance and respect for other people'). Each authoritarian response is scored as 1, and each non-authoritarian response is scored as −1. The five remaining responses, which do not directly measure authoritarian or non-authoritarian values (hard work, feeling of responsibility, thrift, determination, and unselfishness), are scored 0. A respondent could thus score from 3 (indicating three authoritarian responses and no non-authoritarian responses) to −3 (vice versa). This variable is rescaled to run from −1 to 1 and is labelled *Authoritarianism*. As per hypothesis 1, this variable should have a positive coefficient, reflecting higher support for PRR parties.

For the analysis of the Austrian, British, and Finnish data, I rely on alternative measures of authoritarianism. Authoritarianism has often been measured using responses to contemporary (or enduring) socio-political questions. For example, the RWA scale (Altemeyer 1996) includes items measuring respondent attitudes towards punitiveness, deviance, conformity, and obedience in society today. While these questions have the disadvantage of potentially being correlated with attitudes towards contemporary political questions, they effectively measure the underlying construct. As this study examines the effects of authoritarianism on party support (rather than political attitudes), the nature of these questions is less likely to contaminate the results. Additionally, I do not attempt to measure an interaction between authoritarianism and threat (e.g. Stenner 2005; Hetherington and Suhay 2011), so it is also less important to distinguish between the disposition and activated attitudes. Importantly, none of the questions used in this study measures attitudes towards immigration or the European Union, which are typically core issues for PRR parties. Thus, these questions should provide acceptable alternative measures of authoritarianism.

The specific questions and measurement scales vary across the surveys. The AES contains six items measured on a five-point scale, the BES contains five questions measured on a five-point scale, and the Finnish National Election Study contains five items measured on a 0–10 scale. In each case, higher values indicate greater endorsement of authoritarianism. As a result, hypothesis 1 predicts a positive coefficient for these measures in each analysis.

I include a number of control variables across the different analyses. First is a measure of the respondent's assessment of the state of the national economy. Negative assessments of the national economy may be associated with increased support for PRR parties. A second independent variable is economic policy preferences. Although the economic positions of PRR parties are often unclear (Mudde 2007; Eger and Valdez 2015), economic preferences are an important determinant of voting behaviour. When possible, I construct a scale of economic preferences using responses to multiple questions. The scale created from the Austrian data contains five items measured on a five-point scale; the BES also includes five items measured on a five-point scale; the Finnish study includes four statements measured on an eleven-point scale; the SES includes three items measured on a five-point scale; and the GLES includes a single question asking respondents to place themselves on an eleven-point scale where 0 indicates a preference for more taxation in order to fund social spending and 11 indicates a preference for reduced spending in order to lower taxes. In each case, items are coded so that higher values indicate support for right-wing economic policies or values. Although the relationship between economic preferences and PRR support is unclear, I include these measures to control for an important determinant of party support.

I include several control variables measuring respondent characteristics. Education indicates self-reported educational attainment, and Income measures household income.[4] Both variables should correlate negatively with support for PRR parties, which often obtain greater support from older, working-class voters (Givens 2005; Ford and Goodwin 2014). I also include a dummy variable for current students, retirees, the self-employed, and unemployed. I include measures for the respondent's age and gender. Older voters and males should be more likely to vote for PRR parties.

---

[4] Due to problems with the coding of the variable measuring household income in the 2015 Finnish National Election Study, I exclude this variable. However, the 2011 election study includes the income measure, which is not significant in the analysis. The substantive results from the analysis of the 2011 study (including income) are identical to those from 2015 (excluding income), suggesting that this finding is robust to its inclusion.

Authoritarianism and PRR Party Support: A First View

I start by examining the broad relationship between authoritarianism and PRR party support in each country. If this chapter's argument is correct, then high authoritarians should be more likely to vote for PRR parties. Such a relationship should be visible in the aggregate data. To do this, I conduct a basic comparison between high and low authoritarians within each country. I divide each electorate into two, separating those scoring above the mean value of authoritarianism from those scoring below, and I summarize the self-reported voting behaviour of each group. A larger share of high authoritarians should support PRR parties, while more low authoritarians should support green or other left-libertarian parties. The results are presented graphically in Figure 6.1.

The results shown in Figure 6.1 suggest a clear relationship between authoritarianism and support for PRR parties. In each country, support for the PRR party is substantially larger among high authoritarians. In Austria, just under 26 per cent of high authoritarians voted for FPÖ compared to 10.1 per cent of low authoritarians. Similarly, 20.7 per cent of high authoritarians support UKIP compared to 6.5 per cent of low authoritarians. The Finns Party has the support of nearly twice as many high authoritarians compared to low authoritarians (22.3 per cent versus 11.2 per cent). In Germany, which had the newest PRR party, 11.4 per cent of high authoritarians supported the AfD compared to 6.3 per cent of low authoritarians. And in Switzerland, 32.7 per cent of high authoritarians voted SVP compared with only 13.8 per cent of low authoritarians. In each case, the gap in support between high and low authoritarians was substantial. A comparable pattern is evident among low authoritarians. In each country, they support green parties in greater proportions than high authoritarians.

In contrast to the patterns surrounding PRR and green parties, no similar patterns exist for the mainstream parties. In several cases, a larger share of high authoritarians supports mainstream centre-right (i.e. Conservative or Christian Democratic) parties. This pattern is evident in Britain and Germany—and, to some extent, Austria—but not in Finland or Switzerland. Similarly, low authoritarians in Britain and Switzerland support mainstream centre-left (i.e. Social Democratic) parties in greater numbers—but not in Austria, Finland, or Germany. This pattern highlights the degree to which is a worldview evolution is occurring. Because authoritarianism was not relevant to historical patterns of party support until recently, there is no consistent relationship between authoritarianism and support for traditional mainstream parties. Radical right and green parties are newer party families formed around recent socio-cultural issues, and so their patterns of support reflect the ongoing evolution of electoral politics. In the process, these new party families are drawing away support from the established parties.

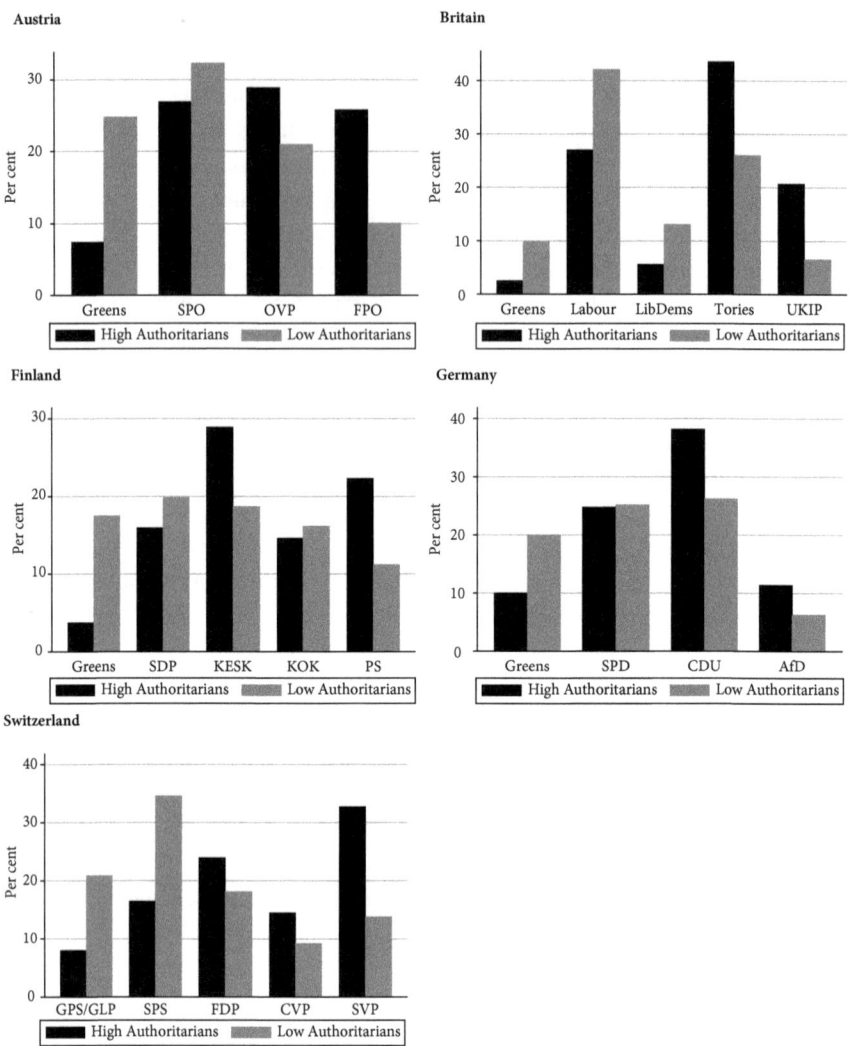

Figure 6.1 Party support by authoritarianism

Sources: Austrian Election Study (Kritzinger et al. 2014), British Election Study (Fieldhouse et al. 2019), Finnish National Election Study (2018), German Longitudinal Election Study (Rattinger et al. 2014), Swiss Election Study (Lutz and Pekari 2015).

The findings of this descriptive analysis suggest a relationship between authoritarianism and PRR party support. However, we cannot have much confidence in these findings as a variety of other factors could be causing this apparent relationship. In the following section, I present the results of multivariate analyses that analyse individual survey responses and include a number of control variables that could possibly account for this relationship.

Multivariate Analyses

In this section, I present and discuss the results of logistic regression analyses of the relationship between authoritarianism and PRR party support in the presence of a wide range of control variables. I present the results in three tables. Table 6.1 shows the results from those surveys including the child-rearing measure of authoritarianism from the German and Swiss election studies, Table 6.2 shows the results from the EVS cross-national data using the child-rearing measure, and Table 6.3 presents those using attitudinal measures. Although I do not expect to

Table 6.1 Authoritarianism and support for PRR parties in national elections

Variable	Germany 2014	Switzerland 2015
Authoritarianism	.58*	.51*
	(.24)	(.12)
Economic Preferences	−.25*	.99*
	(.06)	(.10)
Retrospective Economy	−.27	−.08
	(.16)	(.08)
Religiosity	.12	−.07
	(.18)	(.09)
Gender	−.89*	−.38*
	(.30)	(.14)
Age	−.28*	.01
	(.14)	(.07)
Education	−.23	−.40*
	(.21)	(.08)
Student	−1.4	−.56
	(.80)	(.43)
Unemployed	−.81	.03
	(1.1)	(.78)
Retired	−.37	−.47*
	(.55)	(.22)
Self-Employed	.53	.15
	(.57)	(.25)
Income	.02	−.08*
	(.06)	(.02)
Constant	1.4	−1.1*
	(.85)	(.55)
N	765	1,900
Pseudo R^2	0.13	0.14

Note: Figures show logistic regression coefficients with standard errors in parentheses, * p < .05.

Table 6.2 Authoritarianism and support for PRR parties

Variable	Coefficient	Standard Error
Authoritarianism	.25*	.10
Immigration	1.2*	.08
Religious Hostility	1.2*	.12
Economic Preferences	.16*	.02
Religiosity	−.12*	.04
Gender	.29*	.07
Age	−.05	.03
Education	−.09	.05
Income	.03	.02
Manager	−.52*	.09
Unskilled	.10	.09
Student	−.46*	.21
Unemployed	.11	.16
Farmer	−1.1*	.34
Locality	−.09*	.03
Constant	−3.2*	.31
N	11,651	
Chi Squared	636.8	

Note: Figures show multilevel logistic regression coefficients with standard errors, * $p < .05$.

Source: EVS 2019.

find differences between these two sets of countries, I present the analyses separately to account for the different measurement of the main independent variable.

The results in all three tables show that *Authoritarianism* is positive and significant in each case. High authoritarians are more likely to support PRR parties, which is consistent with expectations. This finding holds across various countries, samples, and different measures of authoritarianism. Also, the results suggest that the link between authoritarianism and PRR party support is stronger in recent elections than it was in earlier years. For example, though, this study finds evidence that authoritarianism predicts support for the FPÖ, which previous studies had not found (Zandonella and Zeglovits 2013; Dunn 2015). These results are suggestive of a stronger relationship between authoritarianism and PRR party support in recent years.

To explore the substantive impact of these findings in greater depth, I generate predicted probabilities of voting behaviour using the 'margins' command in Stata. This command simulates the predicted probability of voting for the radical right party in each country case at different levels of authoritarianism, along with the associated 95 per cent confidence intervals, while holding control variables constant at their means. The results of these simulations are presented graphically in Figure 6.2. The results in each figure show a positive relationship between

Table 6.3 Authoritarian attitudes and support for PRR parties

Variable	Austria 2013	Britain 2015	Finland 2015
Authoritarianism	1.0*	.76*	.34*
	(.23)	(.05)	(.06)
Economic Preferences	.03	−.17*	.10
	(.25)	(.04)	(.07)
Retrospective Economy	−.23	.07	−.19
	(.14)	(.05)	(.10)
Religiosity	−.17	−.11*	−.16
	(.16)	(.07)	(.10)
Gender	.16	−.32*	−.14
	(.27)	(.07)	(.17)
Age	−.08	.06	−.35*
	(.12)	(.03)	(.08)
Education	−.52*	−.32*	−.62*
	(.23)	(.05)	(.12)
Student	−1.0	−.26	−.85*
	(.83)	(.84)	(.36)
Unemployed	1.1	.16	.24
	(.62)	(.10)	(.32)
Retired	−1.1*	−.03	−.02
	(.41)	(.10)	(.27)
Self-Employed	.29	.31*	−.32
	(.48)	(.12)	(.38)
Income	−.06*	−.01	–
	(.03)	(.01)	
Constant	−1.2	−4.2*	.00
	(1.4)	(.30)	(.67)
N	775	14,990	1,135
Pseudo R^2	0.13	0.07	0.11

Note: Figures show logistic regression coefficients with standard errors in parentheses, * $p < .05$.

authoritarianism and the probability of voting for a radical right party, though the strength of that relationship varies in each country (readers should note that the y-axis is not scaled uniformly). The relationship is particularly strong in Austria and Finland, where moving from moderately low to moderately high authoritarianism (i.e. from 2 to 4 in Austria, and from 2 to 6 in Finland) increases the probability of voting for a PRR party from under 0.1 to nearly 0.3 in both cases. The relationship is weakest in Germany, where the relatively low slope hints at a weaker relationship in which the difference between high and low authoritarians is only statistically significant for the poles of the authoritarian

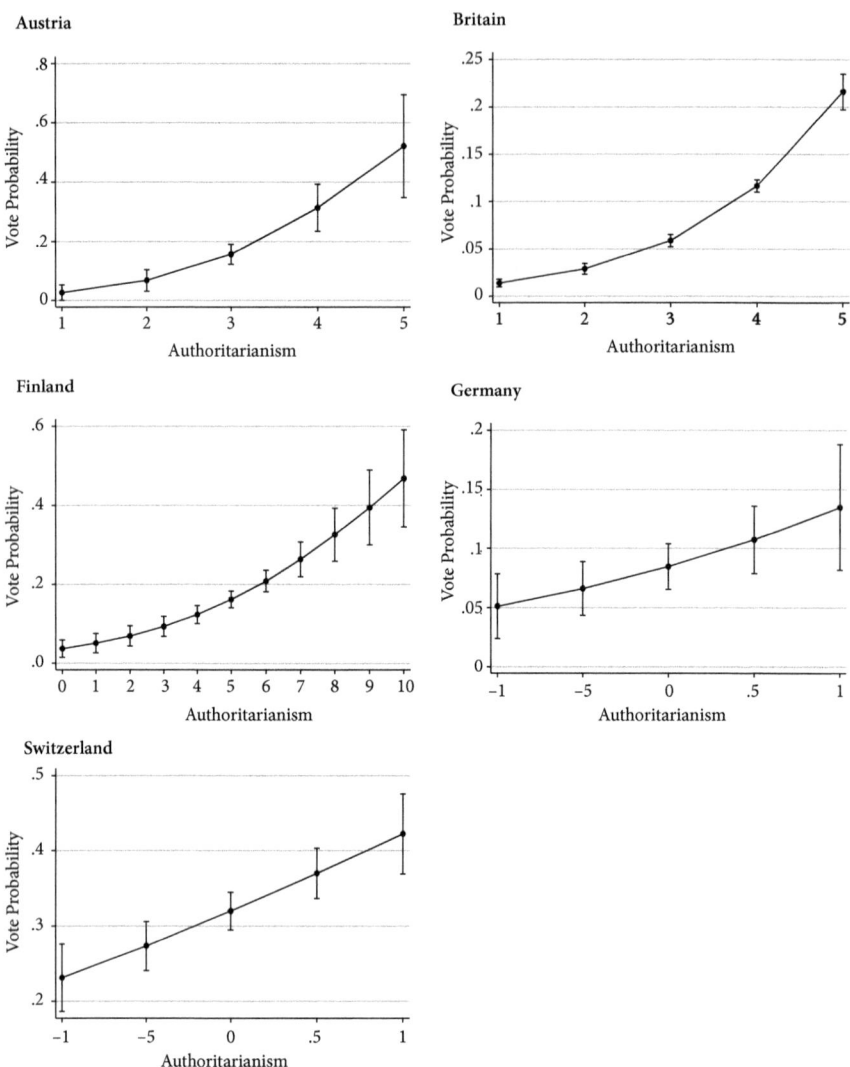

Figure 6.2 Authoritarianism and PRR party support

Note: Each plot shows the predicted probability of voting for a PRR party for the given level of authoritarianism. The bars show the 95 per cent confidence intervals.

Sources: Austrian Election Study (Kritzinger et al. 2014), British Election Study (Fieldhouse et al. 2019), Finnish National Election Study (2018), German Longitudinal Election Study (Rattinger et al. 2014), Swiss Election Study (Lutz and Pekari 2015).

scale. The relationship is also relatively strong in Britain and Switzerland. In short, there is a significant difference in the likelihood of voting for a PRR party between low and high authoritarians. Thus, the evidence from this first study is consistent with the research hypothesis.

Authoritarianism and Mainstream Political Attachment

The discussion earlier in this chapter noted that the relationship between authoritarianism and PRR party support might not be straightforward. Though high authoritarians should be drawn to PRR parties' ideologies, they may also be less likely to abandon established mainstream parties for new, 'outsider' parties. Instead, they should be more likely to stay loyal to established parties instead of switching their voting behaviour. This argument suggests that high authoritarians are less likely to support PRR parties, but only if they are already more attached to the political mainstream. In this section, I examine this possibility by comparing the behaviour of high authoritarians who are more attached to the political establishment with those who are not.

One challenge is finding survey questions that can measure respondents' level of attachment to the political system. I compare high authoritarians according to their degree of satisfaction with democracy in their country. Those who report greater satisfaction with democracy should be more attached to the national political system, which includes the established political parties. Thus, it is more likely such voters would be habitual supporters of a mainstream party, which would make them less likely to vote for a PRR party that positions itself as 'anti-establishment'. By contrast, those with less satisfaction with democracy should be less attached to the political mainstream and more likely to switch their support to a PRR party. Finally, I include a measure of trust in national political institutions, which was available in Germany. I expect that high authoritarians who trust national institutions should be less likely to vote for a PRR party than those who do not. Therefore, I focus on these two questions, which are available in the Austrian, Finnish, German, and Swiss data, allowing a broad analysis.

I estimate logistic regression models including the relevant variable (e.g. satisfaction with democracy) as a constituent variable and as an interaction term with authoritarianism.[5] This method of analysis combined with post-estimation analyses allows for a test of whether the variable affects the relationship between authoritarianism and PRR party support. After estimating each model, I simulate predicted probabilities of voting for a PRR party given different values of authoritarianism and satisfaction with democracy, while the control variables are held at mean values. I simulate these values using the 'margins' command in Stata 15, and the results for the interactions with satisfaction with democracy are shown in Figure 6.3. The results of these analyses are given in Table 6.4, and graphical representations of the predicted probabilities are shown in Figure 6.3.

---

[5] I drop the occupational variables in these models. In addition to simplifying the analyses, these omissions avoid any confounding effects that would come—particularly in the models including age, which correlates with one's likelihood of being a student or retired in particular. The substantive results do not change if these variables are included.

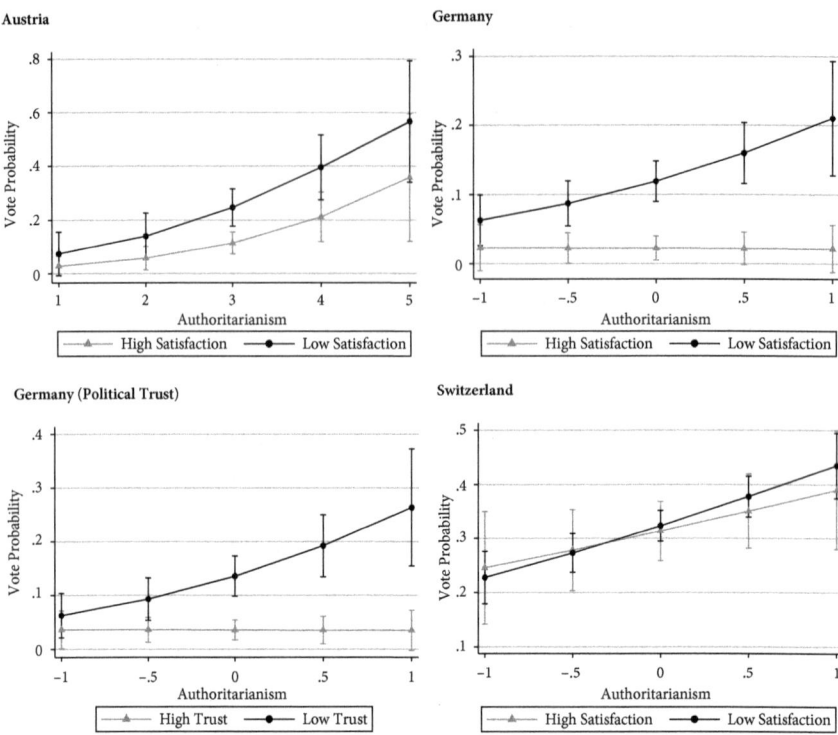

Figure 6.3 Authoritarianism, satisfaction with democracy, and PRR party support

Note: Each plot shows the predicted probability of voting for a PRR party for the given satisfaction with democracy and level of authoritarianism. The bars show the 95 per cent confidence intervals.

Sources: Austrian Election Study (Kritzinger et al. 2014), British Election Study (Fieldhouse et al. 2019), Finnish National Election Study (2018), German Longitudinal Election Study (Rattinger et al. 2014), Swiss Election Study (Lutz and Pekari 2015).

The results are mixed. In Germany, high authoritarians who are dissatisfied with democracy (or who have less trust in national political institutions) are more likely to vote for the radical right AfD than those who are satisfied with democracy (or who trust national political institutions). This finding is consistent with expectations. However, the results are not significant in Austria or Switzerland, indicating that satisfaction with democracy does not affect PRR party support in those contexts. In short, the evidence does not support the claim that those with weaker attachments to the established political system are more likely to vote for PRR parties—except perhaps in Germany.

What does this mixed finding indicate? One possibility is that voters no longer view radical right as political outsiders, so that high authoritarians would not be deterred from supporting PRR parties. One piece of evidence

Table 6.4 Authoritarianism, satisfaction with democracy, and PRR party support

Variable	Austria	Germany	Germany (Political Trust)	Switzerland
Authoritarianism	.76	−.03	−.02	.38
	(.30)	(.69)	(.47)	(.26)
Satisfaction with Democracy	1.1	1.9*	1.5*	.05
	(1.3)	(.45)	(.34)	(.17)
Auth. X Satisfaction	−.04	.77	.92	.16
	(.39)	(.74)	(.55)	(.28)
Economic Preferences	−.01	−.26*	−.24*	.98*
	(.24)	(.06)	(.06)	(.10)
Retrospective Economy	−.16	−.13	−.07	−.08
	(.14)	(.16)	(.17)	(.08)
Religiosity	−.15	.14	.10	−.08
	(.16)	(.18)	(.18)	(.09)
Gender	.02	−.96*	−.91*	−.37*
	(.28)	(.30)	(.30)	(.14)
Education	−.28	−.09	−.00	−.39*
	(.24)	(.19)	(.19)	(.09)
Income	−.06	.06	.06	−.07*
	(.03)	(.06)	(.06)	(.02)
Constant	−2.1	−2.0*	−2.0*	−1.1*
	(1.6)	(.92)	(.89)	(.53)
N	775	764	765	1,888
Pseudo R^2	.10	.17	.17	.14

Note: Figures show logistic regression coefficients with standard errors in parentheses, * p < .05.

supporting this conclusion is that the only significant findings were in Germany, which has a new radical right party among the countries examined here. In those contexts, it could be that high authoritarians who are more satisfied with democracy remained loyal to established parties. By contrast, the PRR parties in Austria and Switzerland have been established in their respective political systems for longer. In Austria, the radical right FPÖ participated in a coalition government from 2000 to 2005 and has been among the three largest parties since the 1990s. Similarly, the radical right SVP has been among the largest parties in Switzerland since the 1990s and part of the governing coalition as well. As such, high authoritarian voters may no longer view them as being anti-establishment or outside of the country's normative political tradition. Moreover, Austrian and Swiss voters have now long been socialized into a political system in which the radical right is an established and major actor. These findings could make sense of why this analysis of elections since 2013 finds stronger results than those analysing earlier years (e.g. Zandonella and Zeglovits 2013; Dunn 2015). Nonetheless, the main conclusion should be that authoritarianism has a significant relationship on PRR party regardless of the level of attachment to the political system—suggesting that PRR parties appeal to high authoritarians because they promise to protect the normative social order.

The Role of Cultural and Economic Attitudes

The evidence so far has pointed to a relationship between authoritarianism and the likelihood of voting for a PRR party. However, these findings come in the wake of a larger body of research showing that attitudes towards immigration affect PRR party support (e.g. Givens 2005; Ivarsflaten 2005, 2007; Lucassen and Lubbers 2012), as well as arguments linking anxieties about economic decline or marginalization to PRR party support (e.g. Ford and Goodwin 2014; Gest 2016; Inglehart 2018). I examine here whether authoritarianism has a significant effect on PRR party support that cannot be explained simply by economic or cultural attitudes.

In addition, recent theories of authoritarianism argue that perceived threats to the normative order activate the authoritarian predisposition, producing authoritarian attitudes (Feldman and Stenner 1997; Stenner 2005; Hetherington and Weiler 2009). It can be difficult to measure perceived threats in practice using observational data. These analyses of economic anxiety and immigration attitudes will provide an indirect attempt, though at least one prior study has used economic anxiety as a measure of threat (Feldman and Stenner 1997). The levels of immigration in recent decades should trigger a sense of threat to the normative order among high authoritarians. Therefore, these analyses will also examine the interaction between perceived threat and authoritarianism.

Attitudes towards Immigration

The relationship between anti-immigration attitudes and PRR party support is well documented (e.g. Givens 2005; Norris 2005; Ivarsflaten 2007; Lucassen and Lubbers 2012). Even those recent studies that emphasize the role of economic marginalization or decline among native-born working-class voters also note the role of ethnocentrism among these voters (e.g. Ford and Goodwin 2014; Gest 2016). Therefore, it is fairly clear that opposition to immigration is an important determinant of support for the radical right. The strength of these past findings might raise the question of whether the analyses in this chapter actually demonstrate anything new—or do they simply produce the same findings with a different measure? Answering this question is complicated by the fact that authoritarianism correlates powerfully with attitudes towards immigration (Altemeyer 1996; Stenner 2005), so simply including a control variable to measure anti-immigration attitudes will confound the analyses.[6] In this analysis, I examine the interaction between authoritarianism and anti-immigration attitudes. Doing so allows me to examine both whether authoritarianism has an independent effect even when anti-immigration attitudes are included in the model and whether anti-immigration attitudes strengthen or reduce that effect.

Each national election study asks a slightly different question about immigration attitudes. The Austrian survey asks respondents whether they are worried about immigration on a four-point scale where answers range from 'not at all' to 'very worried'. The British Election Study asks respondents to place themselves on an eleven-point scale where one pole indicates a desire to reduce immigration and the other to increase it, and the German survey asks a nearly identical question. The Finnish survey asks a similar question on an eleven-point scale, though it prompts respondents to consider whether it would be good or bad if Finland had more immigration. The Swiss survey does not ask directly about immigration; rather, it asks respondents whether Swiss law should make it easier for third-generation immigrants to naturalize. Although this question is substantively different, it should measure the same underlying preferences about allowing those of non-native backgrounds to join Swiss society. The analyses in this section include the measure of anti-immigration attitudes in interaction with authoritarianism. The statistical results are given in Table 6.5. Graphical results showing the interactive effects of anti-immigration attitudes and authoritarianism on the predicted probability of voting for a PRR party are shown in Figure 6.4.

Logistic regression models including interaction terms are difficult to interpret, so the graphs in Figure 6.4 are more useful for understanding the results. The results point to the importance of the interaction between authoritarianism and anti-immigration attitudes in every case but Switzerland. In Austria, Britain, Finland, and Germany, only high authoritarians with anti-immigration attitudes are more significantly more likely to vote for PRR parties. High and low authoritarians do not differ in their propensity to support the radical right when they hold favourable attitudes towards immigration, as can be seen by examining the slope of the line for the pro-immigration respondents. Because the slope in each case is nearly flat, there is no statistically significant difference in the likelihood of voting for a PRR party among those with pro-immigration attitudes. Also, low

---

[6] This is a statistical problem known as multicollinearity, in which two predictor variables are themselves highly correlated. Because authoritarianism shapes attitudes towards immigration, with both in turn shaping voting behaviour, any model that simply includes both variables will find stronger results for anti-immigration attitudes given their closer 'proximity' to voting behaviour.

Table 6.5 Authoritarianism, attitudes towards immigration, and PRR party support

Variable	Austria	Britain	Finland	Germany	Switzerland
Authoritarianism	.54	.03	.21*	−1.8	−.17
	(.87)	(.37)	(.09)	(1.0)	(.34)
Immigration	.65	−2.1	−.21	.37*	−.71*
	(.83)	(1.1)	(.11)	(.08)	(.08)
Auth. X Immigration	.07	.29	.01	.23*	.24*
	(.26)	(.24)	(.02)	(.11)	(.12)
Economic Preferences	.05	−.13	.11	−.17*	.71*
	(.26)	(.24)	(.07)	(.07)	(.11)
Retrospective Economy	−.13	−.28*	−.20	−.17	−.06
	(.14)	(.07)	(.10)	(.17)	(.08)
Religiosity	−.20	−.10	−.09	.17	−.12
	(.16)	(.15)	(.10)	(.19)	(.10)
Gender	.07	−.46*	−.12	−.86*	−.21
	(.28)	(.14)	(.17)	(.31)	(.15)
Age	−.08	−.10	−.33*	−.31*	.08
	(.13)	(.07)	(.08)	(.14)	(.07)
Education	−.65*	−.26*	−.55*	−.05	−.32*
	(.24)	(.10)	(.12)	(.22)	(.10)
Student	−.74	.58	−.74*	−1.3	−.32
	(.92)	(.65)	(.36)	(.82)	(.43)
Unemployed	1.2*	.63*	.25	−.31	.09
	(.58)	(.23)	(.33)	(1.1)	(.99)
Retired	−1.1*	.30	.01	−.19	−.44
	(.41)	(.20)	(.27)	(.65)	(.23)
Self-Employed	.29	.40	−.26	.72	.39
	(.47)	(.21)	(.38)	(.62)	(.26)
Income	−.04	.01	–	.03	−.06*
	(.03)	(.02)		(.07)	(.02)
Constant	−2.4	1.4	.93	−2.9*	.82
	(3.2)	(1.7)	(.79)	(1.3)	(.61)
N	766	3,716	1,135	755	1,830
Pseudo R^2	.19	.14	.14	.20	.21

Note: Figures show regression coefficients with standard errors in parentheses, * $p < .05$.

authoritarians are very unlikely to vote for a PRR party, regardless of whether they hold pro- or anti-immigration attitudes, as shown by the overlapping confidence intervals between the two lines at the left of each panel. Rather, it is the combination of high authoritarians who hold anti-immigration attitudes who are significantly more likely to vote for a radical right party.

The results are different in Switzerland. Here, there is a substantial and consistent gap in the likelihood of voting for the radical right SVP based on attitudes towards the naturalization of third-generation immigrants. For all levels of

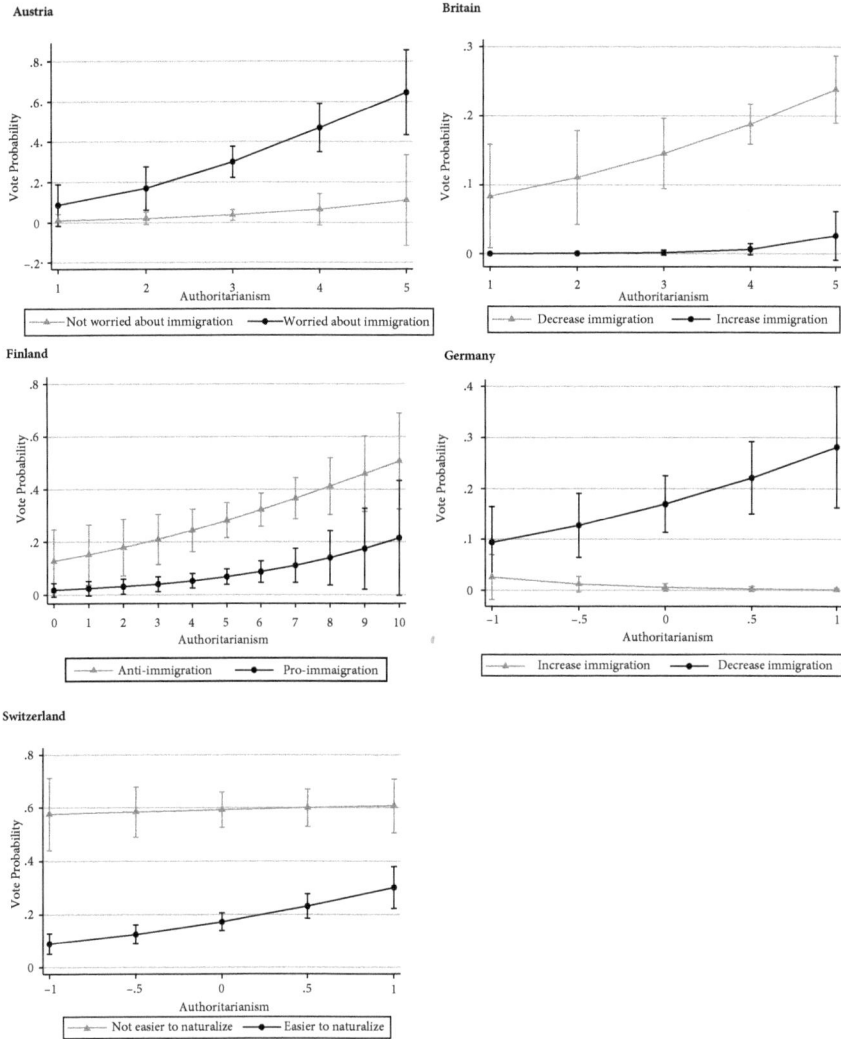

Figure 6.4 Authoritarianism, attitudes towards immigration, and PRR party support

Note: Each plot shows the predicted probability of voting for a PRR party for the given immigration attitudes and level of authoritarianism. The bars show the 95 per cent confidence intervals.

Sources: Austrian Election Study (Kritzinger et al. 2014), German Longitudinal Election Study (Rattinger et al. 2014), Swiss Election Study (Lutz and Pekari 2015).

authoritarianism, those who oppose naturalization are more likely to vote SVP than those who support it. Among those who support easing naturalization laws, high authoritarians are significantly more likely to vote SVP than low authoritarians, as can be seen from the slope of the corresponding line moving from left to right across the graph. This finding might suggest that other concerns relevant to high authoritarians—such as the preservation of traditional values or tough law-and-order policies—also influence SVP support. Why are the results different in Switzerland? One possibility is that the question measures a distinct political issue, over which attitudes are more crystallized, rather than general orientations towards immigration. As a result, the link between attitudes on this issue and party support may be stronger as a function of knowledge and opinion about this particular issue. However, authoritarianism still has an effect among those with more favourable attitude towards immigration.

These findings generate two broader conclusions. The first claim, which is crucial for this book's argument, is that authoritarianism matters—even when immigration attitudes are included in the analysis. Among those who oppose immigration in the first four countries, high authoritarians are more likely to vote for PRR parties than low authoritarians. Nonetheless, this relationship is not universal; the effect of authoritarianism is strongest among those who oppose immigration. Second, this finding adds nuance to our understanding of how anti-immigration attitudes predict PRR party support. It is not sufficient simply for a voter to oppose immigration; he or she is only more likely to vote for the radical right if she also scores higher in authoritarianism. Low authoritarians who oppose immigration are very unlikely to vote for a PRR party. This finding suggests that the combination of opposing immigration and being attentive to threats to social cohesion increase support for the radical right. It also highlights the distinction between authoritarianism and conservatism raised by Stenner (2005, 2009). In Stenner's formulation, conservatives seek to slow the pace of social or cultural change, but high authoritarians support punitive or reactionary policies in order to stop or reverse such changes when they perceive a threat to the normative order. Because PRR parties take stronger anti-immigration positions while mainstream centre-right parties typically promise more moderate approaches, high authoritarians may gravitate towards PRR parties while those scoring lower in authoritarianism may prefer mainstream parties even if they hold anti-immigration attitudes.

Economic Anxiety

Does economic anxiety moderate the relationship between authoritarianism and PRR party support? In some popular accounts, the radical right draws support from workers who have suffered job or income losses as a result of global economic competition and immigration (e.g. Mounk 2018). This sense of economic anxiety makes such voters more receptive to the messages of PRR parties, which promise to protect workers from the harmful economic effects of foreign trade competition and immigration. Careful academic versions of this argument emphasize that this is part of a broader process of social and cultural alienation, in which the native-born working class has seen its jobs, values, and social standing degraded by the mainstream political elite (e.g. Ford and Goodwin

2014; Cramer 2016; Gest 2016). Those arguments bear greater similarity to this book's argument by emphasizing the effect of value change and demographic change on the political attitudes of native-born working-class voters. The difference is that those other works do not shed much light on the individual dispositional traits leading some of these voters (as well as others that do not fit that socio-economic profile) to move towards the radical right. Nonetheless, the question here centres on the more straightforward 'economic anxiety' argument. Simply put, are voters who are more anxious or pessimistic about their economic future more likely to support PRR parties? And, more importantly to this book's argument, does economic anxiety moderate the relationship between authoritarianism and PRR party support?

It is difficult to determine what a good measure of economic anxiety would look like. It is not clear whether economic anxiety should be understood to reflect current struggles with income security or longer-term pessimism about financial prospects, so I use both types of questions in the following analysis. The AES asks respondents whether they are able to get along well or with difficulty given their current income situation. Responses range from 'with great difficulty' (1) to 'very well' (5). The Finnish National Election Study includes two relevant questions. The first asks respondents whether they believe that their standard of living will improve over the next ten years. Answers range from 'very unlikely' (1) to 'very likely' (4). The second question asks respondents about the perceived risk that their income could be severely reduced in the next twelve months. Answers range from 'very likely' (1) to 'very unlikely' (5). Finally, the BES includes three relevant questions. The first asks whether respondents consider it a good time to make a major purchase. Respondents could indicate that it was (1), it was not (3), or that they were uncertain (2). The second and third questions ask respondents about their perceived risk of poverty and unemployment, respectively, in the near future. Respondents could indicate on a five-point scale that they considered such a risk very unlikely (1) to very likely (5) or somewhere in between. I combine the answers to these last two questions to create an index of economic anxiety. Higher values (indicating more economic anxiety) should correspond with higher support for PRR parties if arguments about economic anxiety are correct. I include these measures as components of an interaction term with authoritarianism. Such a model examines whether the level of economic anxiety among respondents moderates the effect of authoritarianism on the likelihood of voting for a PRR party. If the economic anxiety argument is correct, then the relationship between authoritarianism and PRR party support should be stronger for those experiencing economic anxiety. If not, then their inclusion will not affect the relationship between authoritarianism and PRR party support shown above. The results are presented in Table 6.6 and Figure 6.5.

Does economic anxiety affect PRR party support? No. As each panel in Figure 6.5 shows, there is no difference in the relationship between authoritarianism and PRR party support among those who are anxious about their economic situation and those who are not. Nor are those who are anxious about their economic situation generally more likely to vote for a PRR party. In every case, the overlapping confidence intervals (shown by the bands surrounding each estimate) indicate that the predicted probabilities are statistically indistinguishable. Furthermore, the gap that appears between the high and low anxiety

Table 6.6 Authoritarianism, economic anxiety, and PRR party support

Variable	Austria	Finland: Standard of Living	Finland: Income Risk	Britain: Major Purchase	Britain: Future Situation
Authoritarianism	1.1*	.13	.49*	.78*	.53*
	(.29)	(.15)	(.19)	(.18)	(.18)
Economic Anxiety	1.4	−.52	.13	.03	−.34
	(1.5)	(.33)	(.26)	(.33)	(.29)
Auth. X Economic Anxiety	−.24	.09	−.04	−.00	.09
	(.44)	(.06)	(.05)	(.08)	(.07)
Economic Preferences	.05	.09	.10	−.09	−.08
	(.24)	(.07)	(.07)	(.10)	(.10)
Retrospective Economy	−.17	−.15	−.18	−.21*	−.19*
	(.14)	(.10)	(.10)	(.07)	(.07)
Religiosity	−.17	−.15	−.15	−.07	−.06
	(.16)	(.10)	(.10)	(.15)	(.15)
Gender	.11	−.15	−.16	−.44*	−.45*
	(.27)	(.17)	(.17)	(.14)	(.13)
Age	−.08	−.36*	−.35*	−.01	−.01
	(.12)	(.08)	(.08)	(.07)	(.07)
Education	−.47*	−.61*	−.60*	−.33*	−.34*
	(.24)	(.12)	(.12)	(.09)	(.09)
Student	−1.1	−.79*	−.81*	.45	.49
	(.81)	(.36)	(.36)	(.68)	(.68)
Unemployed	.84	.28	.25	.62*	.62*
	(.66)	(.32)	(.32)	(.22)	(.22)
Retired	−1.0*	.01	01	.21	.24
	(.40)	(.27)	(.27)	(.20)	(.21)
Self-Employed	.28	−.30	−.30	.32	.32
	(.50)	(.38)	(.38)	(.22)	(.22)
Income	−.04	–	–	.02	.02
	(.03)			(.02)	(.02)
Constant	−2.2	1.3	−.60	−3.6*	−2.8*
	(1.5)	(1.0)	(1.2)	(.82)	(.90)
N	775	1,124	1,135	3,716	3,716
Pseudo R²	.14	.11	.12	.08	.08

Note: Figures show logistic regression coefficients with standard errors in parentheses, * p < .05.

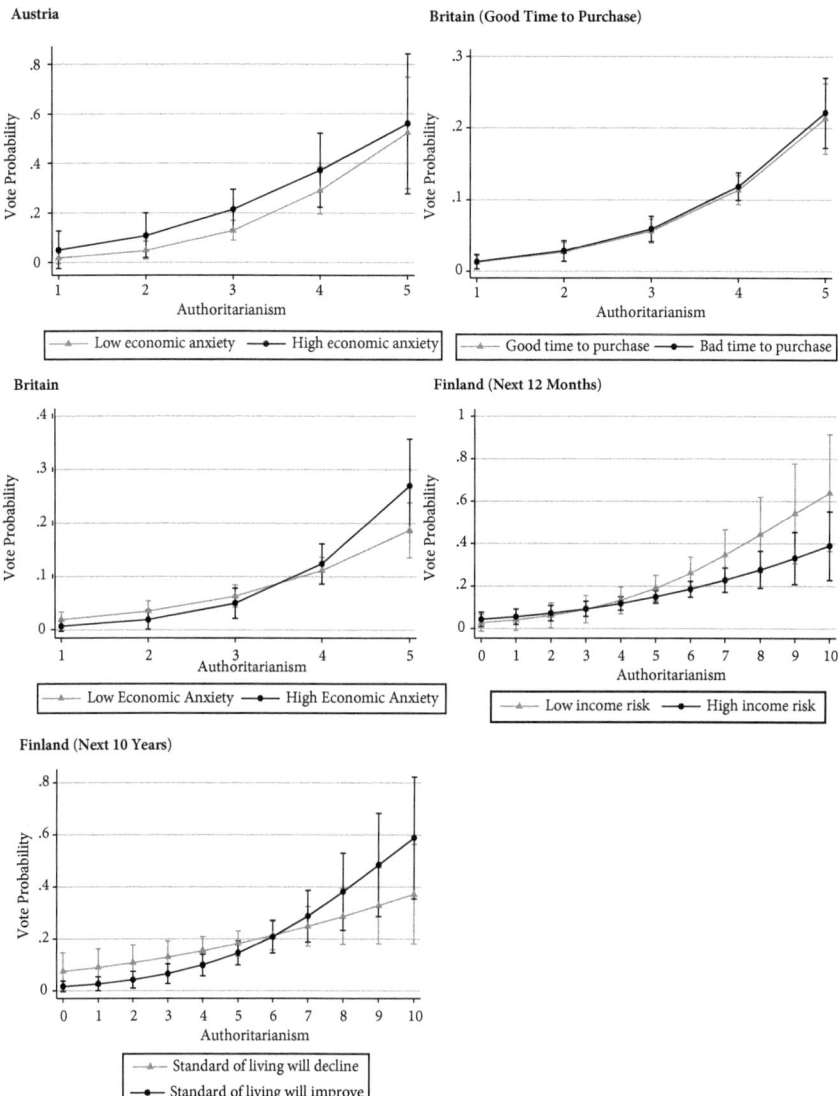

Figure 6.5 Authoritarianism, economic anxiety, and PRR party support

Note: The plots show the predicted probability of voting for a PRR party for the given level of economic anxiety and authoritarianism displayed on the horizontal axis. Bars display the 95 per cent confidence intervals.

Sources: Austrian Election Study (Kritzinger et al. 2014), British Election Study (Fieldhouse et al. 2019), Finnish National Election Study (2018), German Longitudinal Election Study (Rattinger et al. 2014), Swiss Election Study (Lutz and Pekari 2015).

groups in Finland is in the opposite direction: high authoritarians who are *less* worried about their economic futures show a modestly (though not statistically significant) higher likelihood of voting for a PRR party. This lack of findings holds true across questions measuring immediate or short-term economic worries (as in Austria and the first models from Britain and Finland, respectively) and longer-term concerns (as in the second models from Britain and Finland). In short, economic anxiety has no relevant effect on PRR party support, at least in the context of authoritarianism.

This (non-) finding speaks to broader arguments about economic development and values change in Western European societies. The rise of the radical right has led to a debate about the relative importance of economic insecurity versus cultural backlash. Advocates of the economic insecurity argument argue that rising inequality and post-industrial economic transformations have fuelled support for PRR parties among the 'losers' of those transformations—those who experience growing insecurity and declining income as a result. By contrast, advocates of the cultural backlash argument see the roots of growing PRR support in the reaction to increasing diversity and values liberalism. The findings presented here weigh against the economic insecurity argument, at least in the direct form that appears in popular accounts. Economic concerns have no bearing on high authoritarians' likelihood of supporting PRR parties, in contrast to their attitudes about immigration. These results suggest that cultural anxieties are driving high authoritarians towards PRR parties rather than economic anxieties. With that said, it is important to remember that these variables may not be effective measures of the broader anxieties created by long-term economic change (such as deindustrialization) or growing economic inequality, which are difficult to measure in surveys. Moreover, thoughtful academic accounts of PRR party support incorporating economic concerns (e.g. Ford and Goodwin 2014; Gest 2016) treat them as being linked to social and cultural anxieties: native-born working-class communities have experienced economic *and* cultural marginalization over the past several decades as West European societies have become more post-industrial and multicultural, generating a broader set of anxieties about their social standing.

Conclusion

This chapter examines the relationship between authoritarianism and support for populist radical right (PRR) parties. Prior research on this question has found mixed results (Zandonella and Zeglovits 2013; Dunn 2015; Vasilopoulos and Lachat 2018), which is surprising given that the PRR parties often emphasize issues that would appeal naturally to high authoritarians. This study re-examined this relationship using election study data from 2013 to 2017. The results show that authoritarianism predicts PRR party support across different national election surveys. Moreover, anti-immigration attitudes strengthen this relationship, suggesting that it is driven at least in part by high authoritarians' desire to preserve social cohesion.

These results contribute to our understanding of the dynamics of PRR party support, though questions remain. One puzzle is why this study found a stronger relationship between authoritarianism and PRR party support than previous studies that employed similar research strategies (e.g. Zandonella and Zeglovits 2013; Dunn 2015; but see Vasilopoulos and Lachat 2018). One possibility is that PRR parties have becoming increasingly normalized over time, making them more socially acceptable to high authoritarians. Because high authoritarians are typically attached to tradition and are sensitive to cues about conventional behaviour (Oyamot et al. 2012), they are less likely to be the first to abandon an established party for the radical right. The evidence from the second analysis lends some support to this claim. In Germany, where the AfD was rather new as of May 2014, attachment to the political establishment (measured as satisfaction with democracy and trust in national political institutions) moderated the relationship. High authoritarians with less political attachment were more likely to vote AfD than high authoritarians with stronger attachments. Those latter high authoritarians are more likely to remain loyal to an established political party. However, this moderating effect was not evident in Austria or Switzerland, where PRR parties have been established in national parliaments and even government for a longer time. This finding suggests that high authoritarians may support PRR parties in greater proportions as they become more established in national politics.

Another contribution of this chapter is to clarify our understanding of why high authoritarians support PRR parties. The third set of analyses showed that anti-immigration attitudes strengthen the relationship between authoritarianism and PRR party support. Although these attitudes are not a direct measure of perceived threat to social cohesion, it is likely that those who hold anti-immigration attitudes are likely to view immigration as a threat given its high levels over recent decades. This finding reinforces arguments that anti-immigration attitudes predict PRR party support (e.g. Ivarsflaten 2005, 2007; Lucassen and Lubbers 2012), but they add an important new dimension by identifying for which individuals—high authoritarians—immigration is most important.

Finally, I found that economic anxieties had no effect on voting for PRR parties. This result runs contrary to conventional wisdom about economic decline and support for the radical right. However, this result is not conclusive. Academic analyses of working-class voters find a complex pattern of marginalization that is both cultural and economic (Ford and Goodwin 2014; Gest 2016). Moreover, the relationship between authoritarianism, education, and attitudes is also complex. Though education is associated with greater support for immigration, this relationship may result from self-selection among more liberal individuals (Lancee and Sarrasin 2015). And research on the cognitive styles of high authoritarians suggests that they would be less inclined towards higher education (e.g. Altemeyer 1996; Lavine et al. 2005; Stenner 2005; Kemmelmeier 2010). The result may be that high authoritarians are more heavily concentrated in occupations that do not require university education and that are more vulnerable to global economic competition. In short, the questions surrounding economic change, authoritarianism, education, and political attitudes merit further investigation.

This chapter makes an important contribution to the book's overall argument. In showing that high authoritarians are more likely to vote for PRR parties, it suggests that at least in some West European states electoral politics has moved towards a worldview realignment. But how has this realignment developed? The next chapters examine different aspects of this question. Chapter 7 examines potential support for a hypothetical PRR party in a country without one. Chapter 8 examines the moderating role of age—and whether growing PRR party support reflects a backlash among older voters or a new alignment of younger voters. Chapter 9 traces the patterns of party support among high and low authoritarians over recent decades.

7
Authoritarianism and Potential Support for the Radical Right in Ireland

Introduction

The previous chapter showed the evolving relationship between authoritarianism and support for populist radical right (PRR) parties. In countries where PRR parties have achieved electoral success, high authoritarians form an important part of their support base. At first glance, this finding could lead to the conclusion that high authoritarians have propelled PRR parties into national parliaments and electoral prominence. However, this conclusion may not be correct. Those who form the electoral base of an established party may not be the same as those who first supported the party before it achieved prominence. In this case, the authoritarian traits that propel individuals to support an established radical right party may also deter them from supporting a new party. In other words, support for PRR parties reflects patterns of electoral competition between PRR parties and the mainstream that have developed subsequent to their emergence. High authoritarian voters may begin to support the radical right only as it becomes established, and as media coverage and its interactions with rival parties gives it credibility. By examining the behaviour of high authoritarians in a context without a PRR party, we can learn more about whether high authoritarians are actually more likely to support a new PRR party—and thus drive the worldview evolution described in this book.

This chapter reports the results of an analysis of a survey experiment carried out in Ireland in February 2019. This survey asks respondents to read about a newly formed party in Ireland and to indicate their likelihood of voting for it. In the control condition, respondents read a description in which the new party holds mainstream positions on immigration and the EU. In the treatment condition, the party holds radical right positions on immigration and the EU. Ireland is an interesting case for studying this question, as it is one of the few West European states that does not yet have an electorally relevant PRR party. This absence could result from Ireland's unique history and political culture, which does not provide a base of potential PRR voters (O'Malley 2008). Alternatively, it may simply be that no such PRR party with sufficient resources or leadership has yet emerged, which would be consistent with a view that Irish voters are as likely as those in other West European states to support the radical

Authoritarianism and the Evolution of West European Electoral Politics. Erik R. Tillman, Oxford University Press.
© Erik R. Tillman 2021. DOI: 10.1093/oso/9780192896223.003.0007

right if provided the opportunity. Ireland provides a unique context in which to observe whether high authoritarian voters would be likely to support a new PRR party, and which mainstream parties would lose support as a result. This analysis can shed light on whether Ireland is a unique case.

The main research question is whether high authoritarians are more likely to indicate support for a hypothetical PRR party. The analyses in this chapter consider two secondary research questions. First, are high authoritarians more likely to fear the disintegration of Irish society, consistent with contemporary theorizing on authoritarianism (e.g. Feldman 2003; Stenner 2005)? Second, from which existing parties would a potential PRR party take support?

The results of this analysis show that high authoritarians are significantly more likely to indicate a willingness to support a PRR party. Despite the possibility that high authoritarians may generally be less likely to change habitual behaviours, they express a greater willingness to vote for a new party that appeals to their needs for social cohesion. By contrast, high authoritarians are no more likely to vote for the hypothetical new party in the control condition—indicating that these findings are not simply the result of frustration with established parties or attraction to new parties in general. Second, high authoritarian voters display little evidence of sorting in the current Irish party landscape. High authoritarians' support is dispersed across the major parties. Thus, a new PRR party would plausibly draw high authoritarians from all of the major establishment parties and help to contribute to an electoral realignment. Third, the evidence further shows that high authoritarians express greater concern about the loss of social cohesion—represented both in opposition to immigration as well as fears that Ireland will lose its shared values and social cohesion. These results are consistent with the argument that high authoritarians support PRR parties due to fears of social disintegration driven by immigration and values change.

Who Supports New Parties?

There are various ways of approaching the question of which individuals are more likely to vote for a new party. One approach would emphasize the congruence of the new party's issue positions and the voter's preferences, while the other approach would emphasize voters' dispositional traits that might influence their likelihood of supporting a new party. Of course, these approaches are neither necessarily contradictory nor exclusive, but they lead to different expectations and are most relevant for this study.

The first approach suggests that new parties are likely to emerge when there is potential electoral demand for a set of issue positions that existing parties do not provide. When such a party does not exist, those dissatisfied voters may demonstrate weak attachments to the existing parties or quit participating in elections. For example, evidence from the United Kingdom shows that new supporters of the UK Independence Party had switched between Labour and the Conservatives in prior elections (Ford and Goodwin 2014). Alternatively, voters may prioritize one set of concerns over another in order to choose between parties that only partially reflect their issue preferences. For example, voters with left-wing economic preferences but conservative socio-cultural attitudes have prioritized the economic over the social in recent decades, thus voting for left-wing parties despite disagreeing with these parties' socio-cultural stances (Lefkofridi et al. 2014). If enterprising leaders of new parties recognize this situation and can formulate a set of issue positions to appeal to these dissatisfied voters, they can exploit the situation to gain new supporters by peeling away supporters of existing parties and mobilizing non-voters to participate again (Kitschelt 1997; de Vries and Hobolt 2013; Hobolt and de Vries 2015). Finally, changing circumstances may lead voters to re-evaluate their loyalties. The global financial crisis (GFC) may have led voters who suffered as a result of the crisis and subsequent austerity policies to lose trust in mainstream parties, leaving them more receptive to the electoral appeals of challenger parties (Hobolt and Tilley 2016). More recently, the migrant crisis of 2014–16 may have aided PRR parties by increasing the salience of socio-cultural and security concerns among voters.

This perspective suggests that the main factor driving voters to support a new party is the congruence between the party's issue positions and voters' preferences. When the new party's positions are closer to the voter's than that of existing parties, then those voters should support the new party. Rooted in spatial theories of voting behaviour (Downs 1957), this perspective offers a reasonable expectation about when new parties will gain voters.

A second approach suggests that the preceding discussion may ignore other factors that structure voting behaviour. Voters vary in their degree of attachment to established parties. Voters with strong attachments to existing parties may be unlikely to abandon that party for a new one, even if that new party takes issue positions closer to the voter's. Voting has a habitual element (Franklin 2004), and individuals vary in their propensity to change habitual behaviour. Voters who are dispositionally less likely to change established behaviours or loyalties may be unlikely to support a new party.

Research in political and social psychology often identifies openness to change or novelty as a key factor explaining political behaviour. Studies using the Big Five personality index (openness to experience, conscientiousness, extraversion, agreeableness, and neuroticism; McCrae and Costa 1987) find that individuals scoring higher in openness to experience are more likely to support left-wing parties (Barbaranelli et al. 2006; Schoen and Schumann 2007; Mondak 2010; Bakker et al. 2015a; Johnston et al. 2017) and European integration (Bakker and de Vreese 2016). Conversely, higher levels of conscientiousness are associated with support for right-wing parties (Mondak 2010), and individuals scoring higher in authoritarianism are more likely to support right-wing parties (Hetherington and Weiler 2009; Johnston et al. 2017). In addition, there is a smaller body of evidence suggesting that personality traits affect the stability of these relationships. Individuals scoring higher in openness are more likely to switch party support, while individuals scoring higher in conscientiousness may be less likely to express a party identification (Bakker et al. 2016b; but see also Gerber et al. 2010).

In short, the tendency both to support a particular party (family) and to switch party support may reflect individual dispositional factors. Individuals who are more open to new experiences are both more likely to support a left-wing party and more likely to switch their party support. Openness to experience correlates negatively with authoritarianism, so these tendencies should extend to low authoritarians. This pattern creates an interesting puzzle when applied to the study of radical right parties. PRR parties are expected to draw support from high authoritarians (Dunn 2015), who will tend to score low in openness. Thus, the very individuals who are more likely to support a PRR party due to the resonance between that party's issue positions and the voter's dispositional tendencies may also be less likely to vote for a new party.

Taken together, these two lines of research produce rival expectations about the likelihood of high authoritarians to vote for a new radical right party. If the tendency to support a new party predominantly reflects demand for its policies, then authoritarianism should have no significant effect. Instead, support for the new PRR party should result from preferences over core issues such as immigration and European integration. However, if personality factors affect support for a new party, then there are two possible relationships. First, authoritarianism could increase support for the new PRR party because it appeals to high authoritarians' desire for social cohesion and security. The second possibility is that authoritarianism reduces the propensity to vote for a new, untested party, in favour of maintaining support for an established party. Because high authoritarians are less willing to take a risk on a new party or to abandon an established party, they should be less likely to support the new party.

Parties and Elections in Ireland

Ireland has often been viewed as something of an outlier in the study of West European electoral politics due to the limited ideological differences between the major parties, particularly on questions of class and redistribution. As a result, the traditional social cleavages of class and religion that traditionally divide party supporters in most West European democracies (Lipset and Rokkan 1967) have little predictive value in Ireland (Whyte 1974; Carty 1983; Marsh et al. 2008; Tilley and Garry 2017). Nonetheless, there were strong patterns of party attachment, though it was often difficult to identify the social bases of these divisions. However, these attachments have faded in recent years as the electorate has de-aligned since the 1980s (Marsh et al. 2008).

Irish party politics features relatively minimal policy differences, particularly between Fianna Fáil (FF) and Fine Gael (FG)—the two largest parties and traditional rivals for control of government (Lutz 2003; Marsh et al. 2008). Both parties have similar centre-right profiles, with only traditionally smaller opposition parties such as Labour, Sinn Féin, and the newer Green Party and Anti-Austerity Alliance/People Before Profit (AAA–PBP) offering a left-wing alternative. As a result, alternations in power between the two parties do not necessarily lead to major policy changes, and campaigns often are more pragmatic and local than ideological (Marsh et al. 2008).

This lack of clear distinction between the major parties extends to the electorate, resulting in a situation described as 'politics without social bases' (Whyte 1974). Although there has historically been evidence of widespread party attachment in the electorate (Carty 1983), these attachments did not have clear links to major social divisions (Whyte 1974; Marsh et al. 2008). And while Irish voters identify themselves and parties along a left–right ideological spectrum, these positions have little apparent linkage to policy issues (McElroy 2017). Moreover, there is evidence of de-alignment since the 1980s, producing an electorate with relatively weak attachments to any of the parties (Sinnott 1998; Marsh et al. 2008). As a result, there is little evidence of major differences in class, religion, or core policy preferences across the supporters of the major parties.

The past decade since GFC has led to some change in the political situation. In what would seem to be an example of retrospective voting, opposition parties gained votes in the wake of the crisis and the austerity associated with the International Monetary Fund bailout while the incumbents (FF and the Green Party) responsible for implementing those agreements lost support (Tillman 2016). In addition, several new parties contested the election, winning small shares of the vote, while independent candidates collectively nearly doubled their vote share. In short, the electorate showed greater volatility in the wake of the crisis without much evidence of an ongoing realignment.

These trends continued into the 2016 election. Now the incumbents, FG and coalition partner Labour saw their vote shares decline from 2011, while FF gained back some of its lost support. Sinn Féin, which had the advantage of being in opposition throughout the entire period, gained votes, as did several new parties and independent candidates. The result was a more fragmented and volatile party system (Barrett 2016). This pattern pointed to an ongoing de-alignment of the Irish electorate, but there was also some evidence of a strengthening class alignment. Namely, FG maintained its strength among middle-class voters, while Sinn Féin gained most among working-class voters, and these trends were stronger among younger voters, suggesting some movement towards a realignment based on class (Tilley and Garry 2017). However, FF, Labour, and Independent candidates continued to show no real class basis of support, so electoral politics remained relatively unstructured (Marsh and McElroy 2017).

By the time of the 2016 election, Ireland remained one of the few West European countries without such a relevant PRR party, despite exhibiting many of the favourable conditions seen in other European countries (O'Malley 2008).[1] While factors such as the electoral system or Ireland's unusual structure of party conflict may play a role, another possibility is that Sinn Féin captures much of the latent electoral support for the radical right. As a nationalist party, albeit with left-wing orientations, Sinn Féin may be a 'tolerant party with intolerant supporters' (O'Malley 2008: 969). Sinn Féin partially meets the criteria of a PRR party insofar as it is nationalist, authoritarian, and populist, but its favourable positions on immigrants' rights do not align with PRR party ideology (Mudde 2007; O'Malley 2008). Nonetheless, Sinn Féin attracts voters who are less tolerant towards immigration, and who would thus be more likely to vote for a PRR party elsewhere (Iversflaten 2007).

This discussion suggests that there is electoral potential for a radical right party to fill. An analysis of the ideological space in the Irish party system suggests room to the right of FG for a radical right party to attract support (Bowler and Farrell 2017). Additionally, 'left-authoritarian' voters who hold left-of-centre economic views combined with conservative/authoritarian socio-cultural positions make up close to one-third of the Irish electorate, yet no Irish party offers a compatible set of policies (Costello 2017). Though the measurement used in this study is different, these voters would seem to overlap heavily with high authoritarians, who value social cohesion. The lack of an existing party appealing to this set of concerns leaves an opening for a PRR party emphasizing in-group protection and social cohesion. To the extent such voters have any representation in Irish politics, it is found among some of the independent candidates that seem to hold such views (see Figure 2 in Costello 2017).

In this respect, Ireland resembles other West European party systems in recent years, which also lacked a left-authoritarian option (van der Brug and van Spanje 2009; Lefkofridi et al. 2014). As long as no such party exists, high authoritarian voters have limited choices: they can continue to support a mainstream party based on either economic or cultural views, they can vote for a protest party (or, in Ireland, an independent candidate), or they can withdraw from political

---

[1] The electoral system has an important effect on whether radical right parties can win legislative seats (Givens 2005). As a result, radical right parties in some countries with single-member district electoral systems (e.g. France, the United Kingdom) have struggled to translate substantial electoral support into seats. In Germany, the radical right Alternative for Germany (AfD) narrowly missed passing the 5 per cent electoral threshold in the 2013 federal election before entering parliament after the 2017 election.

participation. However, a PRR party could mobilize such voters by appealing directly to their predispositions for social cohesion.

Drawing on this discussion, the following section also examines the patterns of party support among high authoritarians and low authoritarians. Given the nature of Irish party politics, there is little reason to expect party sorting by authoritarianism. If this expectation is correct, then the movement of high authoritarians towards a hypothetical new PRR party would distribute electoral losses across the existing parties.[2]

Analysis

Data and Variables

The survey data used in this analysis were collected from a representative sample of 416 Irish respondents in February 2019. In the survey, respondents first answer questions about demographics, political and social attitudes, economic assessments and worries, concerns about the future, and prior voting behaviour. Afterwards, respondents read an article containing an experiment designed to assess potential support for a PRR party in Ireland and subsequently answer four additional questions.

In this experiment, respondents read a two-paragraph article about the electoral programme of a new party called the 'Irish People's Party'. Respondents were assigned randomly to a control or treatment condition. In both conditions, the first paragraph is the same as it contains a mixture of mainstream economic and social pledges (drawn from those of mainstream parties) along with a broadly populist pledge to 'make government work for the people again'. The second paragraph contains the experiment that describes the party's position on immigration and European integration. In the control condition, the party holds a mainstream pro-immigration and pro-EU position. The treatment condition describes the party as holding anti-immigration and anti-EU positions. The full text of the treatments is available in Appendix I. After reading this treatment, respondents answer four questions.

The first three questions ask respondents about their perceptions of the hypothetical new Irish People's Party (IPP). The first question asks whether respondents view the party as 'extreme' or 'moderate'. The second asks whether the respondent believes that the IPP 'speaks for people like me' or 'does not speak for people like me'. The third question asks whether the IPP 'offers new ideas' or

---

[2] Ideally, the analysis would also examine whether a new PRR party could mobilize new voters. However, the survey sample included only respondents who indicated having voted in the 2016 general election, so it is not possible to examine the potential behaviour of previous non-voters.

'offers the same ideas as other parties'. All three of these variables are binary, with 0 indicating the unfavourable option (extreme, does not speak for people like me, and offers the same ideas as other parties) and 1 indicating the favourable view (moderate, speaks for people like me, and offers new ideas). Perceptions of the IPP should vary by authoritarianism and experimental condition. High authoritarians in the treatment condition should be less likely to view the IPP as extreme and more likely to view it as speaking for people like them than low authoritarians or high authoritarians in the control condition. It is less clear whether authoritarianism should affect perceptions of the IPP offering new ideas or not.

Finally, respondents indicate their propensity to vote (PTV) (van der Eijk et al. 2006) for the IPP and the other major parties in Ireland. This item asks respondents to evaluate their likelihood of voting for each party on a 0–10 scale, where 0 indicates they would 'never' vote for that party and 10 indicates they would 'definitely' consider voting for it. Respondents answered this question for the IPP plus each of the major existing parties: FF, FG, Labour, Sinn Féin, AAA–PBP, Social Democrats, and the Greens. I derive two measures from these questions. First, I examine the PTV for the Irish People's Party, called *IPP Vote*. This is the main dependent variable and shows the respondent's propensity to vote for this hypothetical new party. High authoritarians in the treatment condition should be more likely to vote for the IPP. Because this measure may be affected by respondents' tendencies to assign higher or lower PTV values in general, I employ a second variable (*IPP Difference*) that measures the difference between *IPP Vote* and the respondent's mean PTV for all other parties. It can range from −10 to +10, with a negative value indicating a lower propensity to vote for the IPP relative to the existing parties and a positive value indicating a higher relative propensity.

Authoritarianism is measured with a five-item measure of child-rearing values (Feldman 2003; Stenner 2005; Hetherington and Weiler 2009). These items ask respondents to choose between pairs of desirable traits in children; they are combined to form a scale. The items, with the low authoritarian option first and high authoritarian option second, are:

- Independence or Respect for Elders
- Self-Reliance or Obedience
- Curiosity or Good Manners
- Being Considerate or Being Well-Behaved
- Creativity or Discipline.

The scale formed from these five items ranges from 0 (low authoritarian) to 1 (high authoritarian). In the administration of the survey, the order of the items was randomized.

A number of questions about political attitudes and values are included. *Tax-Spend* measures respondents' self-placement on a scale where 0 indicates that the government should spend more on social services even if it means increasing taxes and 10 means the government should cut taxes even if it means cutting spending. *Crime* ranges from 1 (protect the rights of the accused), 2 (keep about the same), to 3 (do more to fight crime). *Political Interest* ranges from 1 (not at all interested in politics) to 4 (very interested). The survey includes two questions about support for immigration. The first asks about immigration from EU countries while the second asks about immigration from non-EU countries. In both questions, responses range from indicating that such immigration is 'very bad' (1) for Ireland to 'very good' (5) for Ireland. I combine responses to these two questions into a scale called *Immigration*, which ranges from 1 (very bad) to 5 (very good). High authoritarians should express more negative attitudes about immigration. Respondents also indicate on a three-point scale whether they believe European integration should go further (3), should stay about the same (2), or has gone too far already (1).

The survey contains four questions asking about economic perceptions. The first is a standard retrospective assessment of the national economy, in which respondents indicate whether the economy has improved or grown worse over the past twelve months. *Retrospective Economy* ranges from 1 ('much worse') to 5 ('much better'). Three questions ask about the economic anxieties of respondents. The first concerns whether members of the respondent's household have had difficulties making a major payment on time in the past year, to which respondents could answer 'yes' or 'no'. The second asks whether the respondent feels financially prepared for unexpected expenses. Respondents could indicate that they felt 'very', 'somewhat', 'not very', or 'not at all' prepared. Finally, respondents were asked to indicate their overall satisfaction with their present financial situation, with answers ranging on a five-point scale from 'very satisfied' to 'very dissatisfied'. I re-scaled and combined these items into an index called *Economic Anxiety*, which ranges from 0 (not anxious) to 1 (anxious). Independent of authoritarianism, higher levels of economic anxiety may increase the propensity to vote for a PRR party.

Respondents answer four questions about their fears for the future. Respondents can express their concern on a 1–4 scale (where 1 means 'not at all' and 4 means 'very' worried) about different potential future developments for Ireland. These scenarios, and the name of the variable are:

- Irish society will lose its shared values and customs that hold it together (*Values*).
- Ireland will become a less safe society with more crime (*Safety*).
- The Irish economy will experience another crisis (*Crisis*).
- Ireland will become a more impersonal society where people can no longer trust each other (*Impersonal*).

Authoritarianism should have the strongest relationship with *Values* and *Impersonal*, both of which measure concerns about the loss of social cohesion. High authoritarians should express greater worries about these two scenarios. High authoritarians should also be more likely to worry about rising crime as another possible market of social disintegration. However, there should be no relationship between authoritarianism and fears of another economic crisis, which do not reflect the trade-off between autonomy and conformity at the heart of authoritarianism. By asking about these different scenarios, these questions provide greater insight into the motivations of high authoritarians, who are theorized to prefer maintaining social cohesion and security to individual autonomy and diversity (Stenner 2005).

Finally, several demographic variables are included. *Education* is measured on a 1 (primary or less) to 5 (university) scale. *Income* measures annual household income and ranges from 1 (under €20,000) to 6 (over €100,000). Binary variables are included for respondents who report being a *Student*, *Unemployed*, or *Retired*. In each case, the variable is coded 1 if the respondent is in that category and 0 otherwise. *Age* is coded in six categories, ranging from 18–24 (1) to over 65 (6). *Gender* is coded 1 for female respondents and 0 for male respondents. *Religious* ranges from 1 (respondent never attends religious ceremonies) to 5 (respondent attends religious ceremonies more than once a week).

Authoritarianism and Potential Support for a PRR Party

Does authoritarianism condition the propensity to vote for a PRR party? Table 7.1 presents descriptive statistics for the full sample and the subsamples receiving the control and treatment conditions. There are a few general patterns worth noting. First, overall enthusiasm for the IPP varied by the experimental treatment. *IPP Vote* is 5.41 and *IPP Difference* is 2.15 for those in the control condition, indicating a moderate willingness to vote for this hypothetical new (moderate) party. However, those numbers drop to 4.18 and 0.87, respectively, among respondents in the treatment condition, indicating less overall enthusiasm among respondents for a hypothetical radical right party. Second, *Authoritarianism* was almost perfectly balanced in the sample with a mean of 0.50, though it is slightly higher among respondents in the control group than the treatment group. The mean responses for *Crime* are in the direction of tougher enforcement, while the mean value of *Tax-Spend* is weakly in the direction of reduced taxation. Mean responses to the question about European integration are almost perfectly at the midpoint, indicating little enthusiasm for changing the speed of integration, while attitudes towards immigration are slightly favourable. Respondents on average indicate modest levels of economic anxiety, while assessments of the national economy are modestly favourable. Finally, among worries about the future, concern about another economic crisis is most prevalent, while worries about rising

Table 7.1 Descriptive statistics

Variable	Full Sample	Control	Treatment
IPP Vote	4.8	5.4	4.2
	(3.1)	(2.9)	(3.1)
IPP Difference	1.5	2.2	.87
	(3.4)	(3.0)	(3.6)
Authoritarianism	.50	.52	.48
	(.29)	(.29)	(.28)
Crime	2.8	2.9	2.8
	(.49)	(.43)	(.53)
Tax-Spend	2.1	2.2	2.1
	(.79)	(.78)	(.80)
EU	2.0	2.0	2.0
	(.67)	(.70)	(.64)
Immigration	3.6	3.6	3.6
	(1.1)	(1.1)	(1.1)
Retrospective Economy	3.1	3.2	3.0
	(1.1)	(1.0)	(1.1)
Economic Anxiety	.45	.45	.44
	(.28)	(.29)	(.27)
Values	2.3	2.4	2.3
	(1.0)	(1.1)	(.99)
Safety	2.9	2.9	2.8
	(.97)	(.99)	(.95)
Crisis	3.0	3.1	2.9
	(.87)	(.86)	(.87)
Impersonal	2.7	2.7	2.7
	(.98)	(1.0)	(.97)
Political Interest	2.8	2.8	2.8
	(.93)	(.95)	(.91)
Religiosity	2.2	2.1	2.2
	(1.2)	(1.2)	(1.2)
Education	3.4	3.4	3.3
	(1.2)	(1.2)	(1.2)
Income	3.1	3.2	3.0
	(1.6)	(1.6)	(1.6)
Student	.04	.04	.05
	(.20)	(.19)	(.21)
Unemployed	.06	.05	.07
	(.24)	(.23)	(.25)
Retired	.17	.16	.17
	(.37)	(.37)	(.38)
Gender	.51	.48	.54
	(.50)	(.50)	(.50)
Age	3.9	3.8	3.9
	(1.4)	(1.3)	(1.4)
N	416	205	211

Note: Figures show mean values for each variable with standard deviations in parentheses, * p < .05.

crime and a more impersonal society are both higher than worries about a loss of shared values.

Figure 7.1 displays mean potential support for the IPP among high- and low-authoritarian respondents in the control and treatment conditions. High authoritarians are those scoring above 0.5 on the 0–1 scale while low authoritarians are those scoring below 0.5. The pattern is in the hypothesized direction. High authoritarians in the treatment condition are significantly (p < 0.01) more likely that low authoritarians to support the IPP, with the mean of *IPP Vote* among high authoritarians being 4.84 compared to 3.54 for low authoritarians. Among respondents in the control condition, low authoritarians average 5.62 compared to 5.17 among high authoritarians. This difference is not statistically significant. The same patterns hold if one examines *IPP Difference* instead (not shown). High authoritarians are significantly more likely to support the IPP in the treatment condition, but there is no significant difference between high and low authoritarians in the control condition. At first glance, higher levels of authoritarianism are associated with a greater likelihood to vote for the hypothetical PRR party but not for a new mainstream party.

Other questions asking about assessments of the IPP yield similar results. Figure 7.2 shows the mean responses to a question asking whether the IPP is extreme or moderate, with each bar showing the percentage who rated the party as extreme. As respondents should be less likely to view a party whose views are consistent with their own as extreme, high authoritarians should be less likely to view the IPP in the treatment condition that way. Consistent with the results in Figure 7.1, fewer high authoritarians (34.6 per cent) in the treatment condition

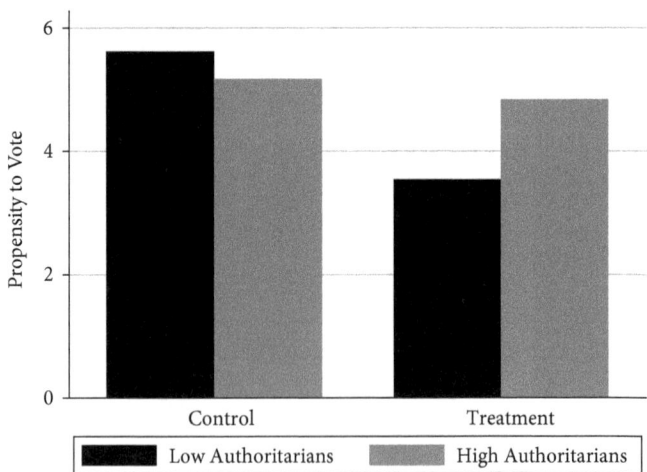

Figure 7.1 Propensity to vote by authoritarianism and experimental condition

Note: Each bar shows the mean propensity to vote on a 0–10 scale for low authoritarians (*Authoritarianism* < 0.5) and high authoritarians (*Authoritarianism* > 0.5) among those who received the control condition and the treatment condition, respectively.

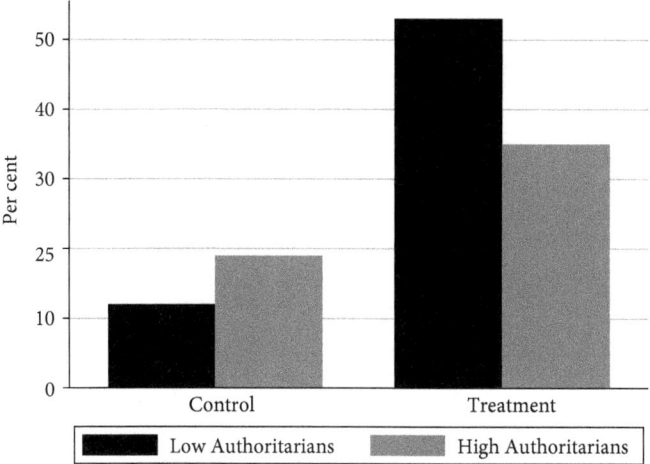

Figure 7.2 Perceptions of extremism by authoritarianism and experimental condition

Note: Each bar shows the percentage of those who rate the Irish People's Party as 'extreme' among low authoritarians (*Authoritarianism* < 0.5) and high authoritarians (*Authoritarianism* > 0.5) who received the control condition and the treatment condition, respectively.

describe the IPP as extreme compared to low authoritarians (53.3 per cent). This difference is significant at the 0.01 level. By contrast, high authoritarians and low authoritarians are statistically indistinguishable in their likelihood of describing the IPP in the control condition as extreme.

A third question asks whether respondents believe that the hypothetical new IPP 'speaks for people like me' or 'does not speak for people like me'. Given high authoritarians' greater preference for maintaining social cohesion and order, they should be more likely than low authoritarians to view the IPP in the treatment condition as speaking for them. The results in Figure 7.3 are consistent with expectations. Just under 57 per cent of high authoritarians in the treatment condition view the IPP as speaking for them, while only about 36 per cent of low authoritarians do. This difference is significant at the 0.01 level. In the control condition, there is little difference between high and low authoritarians with close to 70 per cent of both believing that the party speaks for people like them.[3] In short, these cross-tabulations show that high authoritarians are more likely to view the treatment version of the IPP—which varies with its mainstream version in the control condition in its position on immigration and European integration—as being less extreme and as speaking for people like them in comparison to low authoritarians. As a result, high authoritarians express greater willingness to vote for the radical right version of the IPP presented in the treatment condition.

---

[3] As a caveat, it is important to note that more high authoritarians view the control version of the IPP favourably than the treatment (PRR) version. This gap could be a reflection of the lack of normalization of PRR dialogue into Irish domestic politics. However, it could also reflect a challenge facing a would-be PRR party seeking to enter Irish politics.

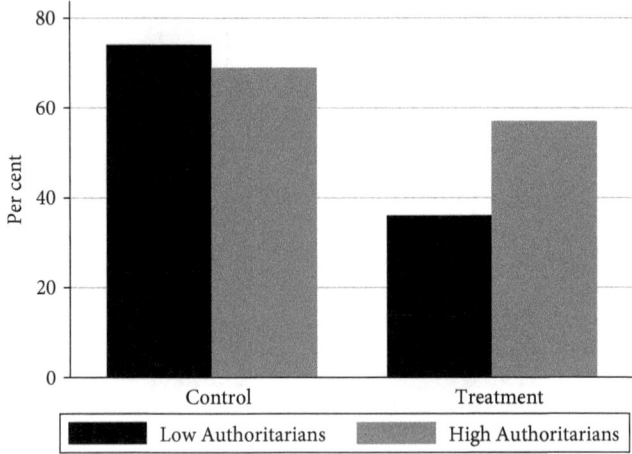

Figure 7.3 Perceptions of representativeness by authoritarianism and experimental condition

Note: Each bar shows the percentage of those who indicate that the Irish People's Party 'speaks for people like me' among low authoritarians (*Authoritarianism* < 0.5) and high authoritarians (*Authoritarianism* > 0.5) who received the control condition and the treatment condition, respectively.

These bivariate relationships between authoritarianism and IPP support are interesting, but will they hold up in a regression model containing other potential predictors of radical right party support? Table 7.2 shows the results of four OLS regression models examining the relationship between authoritarianism and IPP support with a range of control variables included. Models 1–3 contain analyses in which *IPP Vote* is the dependent variable, while Model 4 uses *IPP Difference* as the dependent variable. Models 1 and 4 include an interaction term between authoritarianism and the experimental condition (control = 0, treatment = 1), while Models 2 and 3 show the results for only those in the control and treatment conditions, respectively. The results point to a significant relationship between authoritarianism and support for the radical right IPP in the treatment condition. *Authoritarianism* is positive and significant in Model 3, indicating that higher levels of authoritarianism are associated with a greater propensity to vote for the IPP in the treatment condition. In Models 1 and 4, the interaction term between *Authoritarianism* and the treatment condition is positive and significant, indicating that authoritarianism is associated with a greater propensity to vote for the IPP in the treatment condition. By contrast, *Authoritarianism* is not significant in Model 2, which examines only those in the control condition. When the hypothetical party takes a favourable position on immigration and the EU, high authoritarians are not more likely to support it. One possible limitation to these results is that many control variables are not significant, including attitudes on

Table 7.2 Authoritarianism and potential support for the radical right in Ireland

Variable	Model 1: All Respondents	Model 2: Control Condition	Model 3: Treatment Condition	Model 4: All Respondents
Authoritarianism	−1.3	−.58	3.1*	−1.8*
	(.76)	(.80)	(.79)	(.84)
Treatment	−3.7*	–	–	−3.7*
	(.59)			(.65)
Authoritarianism Treatment	4.8*	–	–	4.8*
	(1.0)			(1.1)
Crime	−.48	−.41	−.63	−.18
	(.30)	(.48)	(.39)	(.33)
Tax-Spend	−.24	−.73*	.21	.03
	(.19)	(.28)	(.27)	(.21)
EU	.08	.57	−.48	−.38
	(.23)	(.31)	(.33)	(.25)
Economic Anxiety	1.3*	1.0	1.7*	.92
	(.58)	(.79)	(.84)	(.64)
Retrospective Economy	.03	.14	−.14	−.22
	(.15)	(.21)	(.21)	(.16)
Religiosity	.05	.17	−.03	−.09
	(.13)	(.18)	(.18)	(.14)
Income	−.23*	−.07	−.34*	−.23*
	(.11)	(.16)	(.15)	(.12)
Education	.07	−.18	.18	.07
	(.14)	(.20)	(.19)	(.15)
Gender	.24	.26	.21	.08
	(.31)	(.43)	(.44)	(.34)
Age	−.30*	−.42*	−.17	−.05
	(.14)	(.19)	(.20)	(.15)
Student	−1.4	−1.9	−.76	−2.1*
	(.77)	(1.1)	(1.1)	(.84)
Unemployed	−.48	−1.3	.31	−.60
	(.65)	(.98)	(.86)	(.71)
Retired	−.20	−.14	−.57	−.19
	(.47)	(.66)	(.66)	(.51)
Constant	8.7*	8.6*	5.7*	5.6*
	(1.5)	(2.1)	(2.1)	(1.7)
N	416	205	211	416
Root MSE	2.9	2.8	2.9	3.2
Adjusted R²	0.12	0.07	0.14	0.10

Note: The dependent variable in Models 1–3 is *PTV*, and in Model 4 it is *PTV Difference*. Figures show ordinary least squares regression coefficients with standard errors in parentheses, * $p < .05$.

crime and European integration. Because authoritarianism has a moderately high correlation with both variables (*EU* −0.19, *Crime* 0.14), the effects of these variables on IPP support may not appear in this model. Due to the stronger correlation between authoritarianism and immigration attitudes, the analyses shown in Table 7.2 exclude the latter variable.

Authoritarianism and Perceived Threats to Social Cohesion

So far, the results suggest that high authoritarians were more likely to consider voting for the hypothetical radical right IPP in the treatment condition. To what extent was this increased willingness driven by concerns over the loss of social cohesion in Ireland? I examine this question through two further analyses. The first approach involves examining respondents' worries about the future of Ireland. Are high authoritarians more likely to fear the disintegration of social cohesion or order than low authoritarians? Figure 7.4 shows the mean responses to four questions concerning Ireland's future—*Values, Crime, Crisis,* and *Impersonal.* High authoritarians should express higher levels of concern about changing values, rising crime, and a loss of community (*Impersonal*), while high authoritarians should not have greater fears about an economic crisis. The results in Figure 7.4 support these expectations. On average, high authoritarians worry more about the loss of shared values (a mean of 2.52 versus 2.18 for low authoritarians), rising crime (3.00 versus 2.73), and society becoming more impersonal (2.83 versus 2.56). All three differences are significant at the 0.01 level. By contrast, high authoritarians and low authoritarians do not differ in their worries about another economic crisis (a worry that is most widespread among respondents). This pattern of differences is consistent with the view that high

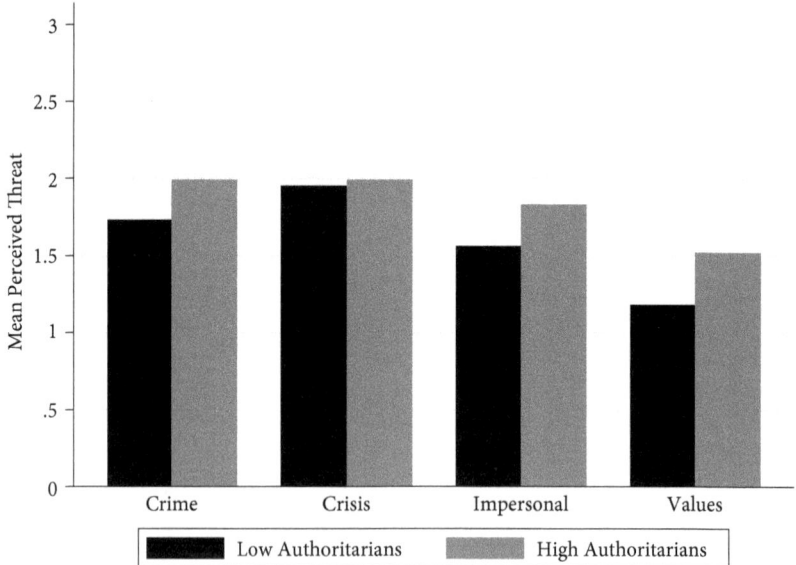

Figure 7.4 Authoritarianism and fears about the future

Note: Each bar shows the mean responses of low authoritarians (*Authoritarianism* < 0.5) and high authoritarians (*Authoritarianism* > 0.5) on a four-point scale where 1 means 'not at all worried' and 4 means 'very worried'.

authoritarians worry more about social cohesion—as reflected in a loss of community, values, or safety—than economic concerns.

The regression analyses presented in Table 7.3 partially confirm this pattern of results. *Authoritarianism* is positively and significantly associated with increased worries about the loss of shared values and the development of a more impersonal society. Both concerns relate closely to high authoritarians' concern with social cohesion. However, authoritarianism does not have a significant effect on fears of more crime, though this may be explained by the inclusion of the variable measuring preferences towards criminal justice. Unsurprisingly, those who prefer more efforts to fight crime rather than protect the rights of the accused are more likely to worry about rising crime in the future. Finally, authoritarianism is not related to fears of another economic crisis. Because an economic crisis does not reflect concerns about social cohesion, it is expected that authoritarianism has no relationship with this fear. In short, high authoritarians show more concern about a loss of social cohesion. However, further analyses (not shown) including interaction terms between *Authoritarianism* and *Values*, *Crime*, or *Impersonal* fails to uncover a multiplicative relationship on the propensity to vote for the IPP. In other words, the effect of authoritarianism on IPP support is not stronger among those who worry more about the future of Irish society. Instead, *Authoritarianism* and *Values* each have independent effects on *IPP Vote*, reflecting the strong relationship between these variables and that fears of social disintegration influence the likelihood of voting for a PRR party.

What about the relationship between authoritarianism and attitudes towards immigration? Prior research has shown that anti-immigrant attitudes are an important correlate of support for PRR parties (e.g. Ivarsflaten 2007), and high authoritarians' concern with maintaining social cohesion should result in greater opposition to immigration (Stenner 2005). Table 7.4 shows a regression analysis of the effect of *Authoritarianism* on support for immigration with the same set of control variables used in prior analyses. Recall that *Immigration* is composed of responses to two questions asking about immigration from EU member states and non-EU countries. These variables are highly correlated ($r = 0.77$) and substituting either of these measures for *Immigration* does not change the results. *Authoritarianism* has a negative and significant coefficient, indicating that high authoritarians are less likely to favour immigration. This result is consistent with expectations. In addition, support for European integration is positively associated with support for immigration, while a preference for increased social spending is associated with higher support for immigration. Other control variables are not significant. In short, authoritarianism is associated with reduced support for immigration in Ireland, even in the absence of an active PRR party.

The results in Table 7.4 highlight the relationship between authoritarianism and attitudes towards immigration. Does authoritarianism still affect the propensity to vote for a PRR party when the measure of immigration attitudes is

Table 7.3 Authoritarianism and worries about the future of Ireland

Variable	Model 1: Values	Model 2: Crime	Model 3: Crisis	Model 4: Impersonal
Authoritarianism	.38*	.23	−.09	.52*
	(.17)	(.17)	(.16)	(.18)
Crime	−.04	.28*	.20*	.10
	(.09)	(.09)	(.09)	(.10)
Tax-Spend	.17*	.13*	.10	.15*
	(.06)	(.06)	(.06)	(.06)
EU	−.56*	−.34*	−.13*	−.27*
	(.07)	(.07)	(.06)	(.07)
Economic Anxiety	.28	.21	.50*	.19
	(.18)	(.18)	(.17)	(.18)
Retrospective Economy	−.07	−.01	−.14*	−.04
	(.05)	(.05)	(.04)	(.05)
Religiosity	.08*	.01	.03	.06
	(.04)	(.04)	(.04)	(.04)
Income	.01	−.03	.01	−.05
	(.03)	(.03)	(.03)	(.03)
Education	.02	−.01	.12*	.01
	(.04)	(.04)	(.04)	(.04)
Gender	−.04	.09	.02	−.06
	(.10)	(.10)	(.09)	(.10)
Age	.03	.11*	.08*	.06
	(.04)	(.04)	(.04)	(.04)
Student	−.27	.29	.05	−.11
	(.24)	(.24)	(.22)	(.24)
Unemployed	−.20	−.10	−.09	−.21
	(.20)	(.20)	(.19)	(.20)
Retired	.06	.01	.07	−.26
	(.15)	(.14)	(.13)	(.15)
Constant	2.8*	1.9*	1.9*	2.2*
	(.45)	(.45)	(.42)	(.46)
N	416	416	416	416
Root MSE	0.91	0.90	0.84	0.92
Adjusted R^2	0.21	0.13	0.08	0.12

Note: Figures show ordinary least squares regression coefficients with standard errors in parentheses, * $p < .05$.

included? Table 7.5 shows the results of four analyses identical to those in Table 7.2 with the addition of *Immigration* (and an interaction term between it and the treatment condition). The results show that authoritarianism affects the propensity to vote for the IPP in the treatment condition—when it is presented as a PRR party. In Model 1 and Model 2, the positive and significant coefficient

Table 7.4 Authoritarianism and support for immigration in Ireland

Variable	Coefficient	Standard Error
Authoritarianism	−.53*	.17
Crime	−.08	.09
Tax-Spend	−.20*	.06
EU	.80*	.07
Economic Anxiety	−.16	.18
Retrospective Economy	.01	.05
Religiosity	.06	.04
Income	.03	.03
Education	.00	.04
Gender	.10	.10
Age	.04	.04
Student	.17	.24
Unemployed	.02	.20
Retired	−.01	.15
Constant	2.5*	.45
N	416	
Root MSE	0.91	
Adjusted R^2	0.33	

Note: Figures show ordinary least squares regression coefficients with standard errors, * $p < .05$.

between *Authoritarianism* and *Treatment* shows that authoritarianism significantly increases the propensity to vote for the IPP in the treatment condition. By contrast, authoritarianism is unrelated to the likelihood of voting for the IPP in the control condition (the coefficient of *Authoritarianism* is not significant, which shows its effect when *Treatment* is 0). Model 3 and Model 4 repeat the analyses separately for the respondents in the treatment and control conditions, respectively. Once again, *Authoritarianism* is significant and positive only for respondents in the treatment condition, in which the IPP is described as a PRR party. By contrast, the coefficient is not significant among respondents in the control condition, which describes the IPP as a mainstream party. In addition, the coefficients for *Immigration* show that individuals with less favourable attitudes towards immigration are more likely to vote for the IPP in the treatment condition. By contrast, the coefficient is positive in the control condition, in which the IPP is described as favouring immigration. Crucially, the results in Table 7.5 show a relationship between authoritarianism and potential support for a PRR party even when the analysis includes attitudes towards immigration. Taken in context with the findings presented above, these results suggest that high authoritarians' potential support for the radical right reflects a desire to preserve social cohesion—but this concern extends beyond immigration.

Table 7.5 Authoritarianism, immigration attitudes, and potential radical right support in Ireland

Variable	Model 1: IPP Vote	Model 2: IPP Difference	Model 3: Treatment	Model 4: Control
Authoritarianism	−.80	−1.3	2.0*	−.62
	(.73)	(.81)	(.79)	(.78)
Treatment	3.4*	3.2*	–	–
	(1.2)	(1.3)		
Authoritarianism Treatment*	3.0*	3.1*	–	–
	(1.0)	(1.1)		
Immigration	.73*	.72*	−1.0*	.70*
	(.20)	(.23)	(.21)	(.23)
Immigration Treatment*	−1.7*	−1.7*	–	–
	(.26)	(.29)		
Crime	−.63*	−.33	−.76*	−.43
	(.29)	(.32)	(.37)	(47)
Tax-Spend	−.27	.00	.03	−.53
	(.19)	(.21)	(.26)	(.28)
EU	.05	−.42	.20	−.08
	(.25)	(.28)	(35)	(.37)
Economic Anxiety	1.4*	1.0	1.6	1.1
	(.55)	(.61)	(.80)	(.77)
Retrospective Economy	.01	−.24	−.12	.15
	(.14)	(.16)	(.20)	(.21)
Religiosity	.10	−.03	.09	.16
	(.12)	(.13)	(.17)	(.18)
Income	−.22*	−.22	−.30*	−.12
	(.44)	(.11)	(.14)	(.16)
Education	.10	.10	.25	−.12
	(.13)	(.15)	(.19)	(.20)
Gender	.17	.01	.21	.10
	(.29)	(.33)	(.42)	(.43)
Age	−.31*	−.06	−.12	−.46*
	(.13)	(.14)	(.19)	(.19)
Student	−1.6*	−2.3*	−.67	−2.2*
	(.73)	(.81)	(1.0)	(1.1)
Unemployed	−.47	−.59	.33	−1.4
	(.61)	(.68)	(.82)	(.96)
Retired	−.22	−.22	−.49	−.08
	(.44)	(.49)	(.63)	(.64)
Constant	6.3*	3.2	8.4*	7.2*
	(1.5)	(1.7)	(2.0)	(2.1)
N	416	416	211	205
Root MSE	2.8	3.1	2.8	2.8
Adjusted R^2	0.21	0.17	0.22	0.10

Notes: Figures show ordinary least squares regression coefficients with standard errors in parentheses. The dependent variable in Models 3–4 is *IPP Vote*. * $p < .05$.

Authoritarianism and the Present Electoral Alignment

The final question that this analysis considers is how authoritarianism relates to voting behaviour in the 2016 Irish general election. To the extent that high authoritarians would gravitate towards a new PRR party, it is important to understand which parties might lose support as a result. Does authoritarianism structure voting behaviour in Ireland? The survey asked respondents to indicate for which party they voted, and Figure 7.5 shows the percentage of respondents choosing each party broken down by authoritarianism. The results show minimal sorting by authoritarianism. High authoritarians are somewhat more likely to support either of the traditional parties of government—FF and FG—both of which hold centre-right ideological positions. By contrast, low authoritarians are modestly more likely to support the left-of-centre parties. Notably, Sinn Féin receives roughly equal support from high and low authoritarians. These results suggest that both of the largest parties, which have stood as rivals for control of government for decades, would stand to lose support to a new PRR party. The patterns in Figure 7.5 suggest that a viable PRR party would be a potential electoral threat to both major parties, along with Sinn Féin.

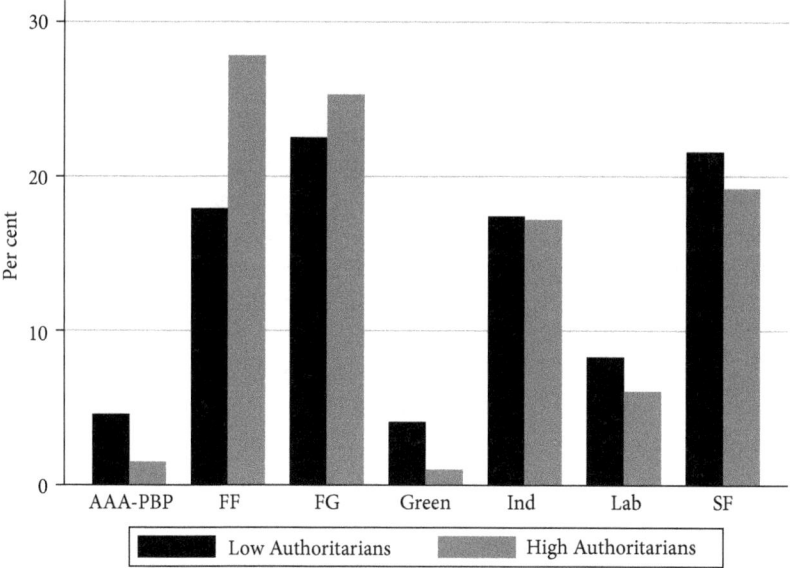

Figure 7.5 Reported voting behaviour in 2016 by authoritarianism

Note: Each bar shows the percentage of those indicating they voted for each party in the 2016 general election among low authoritarians (*Authoritarianism* < 0.5) and high authoritarians (*Authoritarianism* > 0.5).

Conclusion

This chapter has sought to build on the analyses of the previous chapter by examining whether high authoritarians would be more likely to vote for a hypothetical new PRR party in a country that does not already have one. The analyses generate four central findings. First, a survey experiment conducted in Ireland shows that high authoritarians are more likely to support a hypothetical new PRR party—but not a hypothetical new mainstream party. This finding is consistent with expectations and suggests that high authoritarians are more likely to form the original core supporters of a new PRR party. Moreover, this finding holds even when attitudes towards crime, the EU, and immigration are included in the analysis. Second, further analyses show that high authoritarians are more likely to worry about social disintegration—the loss of shared values and an increasingly impersonal society—consistent with contemporary theorizing about authoritarianism (Feldman 2003; Stenner 2005). By contrast, high authoritarians are not more likely to worry about another economic crisis, which does not relate as clearly to the preservation of social cohesion. Third, high authoritarians are more likely to oppose immigration, but their tendency to support a new PRR party is not simply the product of anti-immigration attitudes. Authoritarianism is still associated with a higher propensity to vote for a PRR party when measures of immigration attitudes are included in the analysis. Finally, there is presently little partisan sorting by authoritarianism in Irish elections. As a result, all of the major established parties would stand to lose votes to a new PRR party if one actually existed.

The findings of this analysis are consistent with this book's broader argument: high authoritarians are more likely to support populist radical right parties. This analysis shows that this pattern holds even in a context with no PRR party. In addition, there is no party sorting by authoritarianism currently, as both high and low authoritarians are distributed across the party spectrum. The emergence of a credible PRR party could therefore draw high authoritarians from various established parties (as well as independent representatives), leading to a worldview realignment of electoral politics in Ireland similar to that observed in other West European states. Of course, this analysis does not suggest that this potential realignment is likely to occur in Ireland in the near or long term.

This finding also suggests that the lack of a PRR party in Ireland at present may reflect a failure of supply more than a lack of demand within the electorate reflecting unique cultural or historical qualities. High authoritarians in Ireland express similar concerns about social cohesion as their counterparts elsewhere, and they are similarly open to supporting a PRR party. Historical contingencies may have prevented the formation of a PRR party thus far, but the results of this analysis suggest that high authoritarians in the Irish electorate would be open to supporting such a party if it were to form. In short, the potential exists for a worldview evolution in Irish politics.

8

Cultural Backlash or Worldview Evolution?

Age, Authoritarianism, and Support for the Radical Right

The Puzzle of Rising Support for the Radical Right

The previous two chapters have demonstrated the relationship between authoritarianism and support for populist radical right (PRR) parties in West European democracies. This relationship exists for established PRR parties that regularly compete in elections and win legislative seats, and it also exists for a hypothetical PRR party in Ireland. The evidence is straightforward: high authoritarians are more likely to support PRR parties than low authoritarians even when one controls for a wide range of political and social attitudes or demographic attributes. These results are consistent with this book's argument that high authoritarians have started to abandon mainstream parties for PRR parties as the structure of political conflict has evolved in the twenty-first century.

How this evolution of high authoritarians' voting behaviour has unfolded is less clear. One important question is whether younger or older high authoritarians are driving this shift in voting behaviour. This question is important for several reasons, with one being that it speaks to the long-term electoral prospects of PRR parties. If older voters have been moving towards PRR parties, then it may be difficult for PRR parties to maintain electoral strength as those voters exit the electorate and are replaced by younger cohorts. However, greater support among younger high authoritarians could suggest more potential support for PRR parties in the coming years, as those younger voters will be part of the electorate for decades and may develop stronger party attachments as they age. Conceptually, this question relates to our understanding of voter realignments. Is the process of older voters abandoning their previous loyalties to mainstream parties driving this realignment, or is it the result of younger voters with no previous party loyalties gravitating to PRR parties?

Why should age be relevant to the evolution of support for PRR parties? Prior research generates competing expectations. One perspective suggests that younger voters should be more likely to fuel increased support for PRR parties.

Authoritarianism and the Evolution of West European Electoral Politics. Erik R. Tillman, Oxford University Press.
© Erik R. Tillman 2021. DOI: 10.1093/oso/9780192896223.003.0008

There are two reasons this might be the case. First, younger voters generally have weaker party attachments, so they are more likely to support new or non-mainstream parties than older voters, who may have developed a lifelong attachment to an established party. Moreover, their views of politics and political conflict have formed in the current era in which the socio-cultural issues fuelling the rise of PRR parties have been salient, so they should be more likely to support the party that best represents their preferences on the important issues. By contrast, older voters' perspectives developed in an era shaped by different conflicts (such as class; Lipset and Rokkan 1967), which may lead them to view politics through this perspective. A second reason, which is relevant to this study, is that authoritarianism may strengthen the tendency of older voters to remain loyal to an established party. High authoritarians display more attachment to tradition (Stenner 2005), manifesting in more habitual behaviour (in this case, voting for the same party). In addition, high authoritarians' tendency towards social conformity may result in less willingness to vote for parties that identify as (or are labelled as) anti-establishment or extreme (Oyamot et al. 2012). As a result, younger high authoritarians should be more likely to vote for PRR parties, because they have weaker attachments to existing parties and to the political mainstream. The pressures of conformity and habit will not operate as strongly on younger high authoritarians, so they should be more likely to support a party that reflects their worldviews on the salient issues of this era. This is the *worldview evolution* hypothesis described below.

An alternative perspective suggests that older high authoritarian voters should be more likely to vote for PRR parties. The *cultural backlash* hypothesis argues that older high authoritarians are more likely to support PRR parties. As recent decades have seen a liberalization of social and cultural attitudes reflecting a values change, older high authoritarians are more likely to perceive a difference between their own values and those of the political mainstream (Norris and Inglehart 2019). In addition, increased levels of immigration in recent decades create a starker demographic contrast between the society of their youths and the present day. These changes are threatening to older high authoritarians' views of social cohesion, as they are able to see how society has changed (and, in their perspective, lost cohesion) during their adult lives. By contrast, younger high authoritarians grew up among increasingly liberal mainstream values and multicultural societies, so they should be less likely to view these conditions as a threat to the normative order. Having grown up in this era, these conditions may form part of the normative order for younger voters. As a result, older high authoritarians should be the ones moving towards PRR parties. Thus, these rival arguments generate opposing claims about whether younger or older high authoritarians should be more likely to support PRR parties.

The remainder of this chapter examines this debate. The next section describes these rival arguments in detail and generates hypotheses. The analyses examine the direct relationship between age and PRR party support as well as the interactive effect of age and authoritarianism on PRR party support. The results of the analyses fail to support the cultural backlash hypothesis. Older voters (whether high authoritarians or not) are not more likely to support PRR parties. However, the evidence is more consistent with this book's worldview evolution hypothesis. When there is a significant relationship between age (either directly or in interaction with authoritarianism) and the likelihood of supporting a PRR party, it is always negative. In other words, the results suggest that younger high authoritarians (or younger voters generally) are more likely to vote for PRR parties, or there is no relationship between age and PRR party support. The concluding section discusses the implications of these findings for our understanding of the worldview evolution in West European politics.

Age, Authoritarianism, and Radical Right Support: Two Arguments

How do age and authoritarianism interact to shape support for populist radical right parties? This section develops two arguments. The first is this book's worldview evolution argument, which argues that age and authoritarianism should have a negative interaction effect. In other words, the effect of authoritarianism should be stronger among younger voters. The second argument is the cultural backlash thesis, which suggests a positive relationship in which the effect of authoritarianism is stronger among older voters. Finally, the null hypothesis predicts no interactive relationship, in which case the effect of authoritarianism on support for PRR parties does not vary by age.

Worldview Evolution: Are Younger Voters Driving PRR Party Support?

There are two reasons to expect that young voters, rather than older voters, are driving support for PRR parties. The first of these reasons derives from the broader literature on party attachment and voting behaviour. The second reason builds on the authoritarianism literature to understand how authoritarianism and age interact.

The first argument draws on our understanding of voting as a process of socialization that is reinforced throughout adult life. Voting has a habitual character (Campbell et al. 1960; Butler and Stokes 1969; Franklin 2004). Early processes of socialization lead to the formation of party attachments, which in turn guide voting decisions. Ongoing experiences with politics often reinforce these attachments so that they become stronger as one ages. Political participation also typically increases with age as individuals become more settled in careers and families, increasing the time and resources they can devote to politics (Brady et al. 1995). Increased participation in politics strengthens party attachments by reinforcing the habit of supporting that same party. Additionally, group attachments linked to religion, occupation, and community strengthen with age. These attachments link to the political cleavages that structure party attachment (Lipset and Rokkan 1967), further shaping political identity. These processes should reinforce party attachment, growing stronger with age. As a result, older voters should be more likely to vote habitually for the same party and thus to be less likely to vote for a new party.

The changing structure of society and politics provides further reason to expect that younger voters are more likely to support PRR parties. The established parties in West European democracies organized around the major political cleavages in the early and mid-twentieth century (Lipset and Rokkan 1967). The most common and important of these cleavages are social class and religion. Older voters were socialized into this party system, with their class and religious affiliations shaping their party attachments. The economic and social changes of the late twentieth century included the shift towards a post-industrial economy and secularization. As a result, class and religious affiliation have had a weaker effect on party attachments in recent decades (Franklin et al. 2009). Younger voters have been socialized into the politics of this era, so their party affiliations are less likely to reflect these traditional political cleavages.

The changing structure of party conflict has generated debates about whether Western democracies are experiencing realignment or dealignment (e.g. Dalton et al. 1984; Kriesi et al. 2008; Franklin et al. 2009). The particulars of this debate are less important for this discussion than the broader claim that established patterns of party attachment have weakened. As a result, younger generations of voters have entered politics in a period in which either party loyalties were less prevalent (dealignment) or a new set of party attachments were emerging around questions of identity and values (realignment). The rise of new political issues centring on values (Inglehart 1997) and the emergence of a cosmopolitan–national divide (Kriesi et al. 2008) led to the rise of new party families reflecting these divisions—namely, the green and the radical right party families. As a result, younger voters grew up with weaker attachments to established mainstream parties based on class or religious cleavages and a greater potential to form loyalties to new parties based around contemporary values and cultural divisions. The result should be that younger voters are more likely than older voters to lead the gains in support for PRR parties.

A second basis for this argument derives from the authoritarianism literature. There are two reasons to expect that the tendency of high authoritarians to vote for PRR parties decreases with age. First, high authoritarians display greater needs for order and certainty (Stenner 2005; Hetherington and Weiler 2009; Johnston et al. 2017). One manifestation of this is a greater attachment to established behaviours and less willingness to embrace new or untested ideas or behaviours. In this context, this tendency towards the familiar should extend to party support, as older high authoritarians who have formed stronger party attachments will be less likely to vote for a new party. By contrast, younger high authoritarians have not formed such voting habits, so they will not be as resistant to voting for a new party. There is evidence consistent with this expectation. Individuals scoring low in the openness personality trait—which correlates negatively with authoritarianism (Stenner 2005)—are less likely to switch party loyalties when dissatisfied with their current party (Bakker et al. 2016b). Because younger voters are less likely to have formed party attachments, they would not need to switch parties in order to support the radical right.

A second set of findings shows that high authoritarians are more sensitive to social norms and seek to maintain attitudes and behaviours consistent with them (Oyamot et al. 2012). Because authoritarianism is oriented towards the maintenance of social conformity, high authoritarians should be sensitive to the values and behavioural expectations of the normative social order. In particular, they should be aware of proscribed behaviour and values, as the authoritarian worldview views deviant behaviour as a threat to social cohesion (Stenner 2005). In this context, older high authoritarians should be reluctant to support PRR parties, which often position themselves as anti-establishment and are described as 'extreme' by rival parties and the media.[1] Voting for such parties should not appeal to older high authoritarians. While younger high authoritarians will also be sensitive to the potential norm violations of supporting PRR parties, their weaker attachments to the political mainstream should reduce their receptiveness to such criticisms of PRR parties.

Taken together, this discussion provides several reasons to expect that younger high authoritarians should be more likely than their older counterparts to support PRR parties. The weaker attachments to mainstream parties and to mainstream social and political norms should cause younger voters to be more receptive to PRR party messages. If this is the case, then the relationship between authoritarianism and the likelihood of voting for a PRR party should be stronger among younger voters.

Cultural Backlash: Are Older Voters Driving PRR Party Support?

A rival perspective suggests that older high authoritarians account for the increased support for PRR parties. The cultural changes of recent decades—increasing liberalization, secularization, and demographic change—pose the greatest threat to

---

[1] PRR parties suffer from media labels or comparisons to fascism. This comparison may be especially troubling for members of older generations who grew up with more connections to the Second World War, making them especially unlikely to support a party with such connotations.

older voters who were socialized during a previous era. By contrast, younger voters have grown up in this new era and so do not perceive these cultural shifts as a threat to the normative order.

Scholars have documented an ongoing 'silent revolution' in Western societies in which social and cultural attitudes have become increasingly liberal and tolerant (Inglehart 1977, 1997; Norris and Inglehart 2019). According to this argument, West Europeans living in the post-war era have experienced unprecedented levels of existential and economic security as they have grown up in a safer and more prosperous world than their predecessors. This security fostered the development of post-materialist values focused on self-actualization and social justice (Inglehart 1997; Norris and Inglehart 2019). Beginning with the student protests of 1968, members of these younger generations have challenged mainstream social and cultural norms, resulting in the liberalization of society and a growing emphasis on questions of environmental and social justice. Two broader developments have contributed to this silent revolution. First, higher levels of educational attainment among post-war generations promoted greater tolerance. Second, the growing secularization of West European societies reduced the influence of traditional religious authorities. Taken together, these factors have led to a values shift that started in the late 1960s and gained influence in the subsequent decades. Older high authoritarians, who were socialized during the earlier era, could perceive these values changes as a threat to the normative social order while having memories of earlier times before these changes occurred (Stenner 2005; Norris and Inglehart 2019).

A second factor that could produce a backlash among older high authoritarian voters is the rise of immigration and multiculturalism in recent decades. West European societies became increasingly diverse in the late twentieth century as immigration from non-Western societies increased and those immigrants and their descendants established communities in major cities. Many of the settlements were in industrial areas previously inhabited by native-born working-class residents, which created potential for conflict (Gest 2016). Increasing immigration led to greater demands for multiculturalism. Older high authoritarians, who grew up before the rise of mass immigration, could see increased diversity and multiculturalism as a threat to social cohesion.

These cultural shifts have generated alarm among older high authoritarians. Because high authoritarians are more sensitive to threats to social cohesion, they should be more likely to oppose the values and demographic changes of recent decades. Studies of older, working-class respondents in the UK have documented feelings of nostalgia and alienation (Ford and Goodwin 2014; Gest 2016; Gest et al. 2018). As liberal and multicultural values gained mainstream acceptance, older high authoritarians may fear that society is reaching a 'tipping point' beyond which traditional values will be lost (Norris and Inglehart 2019). Moreover, older high authoritarians were socialized prior to these social and cultural changes, so they can perceive the difference between the society they remember and society as it is today. To the extent that they are nostalgic for the society of their youth (Gest 2016), they may believe that these socio-cultural changes are causing social decay. Such a belief that the normative social order is under threat would justify a strong reaction among high authoritarians, including voting for PRR parties promising tough measures to reverse these social changes (Stenner 2005, 2009).

But would these developments not equally threaten younger high authoritarians? The reason why younger high authoritarians would not respond similarly is that they have been socialized into this socio-cultural environment in which liberalism and multiculturalism are mainstream values. Younger voters would associate these values with the normative order rather than as a threat to the normative order. Thus, they should be less motivated to support PRR parties.

A recent study claims that older high authoritarians are more likely to support PRR parties (Norris and Inglehart 2019). Using a measure of authoritarian values derived from the Schwartz Human Values Scale (Schwartz and Bilsky 1987; Schwartz 1992, 1994), this study finds that voters scoring higher in authoritarian values are more likely to support parties that are more authoritarian populist (though not necessarily populist radical right). It also finds a direct and positive relationship between age and support for authoritarian populist parties; members of older generations are more likely to support these parties than members of younger generations. In addition, it finds that age and authoritarian values correlate positively, and that authoritarian values and support for authoritarian populist parties correlate positively.[2] These findings should lead to the expectation that older high authoritarians are more likely to support PRR parties. This discussion generates two rival hypotheses, which the following sections will test:

Worldview Evolution Hypothesis: The relationship between authoritarianism and support for PRR parties is stronger among younger voters.

---

[2] There are several methodological choices that make it difficult to claim that age and authoritarianism have a positive interactive effect on support for PRR parties based on Norris and Inglehart's (2019) analyses. First, their measure of authoritarian values draws on a limited number of items from the Schwartz Human Values Scale. Interestingly, it does not include any of the items measuring Universalism even though a preference for the maintenance of social cohesion is at the core of the concept of authoritarianism. It is unclear how sensitive their measure of authoritarian values is to the inclusion or exclusion of particular items from the Human Values Scale, nor how well it correlates with child-rearing measures of authoritarianism. Second, the analysis groups respondents into broad generational cohorts rather than measuring age directly. Finally, the analyses do not support the conclusion of a positive interaction effect between age and authoritarianism. Rather, a bivariate analysis shows that members of older generations are more likely to support authoritarian populist parties. However, this relationship flips direction when the measure of authoritarian values is included in the model, such that members of the two youngest generations are more likely to support authoritarian populist parties when authoritarian values are included in the model (Norris and Inglehart 2019: 275–6; see also Table 8.2 below). This analysis does not include a test of an interaction between generation and authoritarian values. Therefore, the correct conclusions from those analyses are that members of older generations are more likely to support authoritarian populist parties on average, and respondents with more authoritarian values are more likely to support authoritarian populist parties on average. However, one cannot draw a conclusion about whether older high authoritarians are more likely to support such parties.

Cultural Backlash Hypothesis: The relationship between authoritarianism and support for PRR parties is stronger among older voters.

Data and Measures

Following the approach in earlier chapters, this chapter's analyses use data from the 2017 European Values Survey (EVS) and recent national election studies in Austria, Britain, Finland, Germany, and Switzerland. This choice of data reflects the availability of appropriate survey questions measuring authoritarianism and party support, as well as the presence of a PRR party. The variable in the analyses that follow are identical to those used in Chapter 6, with the exception that age is measured in years rather than in bands.

Because this chapter tests an implication of the cultural backlash hypothesis, it is important to note several differences in measurement strategy in comparison to Norris and Inglehart (2019). The first, and perhaps most important, difference concerns the measurement of authoritarianism. When possible, this book follows the state-of-the-art in measuring authoritarianism using child-rearing questions (see Stenner 2005; Hetherington and Weiler 2009; Johnston et al. 2017). This approach is preferable as the child-rearing measures more effectively measure the fundamental trade-off between individual autonomy and social conformity at the heart of authoritarianism, and political attitudes are less likely to contaminate these measures in comparison to attitudinal questions. However, the analysis of data from Austria, Britain, and Finland uses attitudinal questions in order to expand the number of available cases. These measures correlate highly with child-rearing measures, but they may also reflect political attitudes. Notably, the results presented in Chapter 6 showing a relationship between authoritarianism and support for PRR parties are consistent across both measures. By contrast, Norris and Inglehart (2019) construct a scale of authoritarian values using items measuring security, tradition, and conformity values drawn from the Schwartz Human Values Scale (Schwartz and Bilsky 1987; Schwartz 1992, 1994), though one of these items is dropped from the index. Notably, this index excludes measures of universalism that are available in the Human Values Scale, despite the importance of in-group cohesion to theories of authoritarianism.

A second difference concerns the measurement of age. The analyses in this chapter measure age in years, ranging from 18 to the highest value recorded in the survey. By contrast, Norris and Inglehart (2019) measure the generational cohort of the respondent. Although this measure effectively captures many dynamics of the era in which respondents grew up, it is rather blunt and may lose important information. Consider members of the 'baby boomer' generation, born between 1946 and 1964. Those oldest members of this generation born during the late 1940s might have experienced the final years of scarcity and rationing following the Second World War as children, though they would have reached adulthood during the low unemployment and growing prosperity of the 1960s. By contrast, the late boomers born in the early 1960s would have been children experiencing the social turbulence of the late 1960s, and they would have reached adulthood during the economic crises and growing social disorder of the late 1970s. Given that the socializing influences on members of the same generation could be so different, it is preferable to measure the respondent's age in years.

A third difference concerns the coding of parties. This chapter follows the common practice in coding parties dichotomously as being PRR parties (1) or not (0). Norris and Inglehart (2019) introduce an interesting new approach that places parties on a scale according to their authoritarian and populist characteristics, with 'authoritarian-populist' parties being those scoring in the top quintile on each dimension. This refined measure allows for more nuanced cross-national analyses, and it generates important insights about the degree to which established centre-right parties may adopt authoritarian-populist positions. For the purposes of this analysis, it is important to note that each of the parties classified here as PRR is coded as authoritarian-populist by Norris and Inglehart (2019: 255).

With these differences in mind, it is important to understand the analyses presented here are not a test of the broader cultural backlash argument. Instead, they test the implications of that argument for a particular question: whether and how age moderates the relationship between authoritarianism and the likelihood of supporting a PRR party. If the evidence does not support the cultural backlash hypothesis that older high authoritarians are more likely to vote for PRR parties, then it would indicate a limitation of the argument in the context of this study's research question. In other words, the goal of this analysis is to test the implications of this book's worldview evolution argument, with the cultural backlash hypothesis serving as a rival claim.

Age and Party Support: A First Look

The first analysis examines the relationship between age and party support in eight West European democracies using the 2017 wave of the European Values Survey. This analysis takes the simple approach of comparing the level of support for each party among respondents under the age of 45 with those aged 45 or over. Doing so provides preliminary evidence for a possible age gap, which might lend support to one of this chapter's rival hypotheses. Additionally, an age gap could foreshadow future electoral evolutions if they reflect generational rather than lifecycle differences. Because this descriptive analysis does not incorporate the role of authoritarianism, it examines only whether there are broad differences by age. The results are shown in Figure 8.1, with the panels showing the results for each country.

Descriptive Analyses

The analysis starts with Austria. The evidence shows moderate differences in party support by age. Consider first the populist radical right Freedom Party of Austria (FPÖ). Younger voters support FPÖ in somewhat greater numbers (24.5 per cent to 18.9 per cent). Similarly, younger voters also support the Green Party in greater numbers (12.7 per cent versus 6.0 per cent). These two results suggest that younger voters are more likely to support the two parties organized around cultural issues central to the worldview evolution—either the cosmopolitan and liberal Green Party or the nationalist and conservative FPÖ. By contrast, older voters are more likely to support the established Social Democratic Party (SPÖ) and Austrian People's Party (ÖVP), which are established around the older class and religious cleavages in Austrian politics. These preliminary results from Austria are therefore consistent with the worldview evolution argument rather than the cultural backlash hypothesis.

The results from Britain show a rather different scenario. Here, there is a major age gap in support for the two traditional parties of government. Younger voters support the centre-left Labour Party in greater numbers, while older voters are more likely to support the Conservative Party (Tory). Support for the radical right UK Independence Party (UKIP) and the left-liberal Green Party is too small to generate meaningful conclusions. This surprising result may be the result of enthusiasm for Labour Party leader Jeremy Corbyn among younger voters and support for Brexit among older voters. If so, one could interpret this as evidence consistent with the cultural backlash thesis: older voters have moved towards the party working to fulfil the desire of Leave voters to 'take back control' of British borders and trade policy.

The results present a slightly different scenario in Denmark. Older voters support the radical right Danish People's Party (DF) in slightly greater numbers than younger voters (14.1 per cent versus 10.4 per cent). Older voters are also more likely to support the Social Democratic Party (SD), which has historically been the largest in Danish politics. By contrast, younger voters provide more support to the Red–Green Alliance and the Social Liberal Party (RV). Overall, the results suggest that younger voters support left-liberal parties more while providing less support to the established parties and the radical right.

Finnish voters show more similarities to Austrian voters. Younger voters are more likely to support the radical right Finns Party (PS) (12.9 per cent to 7.1 per cent), and they support the Green League in much greater numbers (31.5 per cent

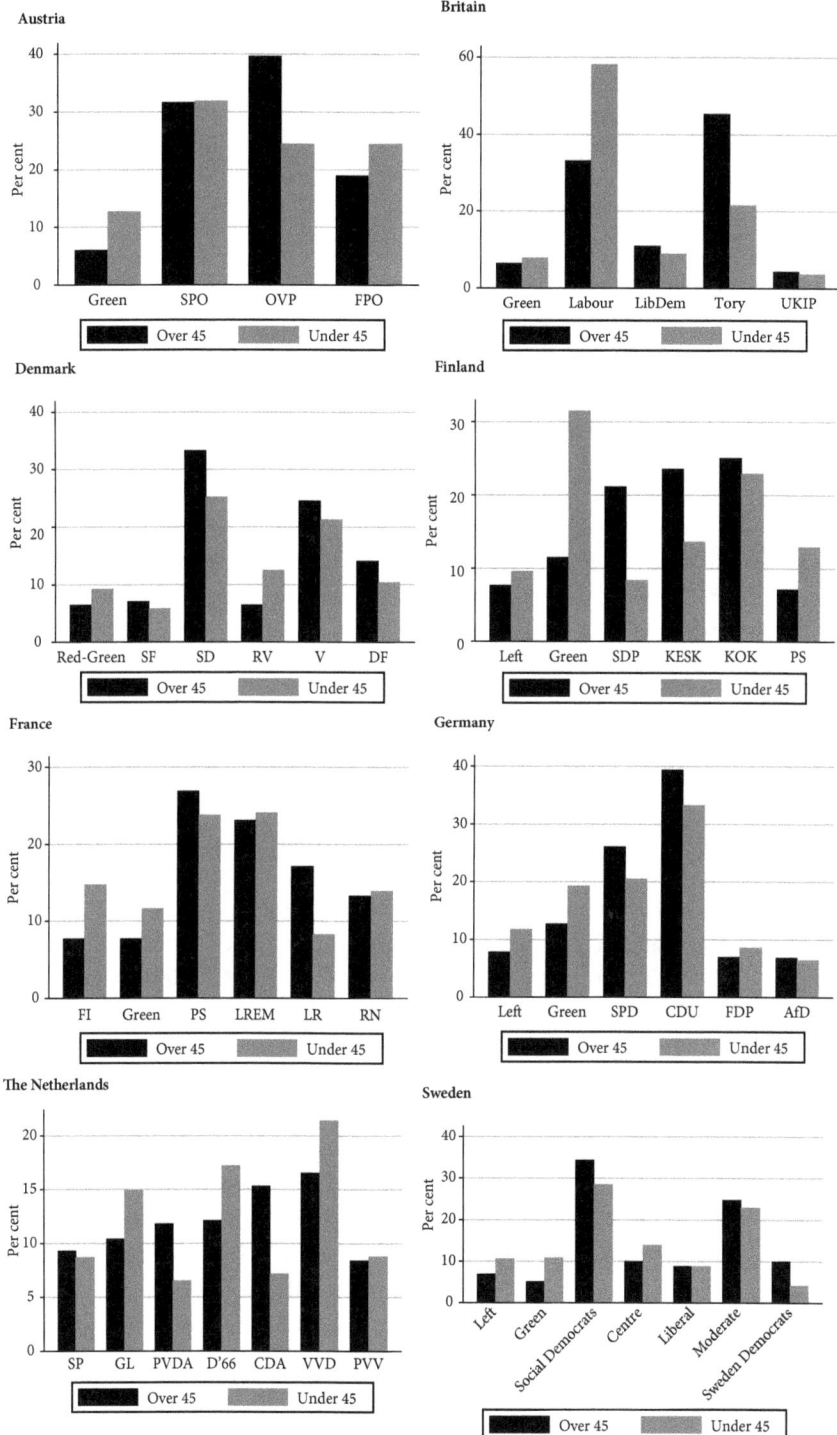

Figure 8.1 Party support by age

Note: Each figure shows the percentage of younger voters (under age 45) and older voters (45 and older) supporting each party.

Source: EVS 2019.

versus 11.5 per cent). However, older voters support the traditional Social Democratic Party (SD) and Centre Party (KESK) in much greater proportion. In Finland, the results suggest that younger voters are less likely to support the parties oriented around traditional class and urban–rural cleavages (SD and KESK), but they are more likely to vote for parties oriented around newer cultural divides (Greens and PS). As with Austria, this evidence is more consistent with a worldview evolution than a cultural backlash among older voters.

By contrast, the results from France and Germany both show little differences by age, particular when PRR parties are concerned. In both countries, younger voters are more likely to support green parties and radical left parties, while older voters are more likely to support the centre-right Republicans (LR) in France and Christian Democratic Union (CDU) in Germany. Older voters also show modestly more support for the traditional centre-left Socialist Party (PS) in France and Social Democratic Party (SPD) in Germany. However, there is minimal difference by age in support for the radical right National Rally (RN) in France or the Alternative for Germany (AfD). In short, there is no evidence of a cultural backlash among older voters, while there is some evidence of younger voters gravitating to the left-liberal parties in both countries.

The evidence from the Netherlands points to a similar set of patterns. Younger voters support the left-liberal Green Left (GL) and Democrats '66 (D66) in greater numbers than older voters. However, older voters provide more support to two of the traditional three major parties of Dutch politics: the Labor Party (PvdA) and the Christian Democratic Appeal (CDA). However, the radical right Party for Freedom (PVV) receives essentially equal amounts of support from younger and older voters. This finding does not support the claim that radical right support is the result of a cultural backlash among older voters, while there is some evidence that younger voters are moving away from traditional class- and religious-based parties towards left-liberal parties.

The evidence from Sweden provides modest evidence of an age difference in voting behaviour. Notably, the radical right Sweden Democrats gain more support from older voters than younger voters, which is consistent with claims of a cultural backlash. As has been the case in most other countries, younger voters also provide more support to the radical-left Left Party and the Green Party. However, there is only a slight age gap in support for the two largest parties, with older voters being modestly more likely to vote for the Social Democrats or the Moderates. In short, the Swedish evidence provides some evidence of a gap between younger, liberal voters and older, traditionalist voters that could be consistent with the cultural backlash thesis.

Taken together, these country analyses do not produce clear evidence of a single pattern. In Austria and Finland, younger voters give more support to PRR parties. By contrast, older voters support PRR parties in greater numbers in

Denmark and Sweden. Finally, PRR parties draw roughly equal support from young and old voters in Britain, France, Germany, and the Netherlands. Thus, this descriptive evidence does not point to a consistent pattern, nor are there are clear regional differences. However, it is notable that younger voters provide greater support to left-liberal parties in most countries, while there is also some evidence that younger voters are less likely to support mainstream parties organized around class or religious cleavages. In short, the evidence thus far should generate scepticism that a backlash among older voters is driving the rise of the radical right (Norris and Inglehart 2019), but a more definitive test requires multivariate analysis.

Multivariate Analyses

Do the findings change in multivariate logistic regression analyses? The descriptive analyses above highlight interesting patterns, but they may fail to account for the true relationship between age and support for PRR parties due to the bluntness of the age measure and the lack of control variables. This next section includes multivariate logistic regression models including age in years and the main independent and control variables shown in Chapter 6. The key difference with those models is the measurement of age in years rather than in age bands. The dependent variable is whether the respondent indicated voting for a PRR party or not. The results from the national election studies are given in Table 8.1, and the results of the EVS data are shown in Table 8.2.

The results in Table 8.1 show that age is negative and significant in three of five cases, and it is not significant in the other two cases. In Austria, Finland, and Germany, older age is associated with a reduced likelihood of voting for a PRR party. In Britain and Switzerland, there is no relationship between age and PRR party support. The analysis presented in Table 8.2 shows that age negatively relates to PRR party support in the EVS data. Older voters are less likely to support PRR parties when controlling for authoritarianism, political and social attitudes, and demographic variables.

What do these results suggest? Most importantly, they weigh against the hypothesis that older voters are primary supporters of PRR parties. Instead, the evidence from most cases suggests that younger voters are more likely to vote for PRR parties. This evidence is consistent with the worldview evolution hypothesis. Because younger voters have weaker attachments to established class- or religious-based parties, they are more likely to vote for newer parties that reflect their worldviews on broader questions of social conformity and individual autonomy. However, the British and Swiss analyses found no direct relationship between age and the probability of supporting a PRR party.

Table 8.1 Age and support for PRR parties in national election studies

Variable	Austria	Britain	Finland	Germany	Switzerland
Authoritarianism	.97*	.77*	.35*	.59*	.51*
	(.24)	(.09)	(.06)	(.24)	(.12)
Age	−.03*	−.00	−.03*	−.03*	−.01
	(.01)	(.01)	(.01)	(.01)	(.02)
Economic Preferences	.07	−.10	.09	−.27*	.98*
	(.23)	(.10)	(.07)	(.06)	(.10)
Retrospective Economy	−.25	−.20*	−.19	−.24	−.09
	(.14)	(.07)	(.10)	(.16)	(.08)
Religiosity	−.15	−.07	−.16	.14	−.07
	(.15)	(.15)	(.10)	(.18)	(.09)
Gender	.15	−.41*	−.12	−.87*	−.36*
	(.27)	(.13)	(.17)	(.30)	(.14)
Education	−.40	−.34*	−.62*	−.35	−.39*
	(.22)	(.09)	(.11)	(.20)	(.09)
Income	−.06*	−.01	–	.06	−.07*
	(.03)	(.02)		(.06)	(.02)
Constant	−.56	−3.1*	−.05	1.5	−1.0
	(1.3)	(.57)	(.64)	(.87)	(.54)
N	775	3,716	1,135	765	1,900
Pseudo R^2	0.10	0.07	0.11	0.12	0.13

Note: Figures show unstandardized logistic regression coefficients with standard errors in parentheses, * p < .05.

Table 8.2 Age and PRR party support

Variable	Coefficient	Standard Error
Authoritarianism	.25*	.10
Age	−.01*	.00
Religious Hostility	1.2*	.12
Immigration	1.2*	.08
Economic Preferences	.16*	.02
Religiosity	−.11*	.04
Gender	.28*	.07
Education	−.10*	.05
Income	.03	.02
Manager	−.50*	.09
Unskilled	.10	.09
Retired	−.12	.12
Unemployed	.09	.16
Farmer	−1.1*	.34
Locality	−.09*	.03
Constant	−3.0*	.32
N	11,651	
Chi-Squared	641.6*	

Note: Figures show unstandardized multilevel logistic regression coefficients and standard errors, * p < .05.

Source: EVS 2019.

Age, Authoritarianism, and Support for PRR Parties

The evidence considered so far does not provide definitive claims about the relationship between age and support for the radical right. However, this analysis has not examined the interaction between age and authoritarianism. It is possible that age mediates the relationship between authoritarianism and PRR party support. This analysis considers two such potential relationships. First, age could *strengthen* the relationship between authoritarianism and PRR party support so that authoritarianism has more effect among older voters. This possibility derives from the cultural backlash argument, which claims that older high authoritarians should perceive more threat to the normative order from cultural and demographic change, making them more likely to vote for PRR parties. Second, age could *weaken* the relationship so that authoritarianism has more effect among younger voters. This pattern would be consistent with the worldview evolution argument advanced in this book, in which PRR parties are more successful among younger voters who lack lifelong attachments to the established parties. Of course, the null hypothesis is that age has no effect on the relationship between authoritarianism and PRR party support.

This analysis tests between these possibilities by estimating the logistic regression models of PRR party support presented in Chapter 6 with the addition of an interaction term between age and authoritarianism. The analysis includes the five national election studies included in Chapter 6 along with the 2017 EVS data (EVS 2019). The results of those national election studies are given in Table 8.3, while the EVS results are shown in Table 8.4. Because the inclusion of an interaction term between age and authoritarianism complicates the interpretation of results, I estimate marginal effects of the interactive effects of age and authoritarianism and show these in Figures 8.2 and 8.3.[3] Nonetheless, it is worth noting that the interaction term is negative and significant in Austria, Finland, Switzerland, and the EVS, suggesting strong negative relationships in these contexts.

Figures 8.2 and 8.3 present the marginal effect of authoritarianism on the probability of voting for a PRR for each age in years between 18 and 80. These marginal effects were estimated using the 'margins' command in Stata 15, including all control variables shown in Table 8.1 or 8.2 set to mean or median values. The darkened circles represent the point estimate for each year, while the surrounding bars show the 95 per cent confidence intervals. For those ages in

---

[3] One cannot directly interpret the coefficients for *Age* and *Authoritarianism* because these now show the effect of that variable on the probability of voting for a PRR party when the other variable equals 0 (Brambor et al. 2006). The sign and magnitude of the interaction term is important, but the interaction may have a statistically significant and substantively important effect for certain values of the component variables even if the coefficient is not significant at conventional levels. Therefore, estimating marginal effects and displaying them graphically provides a more useful test and illustration of the interactive effect of age and authoritarianism on PRR party support.

Table 8.3 Authoritarianism, age, and PRR party support in national election studies

Variable	Austria	Britain	Finland	Germany	Switzerland
Authoritarianism	2.1*	.83*	.70*	.93	1.4*
	(.68)	(.31)	(.16)	(.75)	(.39)
Age	.05	.00	−.01	−.03*	−.01
	(.04)	(.02)	(.02)	(.01)	(.02)
Auth. X Age	−.02*	−.00	−.01*	−.01	−.02*
	(.01)	(.01)	(.00)	(.02)	(.01)
Economic Preferences	.10	−.10	−.09	−.27*	.96*
	(.24)	(.10)	(.07)	(.06)	(.10)
Retrospective Economy	−.23	−.20*	−.18	−.24	−.09
	(.14)	(.07)	(.10)	(.16)	(.08)
Religiosity	−.16	−.07	−.16	.14	−.07
	(.15)	(.15)	(.10)	(.18)	(.09)
Gender	.15	−.41*	−.11	−.87*	−.37*
	(.27)	(.13)	(.17)	(.30)	(.14)
Education	−.45*	−.34*	−.65*	−.34	−.38*
	(.23)	(.09)	(.11)	(.20)	(.09)
Income	−.06*	−.01	–	.06	−.07*
	(.03)	(.02)		(.06)	(.02)
Constant	−4.3	−3.4*	−1.8	1.5	−1.1
	(2.5)	(1.3)	(.98)	(.87)	(.54)
N	775	3,716	1,135	765	1,900
Pseudo R^2	0.11	0.07	0.11	0.12	0.14

Note: Figures show unstandardized logistic regression coefficients with standard errors in parentheses, * $p < .05$.

which the lower confidence interval is above the horizontal line denoting 0, the effect of authoritarianism on the probability of voting for a PRR party is positive and statistically significant. If the confidence interval includes the 0 line, then the effect of authoritarianism is not significant for respondents of that age.

The results from Austria, Finland, and Switzerland have a shared pattern. In each, *Authoritarianism* has a positive and significant effect on PRR party support among younger respondents, which declines with age. Starting at an age above 60, the effect is no longer significant and remains so until the maximum of age 80 or higher. The analysis of the EVS data produces the same result, except that *Authoritarianism* is no longer significant above age 55. The analysis of the German data produces unusual results. The marginal effect of authoritarianism decreases with higher age, but the estimates are relatively imprecise as shown by the large confidence intervals for young voters. Therefore, authoritarianism only has a positive and significant effect on respondents aged between 25 and 44 as per the

Table 8.4 Authoritarianism, age, and PRR party support

Variable	Coefficient	Standard Error
Authoritarianism	1.2*	.27
Age	−.01*	.00
Auth. X Age	−.02*	.01
Religious Hostility	1.2*	.12
Immigration	1.2*	.08
Economic Preferences	.16*	.02
Religiosity	−.11*	.04
Gender	.28*	.07
Education	−.12*	.05
Income	.03	.02
Manager	−.50*	.09
Unskilled	.10	.09
Retired	−.12	.11
Unemployed	.07	.16
Farmer	−1.1*	.34
Locality	−.09*	.03
Constant	−2.8	.33
N	11,651	
Chi-Squared	654.0	

Note: Figures show unstandardized multilevel logistic regression coefficients and standard errors, * $p < .05$.

Source: EVS 2019.

results shown here. The marginal effect of authoritarianism approaches 0 for older voters. Thus, the general trend shown in the German data is negative as in the cases discussed above, but less precision in the estimates of younger voters' behaviour limits the strength of the conclusions.

Only the British data do not fit this pattern. The effect of authoritarianism on the probability of voting UKIP varies minimally by age, remaining positive and significant for all adult ages. This result does not support either hypothesis considered here. Across all ages, high authoritarians are more likely to vote for a PRR party than low authoritarians.

What do the results of these analyses suggest? In every case, authoritarianism has a positive and significant effect on the likelihood of voting for PRR parties among voters younger than 45 (with the exception of Germany as noted above). In every case but Britain, this positive effect becomes statistically insignificant among older voters. Finally, the previous section failed to uncover a consistent relationship between age and PRR party support. However, the direct relationship between age and PRR party support was either negative (i.e. younger voters were more likely to support a PRR party) or not significant. The evidence does not

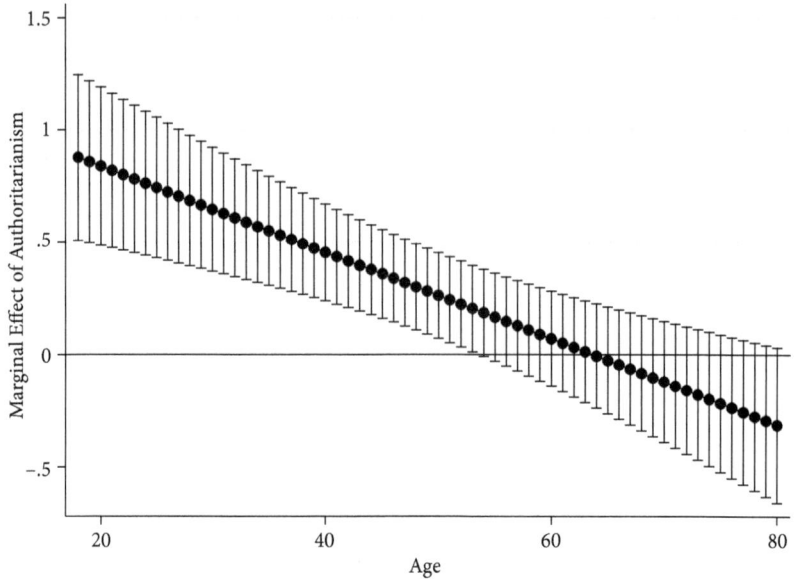

Figure 8.2 Marginal effect of authoritarianism by age on PRR party support

Note: Each circle shows the marginal effect of authoritarianism on the probability of supporting a PRR party for the age indicated on the horizontal scale. The bars show the 95 per cent confidence intervals. Each figure shows the difference in the percentage of younger voters (under age 45) supporting a given party compared to older voters (45 and over). Thus, a bar that is greater than 0 indicates that a greater proportion of young voters support that party.

Source: EVS 2019.

support the claim that older voters or older high authoritarians are more likely to support PRR parties.

This combination of results leads to a rejection of the cultural backlash hypothesis: older voters are not driving increased support for PRR parties. In no case are older high authoritarians more likely to support PRR parties than younger voters. In many cases (excluding Britain and, to an extent, Germany), older higher authoritarians are *less* likely than young high authoritarians to support PRR parties. And the cross-national analysis of the EVS data also finds a negative interaction between age and authoritarianism. In short, the evidence does not support the cultural backlash hypothesis that older voters are driving support for PRR parties across Western Europe.

The evidence in this chapter is more (though not universally) consistent with this book's worldview evolution argument. Younger high authoritarians are more likely (in every case but Britain) to support PRR parties in comparison to their older counterparts, and younger voters generally are equally or more likely than older voters to support PRR parties. This result holds in the cross-national analysis of the EVS data.

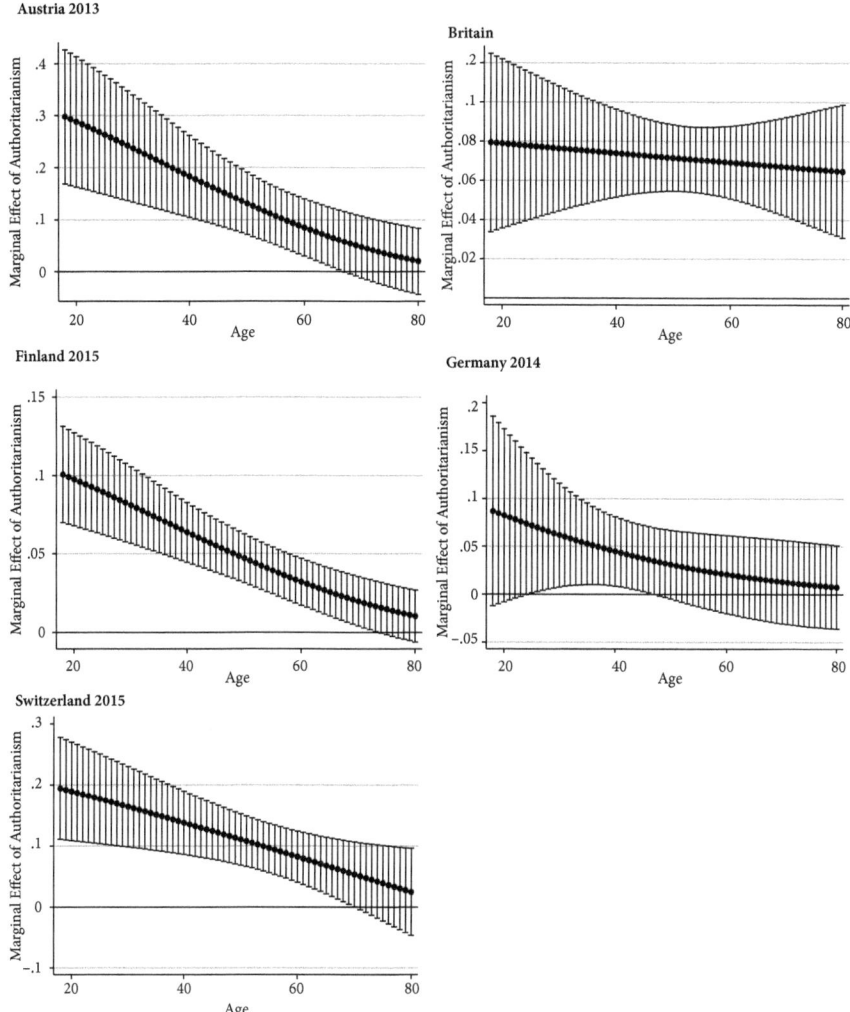

Figure 8.3 Marginal effect of authoritarianism by age on PRR party support

Note: Each circle shows the marginal effect of authoritarianism on the probability of supporting a PRR party for the age indicated on the horizontal scale. The bars show the 95 per cent confidence intervals.

Source: EVS 2019.

Conclusion

This chapter has built on the analyses of the previous two chapters to examine an important question at the heart of this book's argument: does age moderate the relationship between authoritarianism and the propensity to support a populist radical right party? The logic of this book's worldview evolution argument is that age should negatively moderate this relationship. The relationship between authoritarianism and PRR party support should be stronger among younger voters. Because older voters grew up in an era where traditional class and religious cleavages linked voters to mainstream parties (Lipset and Rokkan 1967; Kriesi et al. 2008; Franklin et al. 2009), they formed strong attachments to the mainstream parties. And the tendency of high authoritarians to adhere to tradition and social norms (Stenner 2005; Oyamot et al. 2012) should make older high authoritarians less likely to switch their support to new PRR parties. Young voters do not face those constraints, so they should be more likely to respond to PRR parties' messaging. As a result, younger high authoritarian voters are more likely to support PRR parties whose ideological programmes resonate with their worldviews.

An alternative argument proposes that the relationship between authoritarianism and PRR party support should be stronger among older voters. This cultural backlash argument also emphasizes the role of socialization. Rather than focusing on changing party attachments, this argument claims that older voters were socialized during an era of traditional social and cultural values, which they internalized as their own. The increasing liberalization of mainstream attitudes in the late twentieth century created a gap between older voters—particularly those higher in authoritarianism—and mainstream political parties. For these older voters, increasing liberalization on issues ranging from gender roles and same-sex marriage to immigration and multiculturalism have not just created a gap between voters and parties; this shift has also generated a sense of threat to the normative social order (Norris and Inglehart 2019). When high authoritarians perceive a threat to the normative order, they are more likely to support policies and parties that will stop and reverse these social changes (Stenner 2005). High authoritarians who are older in age see mainstream liberalism and multiculturalism as a threat to traditional shared national values into which they were socialized. Younger voters—even high authoritarians—are less likely to see these new mainstream values as a threat because they were socialized into this new political order. As a result, older high authoritarians should be more likely to support PRR parties that promise to reverse the values and demographic changes occurring in their societies.

The analysis in this chapter considers two questions. The first is simply whether high and low authoritarians vary by age in their party support, respectively. These analyses find mixed evidence of such differences. Younger voters are more or equally likely than older voters to support PRR parties—but never less likely. The second set of analyses includes an interaction between age and authoritarianism to examine whether age moderates the relationship between authoritarianism and PRR party support. These analyses allow for a test of the rival worldview evolution and cultural backlash hypotheses, and they generate two findings. First, the evidence is generally (though not fully) consistent with the worldview evolution hypothesis. The relationship between authoritarianism and the likelihood of supporting a PRR party is stronger among younger voters in most of the analyses. The notable exception is Britain, where age has no moderating effect. In addition, the results are noisy in Germany. While the coefficients are in the expected direction, the larger confidence intervals surrounding the estimated marginal effects do not fully support rejecting the null hypothesis. This noisiness could reflect the fact that the radical right AfD was still very new at the time of the survey (May 2014), leading to less predictable behaviour among voters as they lacked familiarity with the party. In the other cases, including analysis of the 2017 EVS (EVS 2019), the evidence is consistent with the worldview evolution hypothesis. The second major finding is that the results lead to a rejection of the cultural backlash hypothesis. There is no evidence that older high authoritarians are more likely to support PRR parties. Instead, the results point to the opposite conclusion in most cases.

What do these findings add to our understanding of West European electoral politics? The first conclusion is that these results are consistent with this book's worldview evolution argument. High authoritarians, who are more likely to perceive a threat to the normative social order from values and demographic change, are moving towards PRR parties. The previous chapters have compiled evidence consistent with that claim. This chapter provides further evidence showing that this worldview evolution is occurring among younger voters, who have not developed habits of supporting mainstream parties. In turn, these younger high authoritarian voters may develop a habit of supporting PRR parties.

A second conclusion is that it is a mistake to continue to view growing support for PRR parties in Western Europe as a revolt among older voters. There may be certain cases, such as the United Kingdom, where older voters are a more important part of the radical right's electorate (Ford and Goodwin 2014). And early support for radical right parties in past decades came from older, blue-collar voters (Betz 1993; Kitschelt 1997). However, the results from recent years point to growing support among younger voters, while older voters are more likely to remain loyal to established parties. More broadly, these findings should steer us away from viewing support for the radical right as a backlash among older voters distressed by demographic and cultural changes (Norris and Inglehart 2019). Instead, scholars might be better advised to consider radical right support as a preference for the protection of the normative social order among younger voters who have grown up in a changing society.

Drawing on the previous paragraph, another implication concerns our understanding of the future of PRR parties. One tempting implication of the cultural backlash thesis (at least, for opponents of the radical right) is that PRR parties will soon experience electoral decline as their ageing voters are replaced by younger generations who have grown up in a liberalized and multicultural society. This chapter's findings should call that claim into question. Continuing support for PRR parties is not inevitable. However, their support among younger high authoritarians—combined with the tendencies of voters to develop party attachments as they age—provides some reason to expect that these parties will remain electorally relevant in coming years. Rival activists and party leaders should not comfort themselves with the idea that PRR parties' supporters will die off in the coming years. Equally, though, the results of this and preceding two chapters should generate scepticism about predictions of the continuing electoral rise of PRR parties. This book's results suggest that PRR parties appeal successfully to high authoritarians, who make up a substantial minority of voters in West European societies. For PRR parties to command electoral pluralities or majorities, they would need to attract a wider share of voters scoring lower in authoritarianism. Theory suggests the most likely scenario for such a victory is if existential threats (posed by terrorism or rising crime) become more salient to voters, in which case low authoritarians would adopt authoritarian attitudes (Hetherington and Suhay 2011; see also Peffley et al. 2015).

Finally, this chapter hints at broader realignments beyond growing support for PRR parties. Though this book does not focus on green and left-liberal parties, the descriptive results presented in this chapter also show that these parties receive more support from younger low authoritarian voters. In short, established mainstream parties face challenges among younger voters from both directions. High authoritarians are more likely to support PRR parties (and some centre-right parties that have adopted similar positions on cultural issues such as immigration), and low authoritarians are more likely to support left-liberal and green parties. Social Democratic and Christian Democratic parties, which were organized around mid-century class and religious cleavages, have less support among younger voters. Although electoral politics is dynamic and subject to manipulation by enterprising political elites (Riker 1982), these findings may hint at future pressures for traditional mainstream parties.

The results presented in this chapter are consistent with the book's argument of a worldview evolution. However, one caveat is that the results shown here may reflect lifecycle effects rather than cohort differences. In other words, younger voters may generally be more likely to support new or anti-establishment parties. In that case, these results might not reflect a worldview evolution as argued in this book, as these voters may return home to mainstream parties as they age. Future analyses can examine this question as new data become available.

9

Authoritarianism and the Evolution of Voting Behaviour

Introduction

The previous chapters have examined the effect of authoritarianism on support for populist radical right (PRR) parties, demonstrating a relationship between authoritarianism and support for PRR parties in the present era. High authoritarians are more likely to vote for PRR parties relative to low authoritarians across various West European countries, and high authoritarians in Ireland are more likely to vote for a hypothetical new PRR party. This relationship holds when various relevant control variables—such as perceptions of economic anxiety—are included in the analysis. The effect of authoritarianism is magnified among those who are concerned about immigration, suggesting that the hypothesized role of perceived threat to social cohesion is driving this pattern. And this relationship does not simply reflect a backlash among older voters: the relationship between authoritarianism and PRR party support is stronger among younger voters in most West European states.

These analyses show the relationship between authoritarianism and PRR party support in the present era. But several important questions remain about the emergence of this new alignment. First, from where did the support of high authoritarians come? Contemporary cross-national research suggests a broader association between authoritarianism (or related concepts) and support for right-wing parties (e.g. Hetherington and Weiler 2009; Jost et al. 2009; Federico et al. 2011; Malka et al. 2014). But, given that much of that research analyses data from recent years, in which the salience of threats to social cohesion have gained importance, these findings may reflect contemporary but not historical patterns. It is unclear whether high authoritarians voted for particular party families prior to the start of the worldview evolution. If high authoritarians have shifted towards PRR parties in recent years, which parties have lost their support? A related question concerns whether and how the voting behaviour of low authoritarians has also shifted during this era.

Understanding the evolution of the relationship between authoritarianism and voting behaviour over the past two decades makes several important

Authoritarianism and the Evolution of West European Electoral Politics. Erik R. Tillman, Oxford University Press.
© Erik R. Tillman 2021. DOI: 10.1093/oso/9780192896223.003.0009

contributions. First, these findings establish whether the sorting of voters by authoritarianism is a recent development. This book's argument is that the effect of authoritarianism on voting behaviour has emerged in the twenty-first century in response to issues concerning social cohesion, but it is possible that authoritarianism structured party support in earlier eras. Second, this analysis improves our understanding of which parties have lost the support of high authoritarian voters to the radical right. Did high authoritarian voters defect from specific party families, or were they previous dispersed across the party system in earlier years when class or religious cleavages structured voting (Lipset and Rokkan 1967)? Third, it is important to understand whether the voting behaviour of low authoritarian voters has similarly evolved. Have they also shifted party support since the 1990s as the structure of party competition has shifted?

The chapter finds mixed evidence of a worldview evolution in voting behaviour since the 1990s. High authoritarians have shifted from mainstream parties towards PRR parties, while they have also shifted towards mainstream centre-right parties in certain cases. Low authoritarians are more likely to vote for left-liberal parties, but their tendency to support green parties was already present in 1990 and has shifted little since. These two findings suggest that the movement of high authoritarians towards the radical right may represent a response to the growth of low authoritarian green parties in the late twentieth century—a continuation of the ongoing worldview evolution in West European politics. There are two factors limiting these findings, however. First, the results do not point to a single pattern of party support among high (or low) authoritarians in earlier years. The relationship between authoritarianism and party support varied across states. As a result, one cannot conclude that high authoritarians' movement towards PRR parties has harmed a particular party family. Instead, the patterns tend to be more country-specific. Second, most traditional parties of the centre-left and centre-right continue to draw support from across the authoritarian spectrum. Though this support has shrunk in many cases since 1990, it shows that many voters continue to support parties anchored in traditional class or religious cleavages. Of particular interest is the social democratic party family, which is thought to be losing voters to the radical right in large numbers. This chapter's findings suggest that this claim is at best half-correct. Although some high authoritarian voters have abandoned social democratic parties since the 1990s—possibly moving to support PRR parties—low authoritarians have similarly moved towards left-liberal parties. Thus, the recent electoral struggles of social democratic parties may be due to their loss of two different parts of their historic electoral base for distinct reasons. In this sense, social democratic parties are suffering because of the worldview evolution, but it is only partially due to the gains of PRR parties.

Voter Defections to the Radical Right

The rise of PRR parties throughout Western Europe led to scholarly interest in the identity of their voters. One natural extension of that interest is the question of which existing parties lost voters to the radical right. Broadly speaking, two possibilities exist. One is that PRR party supporters tended to support particular party families prior to the rise of the radical right, so PRR parties drew voters away from those former party families. The other possibility is that PRR parties drew supporters from across the existing parties by activating previously dormant concerns about social cohesion and security, leading to a (partial) electoral realignment.[1] In this scenario, PRR party supporters previously voted for established parties based on the factors structuring politics in that earlier era, such as class and religion (Lipset and Rokkan 1967; Franklin et al. 2009), but they now vote for PRR parties based on issues concerning identity and culture.

There is reason to imagine that the second scenario is more likely. Theories of issue evolution and political entrepreneurship argue that new parties seek to enter established party systems by introducing new issues that cut across the dominant axes of party conflict (Riker 1982; Carmines and Stimson 1989; de Vries and Hobolt 2012). In an established party system, parties cultivate loyalties among various groups of voters based on the dominant issues and social identities structuring politics at the time. In a system defined by class, for example, social democratic parties maintain the support of working-class voters while centre-right parties cultivate the support of middle-class voters. For a new party to gain supporters at the expense of established parties, it must find a new issue (or set of issues) that leads voters to rethink their political loyalties. It is unlikely that this issue will exist within the established structure of party conflict. For example, in an era of class-based conflict, a new party is unlikely to gain the support of working-class voters simply by introducing new issues relating to class interests. A social democratic party would likely adopt those new issue positions quickly and undermine the new party's threat to its electoral base. Importantly, the social democratic party would be able to do this without undermining its electoral support, since this issue did not divide its voters. Instead, a new party must introduce issues that encourage those working-class voters to reconsider their political identity through the prism of something other than class so that voting for a party that is not based on class becomes possible. For this new party to enjoy electoral success, this appeal must also extend to voters beyond the working classes. If so, then the new party can build a new coalition of voters that cuts across the traditional class divide. Because the issues driving the new party's appeal are not based on the old class divide, the established parties cannot

---

[1] In this scenario, PRR parties might also mobilize previous non-voters.

respond effectively without risking divisions within their traditional electoral base. Thus, the new party draws voters from each of the major class-based parties, triggering a broader electoral realignment. As voters begin shifting to this new party, other parties respond by changing their appeals in order to attract new voters in a changing electoral landscape.

Several perspectives exist on the factors leading to the rise of the radical right in Western Europe. Some arguments emphasize the role of the economic transformations of the late twentieth century. One reason is that the shift from manufacturing to service economies, combined with globalization, created distinct economic winners and losers. According to this argument, PRR parties heavily represent the losers of these economic transformations. In Western democracies, winners included professional classes, those with university degrees, and immigrants who benefited from access to high-paying job markets. The losers included members of the working class and those with less education (Gabel 1998; Kriesi et al. 2008). The movement of Western economies from manufacturing to service and technology led to reduced employment opportunities, weakening of unions, and more competition with immigrant and overseas labour (Betz 1993; Kriesi et al. 2008). PRR parties were able to gain support among members of these communities by addressing these economic grievances. This argument suggests that PRR voters came primarily from social democratic and labour parties.

A related argument emphasizes the diminished social standing and perceived marginalization of the native working class. Late twentieth-century policy increasingly emphasized higher education and the creation of a meritocratic society as part of the shift to a post-industrial 'knowledge' economy. An unintended consequence of this shift was to diminish the perceived social status of the native working class (Ford and Goodwin 2014; Gest 2016; Gidron and Hall 2020), whose declining economic circumstances could be attributed to a lack of 'merit'. Additionally, members of the political elite increasingly come from middle-class backgrounds with university education, meaning that they have less connection to working-class constituents. This disconnect between representatives and constituents fuels resentment among the latter (Cramer 2016; Gest 2016). As a result, members of the native working class came to see themselves as a marginalized or 'left behind' constituency that mainstream parties no longer represent (Ford and Goodwin 2014), leaving them more receptive to radical right parties' messages. Though this argument might suggest that these PRR voters came from social democratic parties, it is more likely that they have shifted between the established parties in response to different leaders and political-economic conditions (Ford and Goodwin 2014; Gest 2016).

A final economic argument emphasizes the shifting nature of work in the post-industrial economy. The rise of the service economy has generated more jobs in knowledge-intensive industries, which reward autonomy and ingenuity among employees. In addition, many new jobs in the public sector also tend to value interpersonal and multicultural skills. By contrast, the remaining industrial jobs and other private-sector fields operate in rules-driven and hierarchical contexts. Workers in this field will be more receptive to parties offering authoritarian leadership styles (Kitschelt 1994). According to this argument, employees in creative and public-sector fields will be drawn to centre-left parties that promote individual autonomy, while workers in the latter fields will be drawn to PRR parties that offer authoritarian policy solutions. In this case, PRR parties are likely to draw voters from across the different mainstream parties.

Voters may have migrated to PRR parties because of cultural rather than economic concerns. The policy shifts of the late twentieth century have led also to increased migration from non-Western countries and wider elite acceptance of multiculturalism. As mainstream parties shifted to positions that are more favourable on immigration, they abandoned their voters who opposed immigration and multiculturalism. This shift opened space for enterprising PRR party leaders to attract these voters by appealing to their cultural preferences. Voters with lower educational attainment and occupational status are more likely to oppose immigration (Betz 1993). Many such voters may also hold culturally conservative positions alongside left-wing economic preferences (Lefkofridi et al. 2014), given their class backgrounds and interests. As a result, PRR parties may draw more such voters from social democratic parties, though it is also possible that they will draw former right-wing voters as well if they perceive that the centre-right parties have shifted towards the centre on immigration.

A related argument sees the rise of the radical right as part of a cultural backlash against values changes in West European societies (Norris and Inglehart 2019). As mainstream political elites have adopted liberal and post-materialist values, voters who hold more traditional social and cultural stances feel increasingly abandoned or marginalized. According to this argument, these voters are typically older and less educated. Radical right parties have successfully attracted these voters by appealing to these voters' values and associating them with traditional national identity and culture. Of course, multiculturalism is one of those values at the core of this cultural backlash, so anti-immigration attitudes correlate with PRR party support.

This review produces two general conclusions. First, radical right parties have drawn support primarily (though not exclusively) from members of the native working-class population. Cross-national and national research provides quantitative and qualitative evidence for these claims across West Europe (Oesch 2008; Mayer 2013; Rydgren 2013; Ford and Goodwin 2014). In their study of support for the UK Independence Party, Ford and Goodwin (2014) describe the party's core support as 'older, blue-collar voters, citizens with few [educational] qualifications, whites, and men' (175), describing these voters as 'left behind' (176) economically by the transformation to a post-industrial economy in the

1990s and 2000s and politically by the convergence of the mainstream parties in the economic and cultural centre. Other research similarly identifies stronger support for PRR parties among the native working-class population (Betz 1993; Givens 2005; Norris 2005). While this demographic profile would suggest that many were former social democratic voters, their political history may be more complicated.

A second general conclusion is that it is hard to distinguish between the economic and cultural explanations. Because anti-immigration attitudes and culturally conservative values are more common among members of the native working class, it is difficult to isolate whether economic or cultural grievances motivate these voters. While quantitative research finds strong associations between anti-immigrant attitudes and PRR party support (e.g. Ivarsflaten 2007; Oesch 2008; Lucassen and Lubbers 2012), qualitative research demonstrates that many working-class voters who support PRR parties or candidates do not distinguish clearly between economic and cultural concerns in their own thinking (Cramer 2016; Gest 2016). Instead, both concerns contribute to a sense of marginalization or lack of social integration among such voters (Gidron and Hall 2020). As such, it is difficult to identify the explanations for PRR voting in demographic or attitudinal accounts.

The preceding discussion suggests why PRR voters may not predominantly be former social democratic party voters. The historical link between working-class voters and social democratic parties was never monolithic. Even at its peak during the middle of the twentieth century, a substantial minority of manual workers voted for conservative or Christian democratic parties. During a time when the majority of the electorate in many West European societies came from working-class households, centre-right parties could not have won elections without working-class support. During the 1950s and 1960s, roughly one-third of British manual workers voted Conservative or Liberal (Stephens 1979), a pattern which continued into the latter decades of the twentieth century (Ford and Goodwin 2014: 174). In other West European countries, class and education were moderately associated with party support in the 1980s and 1990s. In Germany, university graduates were split relatively equally between the centre-left and centre-right, though they favoured the centre-right by about 13–16 percentage points in Austria. Occupational status provided a somewhat sharper distinction, as blue-collar workers favoured centre-left parties by clearer margins in Austria and Germany, though not in France. The largest gaps were among groups such as farmers and the self-employed, who favoured centre-right parties by bigger margins (Givens 2005).

The evidence showing that many PRR party voters are working class does not necessarily imply that they are former social democratic voters. Many working-class voters hold 'left-authoritarian' values (i.e. favouring redistributive economic policies alongside traditional/authoritarian social and cultural attitudes) (Lipset 1959; Napier and Jost 2008; Lefkofridi et al. 2014). Such voters are cross-pressured as they prefer the economic policies of social democratic parties but the cultural policies of right-wing parties, meaning that they were not necessarily reliable social democratic voters. In earlier decades, religious identities may have led working-class voters to support Christian democratic or conservative parties, despite their class identities, while higher levels of nationalism may have similarly induced greater support for conservative parties. Even among working-class PRR party supporters, many may have supported centre-right parties rather than social democratic parties.

Authoritarianism and Party Support

A separate literature examines the relationship between individual personality dispositions and party support (see Federico and Malka 2018 for a recent review). Understanding this relationship is important for this chapter's analysis: to what extent should one expect high authoritarians to support right-wing parties in general (and not specifically PRR parties)? The potential relationship between authoritarianism and support for right-wing parties is conditional on the relationship between issues, elite conflict, and the political context. In short, high authoritarians were less likely to support right-wing parties before the recent growth of elite conflict over immigration, European Union, and the defence of national community.

The interest in a relationship between authoritarianism and right-wing party support emerged in the earliest research on political psychology (e.g. Adorno et al. 1950; Eysenck 1954). Because authoritarianism reflects a desire to maintain social conformity with traditional social values and identities, high authoritarians should feel an affinity towards right-wing parties that similarly tend to resist change and preserve traditional values and norms. The evidence shows a correlation between authoritarianism and conservative self-identification (e.g. Jost et al. 2003, 2009; Federico et al. 2011).

The linkage between authoritarianism and conservatism is natural on socio-cultural issues, but it is less obvious on economic issues. While high authoritarians may support the maintenance of traditional social hierarchies or reject radical economic change (as implied by left-wing welfare programmes), they are also likely to desire protection against the uncertainty of the free market and of atomistic market competition. As a result, there is no natural affinity between authoritarianism and right-wing economic positions. Various cross-national studies find that authoritarianism correlates with socially conservative positions but not with right-wing economic positions (Thorisdottir et al. 2007; Napier and Jost 2008; Malka et al. 2014).

The translation of conservative self-identification into party support will be conditional on contextual factors. A key determinant is how parties bundle economic and social messages and the resulting extent of party conflict on the economic and socio-cultural dimensions. If parties take divergent positions on economic issues while holding similar positions on social issues, then high authoritarians are unlikely to gravitate towards a particular party. By contrast, sharp divergence on social issues will more likely attract high authoritarians towards the right-wing (or culturally traditionalist) party and low authoritarians towards left-wing party. Evidence from the past several decades supports this interpretation in the United States. As the Republicans and Democrats began to diverge on socio-cultural questions from the 1960s onwards, high authoritarians moved towards the Republicans while low authoritarians shifted to the Democrats (Hetherington and Weiler 2009; Cizmar et al. 2014).

Based on this discussion, the relationship between authoritarianism and party support should be modest throughout Western Europe prior to the twenty-first century. In some cases, high authoritarians may have supported Christian democratic or conservative parties due to religious or national identification. However, authoritarianism should have a modest association with party support prior to the emergence of party conflict over national community issues such as immigration and the EU. When party conflict reflected social class interests more than cultural issues, there would have been little reason for authoritarianism to affect party support. In many cases, this emergence of a radical right party will drive the growth of this conflict. As this conflict grows, high authoritarians should be drawn towards those parties promoting the defence of national community, while low authoritarians move towards parties emphasizing cosmopolitanism and individual autonomy (typically, green and other left-liberal parties). However, the starting point of party attachments for each country will depend on earlier patterns of party conflict. Thus, it is unlikely that one party family will have absorbed the bulk of vote losses to the radical right cross-nationally.

Data and Analysis

The analyses examine changes in party support between 1990 and 2017, comparing the different patterns of party support among high and low authoritarians, respectively. The goal in these analyses is to understand the structure of party support by authoritarianism in the 1990s as the hypothesized worldview evolution was beginning, and then to examine how these patterns of party support evolved cross-nationally. These analyses are descriptive due to the limitations of working with cross-sectional data collected at nine-year intervals. Thus, the findings merit caution and should be viewed as suggestive.

The analysis uses data from the European Values Study (EVS) (covering the years 1990–2017) (EVS 2011a, 2011b, 2016, 2019). The choice of data and years reflects the availability of appropriate questions to measure authoritarianism and party support during the relevant years. The EVS has the best survey measures of authoritarianism in each wave, though its disadvantage is limited time coverage. The survey is administered every nine years, meaning that the data only provide snapshots of electoral behaviour in 1990, 1999–2000, 2008–9, and 2017. In addition, the availability of data from 1990 is valuable for examining the relationship between authoritarianism and party support before the start of the worldview evolution. Other national and cross-national surveys were not appropriate for various reasons. Although other scholars have used measures of values appearing in the European Social Survey (ESS) as a substitute for the child-rearing questions (Norris and Inglehart 2019), this approach introduces various problems—including whether these measures are conceptually distinct from the political behaviour they purport to predict, and questions about the appropriate value measures to include in a scale of authoritarianism. In addition, the ESS survey only started in 2002, omitting crucial early years before the start of the worldview evolution. Most national election survey series do not contain measures of authoritarianism, so they are not appropriate for inclusion in this analysis.

The analysis examines the changing patterns of party support in Austria, Denmark, Finland, France, Germany, Great Britain the Netherlands, and Sweden.[2] One can broadly categorize these countries in three groups. Austria and Denmark already had a PRR party in their national parliaments in the 1990s, meaning that these parties had a core electoral support at the start of the hypothesized worldview evolution. Similarly, France had an electorally successful PRR party, though it had little representation in parliament due to French electoral laws (Norris 2005). The question in these countries will be whether or how PRR party support evolved in the subsequent years. In Finland, Great Britain, and Sweden, a PRR party existed before the twenty-first century but remained electorally marginal before experiencing an electoral breakthrough in the second decade of the century. In each case, the party undertook leadership and programmatic transformations in the years before their electoral breakthroughs, which may have changed their appeal to voters. Finally, Germany and the Netherlands witnessed the formation of a new PRR party in the twenty-first cen-tury, which then quickly established itself electorally. (Both countries had had radical or far-right parties previously, but none had established itself in a national parliament). In these latter two groups of countries, the focus will be on whether high authoritarians abandoned mainstream parties for the radical right, and from which parties those voters came.

The analyses compare the reported party support of respondents above the mean for authoritarianism with those below the mean for each country and year using the child-rearing values measurement of authoritarianism in the EVS. This

---

[2] Other countries are not included due to the lack of inclusion in each survey wave.

method of comparison produces conservative results insofar as it compares roughly one-half of the respondents to the other, including many who are close to the midpoint of the scale. Setting the cut-off points higher (e.g. comparing those in the highest and lowest quintiles of authoritarianism) would produce starker findings at the expense of reduced relevance. As shown in Chapter 3, authoritarianism is distributed normally, so a comparison of only the more extreme parts of the scale would include a relatively small portion of the electorate. Readers wishing to see such an analysis can consult Appendix II, which defines high authoritarians as those scoring 0.33 or higher and low authoritarians as those scoring −0.33 or lower. The analyses presented in Appendix II produce similar (though occasionally more dramatic) results to those presented in this chapter on the smaller subset of voters who score more distinctively as high authoritarians or low authoritarians. The analysis considers each country in turn.

Austria

During the era under consideration, the Austrian party system had four major parties. On the left, the Green Party has been the third or fourth largest party while remaining in opposition throughout this era. Its positions are fairly standard for a European green party, with emphases on environmental protection, social justice, multiculturalism, and participatory democracy. It should attract low authoritarian voters. The Social Democratic Party of Austria (SPÖ) is the major social democratic party and one of the two dominant parties in post-war Austria. It has historical ties to the major unions and the urban working-class vote, but like most social democratic parties has moved to capture urban, middle-class voters in recent decades. The Austrian People's Party (ÖVP) is the other major party in post-war Austria. It operates as a Christian democratic and conservative party, which historical ties to conservative, religious, and rural voters. It has often participated in grand coalition governments with the Social Democratic Party, including during much of the era considered here. As broad catch-all parties of the centre-left and centre-right, SPÖ and ÖVP are likely to have a mix of high and low authoritarian voters, and they should be most vulnerable to losing voters to rival parties. Finally, the Freedom Party of Austria (FPÖ) underwent a transformation in the 1980s from a liberal party to a PRR party under the leadership of Jörg Haider, after which it increased its vote share and become the third-largest party. After a period of internal conflict during the early twenty-first century, the party has consolidated its position as the third largest in Austria. As this party also adopted a radical right programme during the time of Haider's leadership, high authoritarians should be more likely to support FPÖ.

Table 9.1 Party support by authoritarianism in Austria, 1990–2017

Year	Voters	Greens	SPÖ	ÖVP	FPÖ
1990	High Authoritarians	3.1	45.9	37.2	13.9
	Low Authoritarians	15.7	40.1	27.0	17.2
1999	High Authoritarians	3.2	33.3	39.9	22.1
	Low Authoritarians	15.3	33.7	25.0	19.3
2008	High Authoritarians	9.4	43.9	28.3	13.0
	Low Authoritarians	25.4	30.0	22.4	15.1
2017	High Authoritarians	5.1	31.2	36.5	24.6
	Low Authoritarians	10.7	32.1	32.4	18.5
Change 1990–2017	*High Authoritarians*	*2.0*	*−14.7*	*−0.7*	*12.7*
	Low Authoritarians	*−5.0*	*−8.0*	*−5.4*	*1.3*

Source: Data from the 1990–2017 waves of the European Values Survey.

The results from Austria are shown in Table 9.1. Several interesting patterns emerge. Notably, authoritarianism does not structure FPÖ support between 1990 and 2008. High and low authoritarians vote FPÖ in roughly equal proportions, consistent with mixed findings from that era (Dunn 2015). Various reasons for this could include the historical roots of FPÖ as a liberal party, its status as one of only two viable opposition parties against the SPÖ–ÖVP grand coalition, and efforts by the SPÖ–ÖVP governments of 2006–8 to strengthen integration laws, which may have alleviated high authoritarians' concerns about social disintegration. In those earlier years, high authoritarians vote in somewhat larger numbers for the centre-right ÖVP. Meanwhile, low authoritarians support the Greens in much higher proportions. This last finding is consistent with expectations and highlights the electoral distinctiveness of low authoritarians. Moreover, it shows that low authoritarians had already moved towards left-liberal parties by the 1990s.

The 2017 survey wave shows some evidence of a worldview evolution. High authoritarians are somewhat more likely to support FPÖ, and their support for the party grows considerably more than among low authoritarians during the 1990–2017 era. Nonetheless, a substantial share of low authoritarians supports FPÖ throughout this era, which is not consistent with expectations. Both groups of voters abandon SPÖ, though the share is higher among high authoritarians. Thus, there is evidence consistent with the claim that the social democrats lost voters to the radical right. By contrast, low authoritarians moved from both major parties towards smaller liberal and left-liberal parties (not shown). These two findings illustrate that SPÖ faced the double challenge of losing high authoritarian supporters to the radical right while losing low authoritarian supporters to left-liberal parties. In short, the evidence from Austria provides mixed evidence for the worldview evolution hypothesis.

Denmark

Denmark resembles Austria in that it has had a PRR party since the 1980s, though the Danish People's Party (DF) was founded in 1995 by members of the disintegrating Progress Party. The Progress Party started as anti-tax party in 1973, but it subsequently moved towards right-wing populism and anti-immigrant policies by the time of its collapse in the early 1990s. DF continued the emphasis on national sovereignty and anti-immigrant policies while providing support to centre-right coalition governments in 2001–11 and 2015–19. High authoritarians should be more likely to support DF. However, centre-right cabinets under the leadership of prime ministers from the Liberal Party (Venstre) have implemented stricter immigration policies in the twenty-first century, so high authoritarians may also be likely to support the centre-right Liberal Party instead. Low authoritarians should be more likely to support the Socialist People's Party (SPP) and the Red–Green Alliance (RG) in recent years, while the centre-left Social Democratic Party (SD) should gain historical support from across the authoritarian spectrum. There are several smaller parties on the centre-right, but these do not factor into this analysis.

Table 9.2 presents the results from Denmark. First, the data point to the gradual development of a gap in support for DF between high and low authoritarians. That gap increased from 2.2 to 7.5 percentage points between 1990 and 2017. This evidence is consistent with the worldview evolution as high authoritarians moved over time to support the party that promises to protect social cohesion. The Social Democrats experienced declining support as high authoritarians abandoned it between 1990 and 2008, though the party gained support from both high and low authoritarians in 2017. In general, high authoritarians shifted from the Social Democrats and Conservative Party towards DF and the Liberal Party. Low

Table 9.2 Party support by authoritarianism in Denmark, 1990–2017

Year	Voters	SPP	RG	SD	Venstre	Cons	DF
1990	High Authoritarians	9.8	–	39.2	16.3	17.7	7.4
	Low Authoritarians	32.4	–	28.3	9.7	13.1	5.2
1999	High Authoritarians	9.4	–	29.4	41.0	10.2	6.2
	Low Authoritarians	23.4	–	26.1	29.2	6.5	4.2
2008	High Authoritarians	11.0	0.9	22.8	37.3	8.9	15.1
	Low Authoritarians	23.7	2.2	22.5	27.6	8.2	6.4
2017	High Authoritarians	4.8	4.6	30.7	26.0	6.4	15.2
	Low Authoritarians	10.6	13.3	30.7	17.8	4.8	7.7
Change 1990–2017	*High Authoritarians*	*−5.0*	*4.6*	*−8.5*	*9.7*	*−11.3*	*7.8*
	Low Authoritarians	*−19.8*	*13.3*	*1.4*	*8.1*	*−8.3*	*2.5*

Source: Data from the 1990–2017 waves of the European Values Survey.

authoritarians seem only to have shifted between parties of the far left, though the Liberals picked up roughly equal shares of high and low authoritarians. In short, the evidence is consistent with the worldview evolution argument, suggesting that high authoritarians moved from the Social Democrats and possibly the Conservative Party to the Danish People's Party.

Finland

Finland is the first of three cases considered here in which a PRR party established in the 1990s contested its first few elections in relative obscurity before surging in popularity after 2010. The Finns Party (PS) (previously known as True Finns Party) was established in 1995, but it received less than 5 per cent of the vote nationally in its first three elections from 1999 to 2007. Its breakthrough came in 2011, when it received 19 per cent of the vote and became Finland's third-largest party. It consolidated this result in the 2015 parliamentary election and joined the centre-right coalition government of Juha Sipilä of the Center Party (KESK). Its platform includes a mixture of nationalism, social conservatism, and anti-crime position.

The Finns Party entered a multiparty system anchored by three larger parties, two of which typically alternate participating in governing coalitions: the centre-left Social Democrats (SDP), the centrist and agrarian KESK, and the centre-right conservative National Coalition Party (KOK). There are a number of smaller parties, but two that are relevant to the study are the far-left Left Alliance and the left-liberal Green League. The electoral bases of these parties are fairly typical. Historically, SDP relies on working-class and middle-class public-sector workers, while KOK relies on middle-class, suburban and conservative voters. KESK typically gets more support from voters in smaller municipalities and outlying areas of Finland. Given the class and urban–rural structure of Finnish politics, each of the three major parties would be at risk of losing high authoritarian voters to PS and low authoritarian voters to the Green League.

Table 9.3 shows the patterns of party support for high and low authoritarians from 1990 to 2017. The results are consistent with the expectation that PS gained support primarily from high authoritarian voters. KOK lost support predominantly from high authoritarians, while SDP lost support from both groups of voters. Meanwhile, KESK continued to receive relatively more support from high authoritarians, while the Social Democrats and KOK received roughly equal support from each group. By contrast, the Green League earned support predominantly from low authoritarians throughout the analysis, suggesting that many low authoritarians had already sorted to this left-liberal party before 1990.

The results in Finland provide some evidence of a worldview evolution. A greater proportion of low authoritarians support the Green League than the

Table 9.3 Party support by authoritarianism in Finland, 1990–2017

Year	Voters	Left	Greens	SDP	KESK	KOK	PS
1990	High Authoritarians	4.3	4.8	27.2	25.8	35.5	–
	Low Authoritarians	5.0	18.2	26.0	16.0	27.1	–
1999	High Authoritarians	6.3	9.5	31.6	33.3	17.5	1.7
	Low Authoritarians	12.6	20.2	22.2	22.8	20.5	1.7
2008	High Authoritarians	5.1	8.9	18.5	20.4	31.5	15.6
	Low Authoritarians	6.5	24.3	21.3	10.6	26.4	10.9
2017	High Authoritarians	6.4	9.5	18.0	24.4	23.3	12.3
	Low Authoritarians	9.8	24.2	16.7	17.3	25.3	5.8
Change 1990–2017	*High Authoritarians*	*2.1*	*4.7*	*−8.2*	*−1.4*	*−12.2*	*12.3*
	Low Authoritarians	*4.8*	*6.0*	*−9.3*	*1.3*	*−1.8*	*5.8*

Source: Data from the 1990–2017 waves of the European Values Survey.

Social Democrats, suggesting more sorting of these voters towards this left-liberal party. However, many low authoritarians also support the centre-right National Coalition, which may reflect that party's urban and professional base. By contrast, the radical right Finns Party has gained high authoritarian voters, while the rural-oriented Centre Party has maintained a greater share of high authoritarian voters. These findings illustrate a worldview evolution in process while highlighting the importance of the established party system.

France

France is something of a hybrid case in that the radical right National Rally (RN)[3] has been a major electoral force in French politics since the 1990s while achieving minimal presence in representative institutions. Because France uses majoritarian electoral rules, RN has struggled to translate vote shares above 10 per cent in the first round into parliamentary seats (Norris 2005), and its presidential candidate has twice lost in the run-off election in 2002 and 2017. Nonetheless, it has been a visible and popular party throughout the period analysed here, and its presence has influenced the strategy of its centre-right rivals on issues such as immigration.

French politics is anchored by two main parties on the centre-left and centre-right, along with a range of smaller parties that have little presence in parliament. The Socialist Party (PS) is the main party of the centre-left. Its electoral base and policy programme is similar to that of other social democratic parties throughout Western Europe. The Republicans (LR) are the main party of the centre-right, having previously been named the Union for a Popular Movement (UMP; 2002–15),

---

[3] Until 2018, its name was National Front (FN).

Table 9.4 Party support by authoritarianism in France, 1990–2017

Year	Voters	PG	Greens	Socialists	LREM	Republicans	RN
1990	High Authoritarians	3.8	13.7	37.9	–	26.8	6.2
	Low Authoritarians	7.8	20.4	47.7	–	12.0	3.2
1999	High Authoritarians	4.6	11.4	32.9	–	18.5	4.4
	Low Authoritarians	4.3	18.3	40.1	–	9.5	2.1
2008	High Authoritarians	4.6	6.0	34.2	–	32.8	4.6
	Low Authoritarians	9.7	10.0	38.2	–	21.5	1.1
2017	High Authoritarians	7.6	6.3	23.8	21.8	18.3	18.9
	Low Authoritarians	12.7	11.9	27.9	25.2	9.6	7.8
Change 1990–2017	*High Authoritarians*	*3.8*	*−6.3*	*−14.1*	*21.8*	*−8.5*	*12.7*
	Low Authoritarians	*4.9*	*−8.5*	*−19.8*	*25.2*	*−2.4*	*4.6*

Source: Data from the 1990–2017 waves of the European Values Survey.

which itself was formed by a merger of the centre-right Rally for the Republic (RPR) and Union for French Democracy (UDF). As the major centre-right party, its support historically comes from middle class and rural voters. Farther to the left, Europe Ecology–the Greens (EELV) gains support from educated, urban voters, while the Parties on the Left (PG) on the far left also gain substantial vote shares.[4] The newest party is The Republic on the Move! (LREM), which is a liberal party established by Emmanuel Macron in 2016. LREM won the presidential and parliamentary elections of 2017, in the final year of this study's data coverage. Though there are other parties in the French party system, the analysis focuses on these six.

Table 9.4 shows the changing patterns of voting behaviour among high and low authoritarians. There is already evidence in 1990 that high authoritarians are more likely to vote for parties of the right while low authoritarians support parties of the left. Until 2017, support for RN is low though high authoritarians are always modestly more likely to support it. In 2017, however, support for RN grows substantially with much of that coming from high authoritarians. Did that support come from the Socialist Party? A definitive answer is not possible, but the evidence does not point to that conclusion. Rather, it seems more likely that high authoritarians left LR for RN, while LREM attracted a mix of high and low authoritarians. Because of the upheavals to the French party system in 2017, patterns of party support are likely in flux. For example, it remains to be seen whether LREM will develop a stable base of supporters. Nonetheless, two patterns emerge. First, high

---

[4] More recently, former co-president of PG Jean-Luc Mélenchon has formed a new movement called *La France Insoumise*, which translates as 'Unbowed France'. It currently sits as a party grouping in parliament. Because this new grouping comes after the dates of this chapter's analyses, I refer to PG throughout.

authoritarians have moved towards the radical right RN in the past decade, consistent with expectations. Second, high authoritarians are split between RN and LR on the right, while low authoritarians split their support between the Greens and far-left parties. Meanwhile, PS and LREM have a mix of high and low authoritarian supporters. Thus, left–right party support correlates with authoritarianism.

Germany

Germany is the first of two countries in this analysis in which a PRR party was established in the twenty-first century. It is also one in which there is already an authoritarian divide in party support, meaning that the rise of the radical right and an evolution of electoral politics will occur in that context. There are two major and several smaller parties in German politics. The centre-left Social Democratic Party (SPD) and the centre-right Christian Democratic Union (CDU)[5] have traditionally been the main rivals to lead governments, though they have formed grand coalitions on several occasions (including 2005–9 and 2013–17). SPD attracts working-class and public-sector workers, while CDU gains support from conservative suburban and rural residents as well as religious voters. On the right, the Free Democratic Party (FDP) attracts urban and educated supporters with a pro-market and social liberal stance. On the left, the Left was originally formed as a post-communist successor to the East German ruling Social Union Party, while the Greens formed in the 1980s in West Germany. The Greens should attract low authoritarian supporters as in other West European societies. The Alternative for Germany (AfD) was formed in April 2013 during the European financial crisis in opposition to the euro and Greek bailouts, but it quickly transitioned as a PRR party in 2015 (Berning 2017; Mudde 2017). Because the AfD has existed for only a few years, evidence of changing party support among high authoritarians should be limited.

Table 9.5 shows the results for Germany. A notable difference between Germany and the prior three countries examined here is that high authoritarians already showed a strong pattern of support for the centre-right CDU in 1990 and thereafter.[6] Low authoritarians were more likely to support the Greens, while SPD, FDP, and the Left received roughly equal support from both groups. During the period of analysis, SPD lost support from both high and low authoritarians, continuing a pattern observed in Austria and Finland. However, it lost

---

[5] The CDU competes outside of Bavaria, while the Christian Social Union (CSU) only competes within Bavaria. The two parties have cooperated continually since the early post-war years, so it is common practice to treat them as a single party for the purpose of analysis.

[6] It is likely that the relationship between authoritarianism and party support results from other factors, such as the role of religion. Thus, a worldview evolution could still restructure German politics as issues of national community and sovereignty become more salient.

Table 9.5 Party support by authoritarianism in Germany, 1990–2017

Year	Voters	Left	Greens	SPD	CDU	FDP	AfD
1990	High Authoritarians	4.2	2.2	34.1	51.8	7.8	–
	Low Authoritarians	1.9	10.4	45.4	33.3	9.0	–
1999	High Authoritarians	8.0	2.3	32.2	55.5	1.9	–
	Low Authoritarians	14.4	8.2	28.8	45.8	2.7	–
2008	High Authoritarians	13.2	8.5	23.4	47.6	7.3	–
	Low Authoritarians	23.4	12.2	24.2	29.5	10.8	–
2017	High Authoritarians	7.7	10.4	24.1	42.4	7.1	8.3
	Low Authoritarians	10.6	19.5	24.5	32.2	8.0	5.3
Change 1990–2017	*High Authoritarians*	*3.5*	*8.2*	*−10.0*	*−9.4*	*−0.7*	*8.3*
	Low Authoritarians	*8.7*	*9.1*	*−19.9*	*−1.1*	*−1.0*	*5.3*

Source: Data from the 1990–2017 waves of the European Values Survey.

considerably more support from low authoritarians than from high authoritarians, with those low authoritarian voters moving primarily towards the Greens and the Left. A surprisingly high proportion of high authoritarians appear also to have moved to the Greens. AfD has limited support in the only survey in which it appears (2017), and its support is modestly greater among high authoritarians.

The results here suggest that CDU, rather than SPD, stands to lose more voters to AfD if the latter continues to consolidate its support among high authoritarians. With almost half of high authoritarians supporting CDU while only a quarter or less supporting SPD by 2017, there is greater potential for high authoritarians to shift from CDU to AfD than from SPD to AfD. While high authoritarians with stronger religious ties are more likely to remain CDU supporters (Arzheimer and Carter 2009), those with weaker religious affiliation may be more likely to switch support to AfD. Alternatively, the strong presence of high authoritarians in the CDU electorate could lead it to adopt positions closer to the radical right, which would mark a substantial programmatic shift.

Great Britain

The development of the radical right followed a similar pattern in Finland and Great Britain, as a PRR party spent years with little electoral support in national elections before experiencing a breakthrough after 2010.[7] The United Kingdom Independence Party (UKIP) was established in 1991 as a single-issue party

---

[7] This analysis focuses on British voters, excluding those in Northern Ireland in which a different party system operates. It also ignores supporters of the Scottish Nationalist Party and Plaid Cymru (the Welsh nationalist party) for simplicity of analysis and presentation.

focused on leaving the EU, but it gained little support until it shifted its electoral strategy after 2006 to incorporate a broader PRR agenda (Ford and Goodwin 2014). Though it had success in the 2004 and 2009 European Parliament elections, it never received more than 3.1 per cent of the vote in a general election until 2015. In that election, it gained 12.6 per cent of the vote, making it the third-largest party in terms of vote share. Because of the plurality electoral rules used in British elections, it still managed to win only 1 of 650 seats in the House of Commons. Nonetheless, the threat that its growing support posed to the Conservative Party likely contributed to the decision of the Cameron government to call the EU referendum (Clarke et al. 2017). Its support subsequently collapsed in the 2017 general election as the Conservative Party committed itself to exiting the EU in the wake of the EU membership referendum. Because of its dramatic rise and fall in support near the end of this study's time frame, any evidence of the worldview evolution is more likely to appear in support for the two major parties as they have shifted their positions in recent years.

Two rival parties have dominated British politics throughout the post-war era. The Labour Party has its roots in the trade union movement and has historically sought support from the working class, and more recently from middle-class public sector and urban voters. The Conservative (Tory) Party represents the interests of the middle class, of owners, and of rural and religious voters. The smaller Liberal Democrats are a centrist party with a socially liberal and moderate platform. They have historically pursued an electoral strategy designed to win seats in Britain's plurality electoral system by targeting vulnerable major-party incumbents and running localized campaigns. Finally, the Greens follow a fairly standard green programme and should gain more support from low authoritarians. Given the historically strong class cleavage in British politics, it is unlikely that high authoritarians would have been more likely to support either major party prior to the emergence of UKIP and the rise of issues concerning social cohesion and security.

Table 9.6 shows the results for Britain. In 1990, there is minimal difference in party support by authoritarianism. All three parties get roughly equal support from both groups. The subsequent years see the emergence of a modest gap. From 1999, the Tories gain a moderately larger share of high authoritarians. By contrast, Labour maintains roughly equal support among both groups. UKIP makes its only appearance in the EVS data in 2017 (EVS 2019). Its support is small but modestly higher among high authoritarians. In contrast, the Greens maintain a small support concentrated among low authoritarians.

What does all this mean? The long-term rise of a new PRR party in Britain is unlikely. The plurality electoral rules will make it difficult for UKIP, or any other new party, to establish a permanent foothold in British politics unless it replaces one of the two established parties. The Liberal Democrats have had some success using an opportunistic, localized strategy that involves targeting vulnerable

Table 9.6 Party support by authoritarianism in Great Britain, 1990–2017

Year	Voters	Greens	Labour	Lib Dems	Tories	UKIP
1990	High Authoritarians	–	54.7	5.8	39.6	–
	Low Authoritarians	–	51.3	6.6	42.0	–
1999	High Authoritarians	2.3	50.5	15.3	31.9	–
	Low Authoritarians	7.3	52.8	17.7	22.6	–
2008	High Authoritarians	4.6	31.5	16.5	47.4	–
	Low Authoritarians	9.4	32.1	17.5	41.1	–
2017	High Authoritarians	3.4	40.6	8.5	42.6	4.9
	Low Authoritarians	9.9	41.1	12.0	33.7	3.4
Change 1990–2017	*High Authoritarians*	*3.4*	*−14.1*	*2.7*	*3.0*	*4.9*
	Low Authoritarians	*9.9*	*−10.2*	*5.4*	*−8.3*	*3.4*

Source: Data from the 1990–2017 waves of the European Values Survey.

incumbents. Though some variation of this might be possible for UKIP, the Liberal Democrats' dramatic decline from 2010 to 2015 (slipping from 57 to 8 seats) is cautionary. In short, British electoral rules are stacked against UKIP or any other new challenger party.

The British radical right may instead follow one of two paths. At first glance, it may resemble that of the National Rally in France, having a substantial amount of electoral support that it cannot translate into effective representation. In this scenario, UKIP could play a spoiler role in general elections by peeling away votes in marginal constituencies without winning many seats, or by influencing policy through its ability to threaten the major parties. To some extent, UKIP (and the Brexit Party of 2019) have followed this latter strategy. However, because the UK does not use two-round electoral systems as in France, smaller parties have less ability to gain expressive votes in the first round that they can then use to influence the parties in the run-off.

A second, and perhaps more likely, prospect is that the British radical right will follow its counterparts in the United States, which have effectively become a dominant faction within the centre-right Republican Party, attracting high authoritarian voters in the process (Hetherington and Weiler 2009; Cizmar et al. 2014). The result has been an electoral realignment between the two major parties structured by authoritarianism. In a similar fashion, enterprising radical right politicians may choose to seek influence within the Conservative Party, attracting high authoritarian voters along the way. If so, a hypothetical radical right Conservative Party could draw away many current Labour supporters, at the cost of losing many of the party's own low authoritarian supporters (particularly university-educated voters in white-collar professions). The results of the 2019 general election suggest some steps in this direction. In short, British electoral rules create a different set of possibilities for a worldview evolution.

The Netherlands

The Netherlands witnessed the dramatic rise of the radical right early in the twenty-first century. The Centre Party and the more moderate Centre Democrats had minor support in the 1980s and 1990s, but both were effectively defunct by 2000. The contemporary radical right started with the establishment of the Pim Fortuyn List (LPF) in 2002, just months before that year's general election. LPF rhetoric focused on the incompatibility of Islam—which it criticized as 'backwards' and conservative—with the liberalism of Dutch society (Rydgren and van Holsteyn 2004), pledging to reduce immigration from Muslim-majority countries and to block Turkey's EU accession. In this sense, LPF deviated from typical PRR party positions by endorsing social liberalism rather than traditional-authoritarian social values. Nonetheless, the party may have appealed to high authoritarian voters concerned about immigration, multiculturalism, and social cohesion. Pim Fortuyn, the leader and founder of LPF, was assassinated shortly before the 2002 elections, and the party disintegrated in the following years (despite participating in the coalition government formed after the election). But the radical right party space would not remain empty for long. Geert Wilders established the Party for Freedom (PVV) in 2006 after leaving the centre-right People's Party for Freedom and Democracy (VVD). PVV continued LPF's emphases on opposing immigration and Islam, while taking a stronger anti-EU position. After receiving just under 6 per cent of the vote in 2006, PVV has obtained more than 10 per cent of the national vote in the three general elections since.

The Netherlands has a multiparty system, so the analysis focuses on those parties more relevant to this study. In recent decades, there have been three major parties—two of which have commonly formed coalition governments together. On the centre-left, the Labor Party (PvdA) is a standard social democratic party. The Christian Democratic Appeal (CDA) attempts to position itself in the centre while embracing religiously informed communitarian policies, while VVD is a liberal party on the centre-right. Smaller parties include the far-left Socialist Party (SP), the Green Left Party (GL), and the socially liberal Democrats '66 (D66). Low authoritarians are likely to support the GL and D66, while high authoritarians may historically support CDA. However, CDA has recently taken favourable stances on immigration compared to PVV and VVD, so high authoritarians may have abandoned it for the latter two parties.

Table 9.7 shows the results for the Netherlands, which are consistent with expectations. In 1990, high authoritarians support CDA in greater numbers, while low authoritarians support GL and D66. PvdA and VVD get roughly equal support from both groups of voters. The radical right PVV appears in 2008, and it draws more support from high authoritarians. PvdA lose support from both groups of voters, suggesting that it was not the main source of PVV supporters. Throughout, GL maintains most of its support from low authoritarians. Interestingly, VVD maintains balanced support from both groups. Thus, low

Table 9.7 Party support by authoritarianism in the Netherlands, 1990–2017

Year	Voters	SP	GL	PvdA	D66	CDA	VVD	PVV
1990	High Authoritarians	0.7	3.2	27.9	12.0	45.7	10.2	–
	Low Authoritarians	0.2	13.6	23.6	27.3	22.1	12.2	–
1999	High Authoritarians	4.1	15.4	24.8	4.4	24.5	26.7	–
	Low Authoritarians	4.7	25.3	28.3	11.1	8.9	21.8	–
2008	High Authoritarians	10.8	2.6	16.6	4.8	36.7	14.5	14.1
	Low Authoritarians	13.9	11.0	17.7	14.0	17.1	17.1	8.7
2017	High Authoritarians	9.0	6.0	7.8	9.6	16.0	18.7	13.3
	Low Authoritarians	9.2	16.4	11.7	17.0	10.0	17.8	4.9
Change 1990–2017	*High Authoritarians*	*8.3*	*2.8*	*−20.1*	*−2.4*	*−29.7*	*8.5*	*13.3*
	Low Authoritarians	*9.0*	*2.8*	*−11.9*	*−10.3*	*−12.1*	*5.6*	*4.9*

Source: Data from the 1990–2017 waves of the European Values Survey.

authoritarians support the left-liberal GL and D66, while high authoritarians support the radical right PVV. Older parties based on class (SP, PvdA, VVD) or religious (CDA) cleavages retain balanced support, though PvdA and CDA have lost a great deal of support since 1990. These results suggest potential for a continuing worldview evolution in which high authoritarians gravitate towards radical right and right-wing parties and low authoritarians towards left-liberal parties. However, the permissiveness of the Dutch electoral system may allow a multitude of parties to survive on a wide range of interests and identities, preventing a coherent worldview evolution.

Sweden

As in Finland and Great Britain, the Sweden Democrats (SDs) were a minor party for two decades before experiencing a breakthrough in the 2010 parliamentary elections. This breakthrough came after efforts to moderate the party and expel members associated with extremism. After winning 5.7 per cent of the vote and gaining parliamentary seats for the first time, the party became the third largest after the 2014 election with 12.9 per cent of the vote. As with most of its counterparts, the party's main emphasis is opposition to immigration and multiculturalism, while it also takes a generally Eurosceptical position.

SDs entered a party system historically dominated by the centre-left Social Democrats (SAP) and a fragmented centre-right. SAP has been the largest party in every parliament for a century, with a fairly similar voter base and ideology as other West European social democratic parties. But after receiving over 40 per cent of the vote in every election from 1932 until 1988, the party has broken 40 per cent only twice in the seven elections since and has seen its vote share fall below 33 per cent in 2010 and 2014. To the left are the Greens and the far-left Left

Table 9.8 Party support by authoritarianism in Sweden, 1990–2017

Year	Voters	Left	Greens	SAP	Liberals	Moderates	SD
1990	High Authoritarians	4.0	7.8	34.9	17.6	22.9	–
	Low Authoritarians	9.2	10.8	23.2	20.1	25.7	–
1999	High Authoritarians	12.6	7.6	29.4	8.7	26.1	–
	Low Authoritarians	18.3	12.2	22.9	12.5	25.9	–
2008	High Authoritarians	7.9	5.6	38.9	6.8	29.8	–
	Low Authoritarians	8.5	11.7	29.9	11.3	30.6	–
2017	High Authoritarians	6.1	5.0	33.2	9.0	26.0	9.8
	Low Authoritarians	11.7	10.7	30.7	8.8	21.0	4.9
Change 1990–2017	*High Authoritarians*	*2.1*	*−2.8*	*−1.7*	*−8.6*	*3.1*	*9.8*
	Low Authoritarians	*2.5*	*−0.1*	*7.5*	*−11.3*	*−4.7*	*4.9*

Source: Data from the 1990–2017 waves of the European Values Survey.

Party. The centre-right is fragmented with the largest being the Moderate Party, which has a broadly liberal orientation and gets its strongest support from urban and suburban white-collar workers and owners. The Centre Party typically derives support from rural voters. The Liberal Party promotes free-market economic positions with socially liberal policies. In short, the established party system prior to SDs' emergence had broad competition on economic questions while sharing a broadly liberal outlook on social questions.

Table 9.8 shows the results for Sweden. The data from 1990 to 2008 show patterns of party support before the rise of the radical right SDs. Given the broad social liberalism in mainstream Swedish politics, it is unsurprising that authoritarianism has little relationship with party support. High authoritarians support SAP in greater numbers, but this is presumably not because of the party's appeal on socio-cultural issues. Instead, the earlier tendency of high authoritarians to support the Social Democrats could result from its commitment to the welfare state, which protects workers from economic insecurity, or it could simply emerge from the association between authoritarianism and lower educational attainment. By contrast, low authoritarians support the Greens and Liberals in somewhat greater numbers, and the Liberals and Moderates gain roughly equal support from both groups. In 2017, the radical right SDs gains more support from high authoritarians. However, little evidence among the established parties of a worldview evolution exists. The Liberals lose support from both groups, while SAP gains low authoritarians while effectively maintaining its support among high authoritarians. This pattern does not support the claim that SDs is taking support primarily from high authoritarian SAP supporters. However, the recent emergence of SDs as an electoral force means that it may be too early to see evidence of a worldview evolution. As in Denmark and the Netherlands, the permissiveness of the electoral system may allow a wide range of parties with different electoral profiles to survive, limiting the extent of a worldview evolution.

Conclusion

The preceding analysis has tracked changing patterns of party support by authoritarianism from 1990 to 2017, examining seven different West European states. These results shed light on several different important questions. First, they show how the voting behaviour of high and low authoritarians has evolved during the first two decades of the twenty-first century. Second, they demonstrate which parties have gained and lost votes as a result of this electoral shift. Third, they examine how the voting behaviour of low authoritarian voters evolved alongside high authoritarians. Finally, they provide indirect evidence about the role of mainstream party strategies in exacerbating or counteracting this evolution.

The first main finding of this chapter is that there was no prior uniform pattern of party support among high and low authoritarians in past decades. In Germany and the Netherlands, high authoritarians supported Christian democratic parties in greater numbers, though Finnish high authoritarians were drawn more to the Centre Party, and in France they supported parties of the right. In the other countries, there was no relationship between authoritarianism and party support—except for the almost universal pattern that low authoritarians supported green parties. Importantly, there is no clear pattern of high authoritarians leaning to social democratic parties in the 1990s. In most cases, high and low authoritarians supported social democratic parties in roughly equal numbers, with the only exceptions being Denmark and Sweden (where high authoritarians supported social democrats in modestly higher numbers). In short, a worldview evolution may be pushing West European electoral politics in a common direction, but from different starting points.

These findings shed light on which parties have benefited and lost as a result of the evolution of West European electoral politics. High authoritarians have shifted towards PRR parties—at different times and at different rates across countries. However, there is no common party family that has lost due to this trend. This finding may seem surprising, given the popularity of commentary suggesting that the radical right has taken voters from social democratic parties (e.g. Downes and Chan 2018). That claim may be true to an extent in Austria, Denmark, and Sweden, where social democratic parties have lost ground among high authoritarians. But the evidence suggests that centre (Finland) and Christian democratic (the Netherlands) parties have also lost support to the radical right in some countries. And the evidence suggests that centre-right parties are more vulnerable to losing high authoritarian voters to the radical right in France, Germany, and Great Britain. In short, there is no clear pattern across Western Europe because there was no common starting pattern, so claims that PRR parties have taken voters from social democratic parties are correct only in particular cases.

Why have social democratic parties suffered broad electoral losses since the 1990s? Answering this question must incorporate the role of low authoritarians. In most countries, social democratic parties have lost support from both groups.

Social democratic parties have been squeezed from both sides—losing high authoritarian voters to the radical right and losing low authoritarian voters to left-liberal parties. This finding suggests a dilemma for social democratic parties. If they are losing both high and low authoritarian voters, then their efforts to recapture one group of voters by reorienting their positions on socio-cultural issues may also drive away the other group.

Finally, these findings highlight the importance of national electoral rules (Norris 2005). The opportunity structures for PRR parties are much different in France and Great Britain—which use majoritarian electoral systems—compared to states such as the Netherlands that use permissive proportional representation (PR) rules. In states with PR rules, PRR parties have successfully established themselves in parliament and occasionally entered governing coalitions. As with green parties and low authoritarian voters, PRR parties have been able to (and will likely continue to) consolidate the support of high authoritarian voters. By contrast, majoritarian electoral rules create a significant barrier to entry for new parties. While PRR parties have had occasional electoral successes in France and Great Britain, they have been unable to establish a presence in national parliaments. The same has been true for green and left-liberal challenger parties. Therefore, enterprising radical right politicians in France or Great Britain face a dilemma of whether to pursue their aims through a new party or by gaining influence within an established party. They may find the latter option more promising.

In short, this chapter's findings point to an important and ongoing evolution in West European politics. Prior to the past decade, authoritarianism had little effect on electoral politics, which was typically structured by enduring class and religious divisions even as electorates de-aligned (Dalton 2018). The rise of issues relating to social cohesion—immigration, multicultural, and social values—have activated high authoritarians' sense of threat to social cohesion and created an opening for PRR parties to gain their support. The concurrent movement of low authoritarians to new left and social liberal parties, which frequently take opposed positions on those issues of social cohesion, has further contributed to this electoral evolution. The result is that authoritarianism increasingly affects West European electoral politics in a way that was not true in previous decades.

This chapter also demonstrates that the contingencies of national politics matter greatly. The existing party alignments create different opportunities for new PRR parties, such as those cases in which high authoritarians already tended to support Christian democratic parties. Centre-right parties have varied in their electoral and policy responses to the rise of the radical right. And electoral rules create different opportunities for new radical right parties to emerge and consolidate (Givens 2005; Norris 2005). In short, there is reason to imagine both that the worldview evolution will continue in West European politics and that it will take different forms and progress to a different extent in each country.

10

A Worldview Evolution?

Conclusions and Implications

Introduction

As a professor of European politics teaching in the United States, I have been fortunate to participate in various events over the years including members of the local European diplomatic community. During these events, a question will arise about the European Union and whether it can survive the various challenges that it faces. Sometimes, one of the panellists will answer the question by telling an anecdote about travel in earlier decades, which goes something like this:

> When I was young, the first thing I would have to do when I travelled to another EU state for business or holiday was to exchange money. Over time, I ended up with a collection of leftover francs, liras, guilders, and pesetas. Now it's much better because I don't have to worry about any of that thanks to the euro.

This type of anecdote is meant to illustrate the vast benefits of European integration. The common market and the Schengen Zone have made it easier for Europeans to travel, work, trade, and invest across borders. These opportunities have brought economic benefits—increasing trade, investment, and tourism. The EU has also brought individual and cultural gains. The increased opportunities for travel, work, and study abroad have increased cultural exchange, broadened worldviews, and given many individuals greater opportunity to pursue their vision of the good life. These are hugely important benefits of EU membership—and of the broader global push towards the opening of borders to trade, investment, and migration. European leaders celebrate these achievements knowing that without them the continent would be poorer and less free for many of its citizens.

But this anecdote may also overlook some of the reasons why Europeans are unhappy with the political mainstream and have turned towards the populist radical right (PRR). The opening of borders to trade and investment has disrupted local economies, as industrial production has moved to other sites or patterns of tourism have changed. These disruptions have often generated feelings of marginalization within communities that have lost jobs (Gest 2016). Social and cultural changes have accompanied these economic changes. That sense of

Authoritarianism and the Evolution of West European Electoral Politics. Erik R. Tillman, Oxford University Press.
© Erik R. Tillman 2021. DOI: 10.1093/oso/9780192896223.003.0010

marginalization is not just about lost jobs; it is about demographic changes driven by immigration. In 'left-behind' post-industrial communities that have experienced job loss and increased immigration, complaints of being a 'stranger in one's own community' or that the state 'no longer takes care of its own' have become more common (Ford and Goodwin 2014; Gest 2016). Add to that the loss of important national symbols: exchanging guilder, franc, and mark notes may have been inconvenient for business travellers and tourists, but they were also powerful symbols of national identity and pride for many citizens who travelled less. In the meantime, values changes within West European societies have reshaped norms about race and ethnicity, gender roles, behaviour, and religion. In many respects, these values changes have benefited society—reducing discrimination and creating new opportunity and freedom—and most West Europeans have embraced these changes. But it is important to reflect on the wide range of economic, social, and cultural changes that have occurred in Western Europe over the past generation.

Who has benefited from the shift from national currencies to the euro? In the stylized anecdote described above, the individual is a member of the business or political elite. In other words, the storyteller has embraced the enhanced individual autonomy offered by European integration—the freedom to move across borders with fewer restraints and transaction costs. But what about those individuals who value social cohesion over diversity, who prefer conformity to individual autonomy, and who prefer stability to change? For these individuals, the adoption of a new European currency is at best a nuisance—requiring familiarity with new coins, notes, and prices—and at worst a threat to the normative political and social order in which supranational authorities have replaced national elected officials. The adoption of the euro is an example of a broader trend, which has seen the political mainstream push for greater atomization and regional integration in society, economics, and politics. The political mainstream's embrace of these developments has created an environment in which such individuals were receptive to new political messengers promising to turn back these changes. This book argues that these developments, and the responses to them, illustrate the broader political evolution occurring in Western Europe.

The Worldview Evolution Revisited

The starting point of this book's argument is the emergence of a new dimension of conflict, which divides those advocating a cosmopolitan worldview of universalism and integration against those wishing to protect national community and demarcation. This new dimension is increasingly displacing traditional class conflict in West European electoral politics. While this trend has been documented in a variety of studies (e.g. Kriesi et al. 2008; Bornschier 2010; Kriesi et al. 2012; Dalton 2018; Norris and Inglehart 2019), I argue that the reasons why it has resonated with voters have not been explained as clearly. Arguments based on economic concerns fail to capture the scope of this process, while arguments based on cultural values do not explain why some voters are drawn towards nationalist messages and others towards cosmopolitan positions. To understand this ongoing realignment of voters, we need a theory rooted in voter psychology.

This book argues that the psychological concept of authoritarianism provides the best understanding of this electoral dynamic. Though there is an extensive literature on authoritarianism (e.g. Adorno et al. 1950; Altemeyer 1981, 1996), this book draws on recent research that sees authoritarianism as a disposition oriented towards social conformity and the maintenance of social cohesion and security at the expense of individual autonomy (Feldman and Stenner 1997; Feldman 2003; Stenner 2005). The social, cultural, and political changes of recent decades have activated the authoritarian disposition by generating perceived threats to the normative order, which PRR parties have blamed on the cosmopolitan and pro-EU mainstream political elites. As radical right parties have intensified political conflict by criticizing mainstream positions on European integration and issues relating to identity, high authoritarian voters have moved towards these parties and their issue positions while low authoritarians support left-liberal parties.

Following Hetherington and Weiler (2009), I describe this as a worldview evolution because it does not reflect group interests such as class or religious community. Instead, it reflects a conflict rooted in broader orientations towards society and politics. At its heart, this new dimension of conflict reflects two different worldviews about the appropriate direction for West European societies to follow. High authoritarians are drawn towards PRR parties that promise to preserve national identity and sovereignty, protect the social order, and promote social cohesion against values and demographic changes. By contrast, low authoritarians have moved towards left-liberal parties that promote individual autonomy, universalism, and multiculturalism. These rival worldviews reflect in voting behaviour, attitudes towards the EU, and a wide range of social and cultural attitudes. As this worldview evolution unfolds, high and low authoritarians are increasingly sorting into different party families and are divided on a wide range of issues. Due to distinctive national political institutions and context, this worldview evolution is unfolding at different speeds and from different starting points. However, its effects are more visible among younger voters who lack attachment to the established parties oriented around older dimensions of conflict based on class or religious affiliation.

This book evaluates several implications of these claims. First, the analyses in Chapter 3 show that authoritarianism structures rival worldviews, leading to differences in social and political (though not economic) attitudes between high and low authoritarians. This evidence lends support to the argument that socio-cultural concerns are at the heart of the worldview evolution. The analyses in Chapters 4 and 5 demonstrate the changing structure of attitudes towards the European Union. Chapter 4 shows that EU attitudes in the present era are structured by authoritarianism. High authoritarians are more likely to oppose further European integration, EU enlargement, and to fear that the EU threatens national sovereignty and culture. Chapter 5 shows the evolution of these attitudes over the past generation. In the 1990s, authoritarianism had no relationship to EU attitudes. Consistent with the argument of this book, EU attitudes have evolved as elite conflict over Europe has intensified, with high authoritarians adopting more anti-EU positions and low authoritarians adopting more favourable attitudes. This evolution in EU attitudes occurred first in those states with more intense party conflict over European integration. Chapters 6–8 examine the evolving relationship between authoritarianism and support for populist radical right parties. Chapter 6 shows that authoritarianism structures support for PRR parties, with high authoritarians being significantly more likely to vote for such parties. Chapter 7 reports the results of an original survey experiment in the Republic of Ireland—one of the few West European states without a parliamentary PRR party. The results reaffirm the findings of Chapter 6—that high authoritarians are more likely to support a hypothetical new PRR party—and further show that high authoritarians express more concern about social and cultural disintegration in Ireland. Chapter 8 demonstrates that this relationship between authoritarianism and PRR party support is stronger among younger voters in most West European societies. This evidence is consistent with the claim that a worldview evolution is underway, as it is stronger among younger voters who lack attachments to established mainstream parties. Thus, we cannot view rising PRR party support simply as a backlash among older voters. Finally, Chapter 9 tracks the evolving relationship between authoritarianism and party support over the past generation. This analysis demonstrates that authoritarianism previously had no consistent effect on party support. However, the movement of high authoritarians towards PRR parties and low authoritarians towards left-liberal parties is reshaping mainstream electoral politics throughout Western Europe. In short, the findings demonstrate several different facets of the ongoing worldview evolution in West European politics.

The Worldview Evolution in Comparative Perspective

Although this book focuses on West European politics, its argument and findings relate to broader trends occurring in other advanced democracies. This section considers in what respects these trends are similar and in what respects they differ. In doing so, I hope that this book will contribute to a broader comparative understanding of the electoral changes occurring in the advanced democracies.

This book's argument resembles that of Hetherington and Weiler (2009), who coined the phrase 'worldview evolution' to describe events in the United States. There are some important similarities. In both contexts, the combination of political events and strategic elite messages are leading to a restructuring of electoral politics in which authoritarianism is a central factor separating voters. Socio-cultural issues are at the heart of both realignments: the perceived threats to social cohesion and security posed by immigration, multiculturalism, and values change have driven this worldview evolution. But there are important differences as well. Hetherington and Weiler (2009) trace the origins of the US worldview evolution to the major issues of the 1960s in US politics—the civil rights movement and the Vietnam conflict—and the strategic choices by the Republican Party to attract support by appealing to white voters who opposed federal efforts to integrate schools, and the anti-war movement. This process continued through the 'culture wars' of subsequent decades, with debates over abortion and gay rights playing a major role, while the responses to the 11 September 2001 terror attacks provided the final steps. In the USA, the conflict between the two major parties led to the sorting of voters by authoritarianism because the Republican Party at each stage took issue positions that appealed to high authoritarians (i.e. strong national security, traditional morality) while the Democratic Party appealed more to low authoritarians (i.e. values change, multiculturalism) (see Hetherington and Weiler 2009, chapter 4). In the United States, this worldview evolution occurred through the realignment of each party's issue positions and voter support rather than through the entry of new parties.[1]

The particular issues at the heart of the ongoing worldview evolution in Western Europe have differed. Immigration, multiculturalism, and mainstream liberalization have been the driving issues, with fear of demographic and values change driving the political responses. Enterprising radical right political elites have sought to gain from these issues by linking them to concerns such as crime and terrorism. The European Union has been an important issue in this conflict as well, though citizens' relatively low understanding of the EU (Anderson 1998) means that changes in EU attitudes have been more a result than a cause of the worldview evolution. Many of the issues particular to the American worldview evolution—civil rights, abortion, gay rights— have played little such role in the West European context. Thus, the broader nature of the worldview evolution is similar in the USA and Western Europe, although there is limited overlap in issue content.

---

[1] Two third-party presidential candidates—George Wallace in 1968 and Ross Perot in 1992—arguably contributed to the worldview evolution by introducing new issue positions, which the two major parties quickly adopted into their own programmes.

Differences in institutional and political contexts have led to divergent results. In the United States, the combination of presidentialism and plurality elections has produced a durable two-party system—though one in which the two parties have sometimes resembled loose coalitions on many key issues and whose issue positions have changed over time. The worldview evolution in American politics has occurred within the two-party system, with the Republicans becoming the party of high authoritarians and the Democrats becoming the party of low authoritarians over time (Hetherington and Weiler 2009; Cizmar et al. 2014). Thus, the two parties remained in place even while their issue positions and the compositions of their electorates changed dramatically. In Western Europe, the worldview evolution is occurring in a diverse set of political systems, though most are parliamentary and have proportional representation electoral systems. As a result, established mainstream parties, which formed around earlier class and religious cleavages (Lipset and Rokkan 1967), are losing high authoritarian voters to PRR parties while losing low authoritarian voters to left-liberal parties. In these systems, the worldview evolution is resulting in the formation or strengthening of new political parties oriented around socio-cultural issues while putting pressure on established parties.

These differences between the American and West European contexts have major implications. In the United States, the two-party system has given high authoritarians major influence within the Republican Party and low authoritarians the same within the Democratic Party. But not all Republican Party voters (or representatives) are high authoritarians. In fact, the Republican Party electorate is a coalition of high authoritarians, 'small-government' neo-liberals, and religiously conservative Christian voters. Donald Trump succeeded in winning the Republican Party nomination for president in 2016 by appealing primarily to the high authoritarians within the party's electorate, who comprised a large enough share to win the nomination. However, his victory over Hillary Clinton in the general election depended on support from those other Republican partisans who had not supported him in the primary elections. The effects of 'negative partisanship' may have been powerful enough to persuade those Republican partisans to support him (Abramowitz and Webster 2016, 2017). Thus, a candidate relying on a radical right message appealing to high authoritarians successfully gained his party's nomination and won a general election (Greven 2016; MacWilliams 2016). In turn, the Trump presidency has probably pushed the worldview evolution further in the USA, as the remaining low authoritarians in the Republican Party abandon it and the remaining high authoritarians in the Democratic Party do likewise.

The same scenario is unlikely to unfold in most West European states, given more permissive electoral rules. Instead, the movement of high authoritarians towards PRR parties will likely impose a practical limit on these parties' electoral support. Traditional conservatives, economic liberals, and other centre-right voters who are not high authoritarians would have less reason to support a PRR party. A likelier scenario is that PRR parties will be a major factor in electoral and parliamentary politics for the foreseeable future as they consolidate the sizeable minority of high authoritarian voters in their electorates. One upshot is that these smaller PRR parties can retain more cohesive ideological programmes as they have less diverse electoral bases. This may limit the influence of these parties on policy as their ability to enter governments and obtain concessions may be limited. Moreover, the established parties are likely to continue to survive in permissive electoral systems, albeit with less electoral support. However, strategic mainstream party leaders may seek to draw away the voters of their PRR or green counterparts by adopting their issue positions strategically, helping to push a worldview evolution along.

A scenario similar to the USA could unfold in France and especially the United Kingdom, both of which have majoritarian political systems and electoral rules (Lijphart 1999; Norris 2005). In those settings, radical right politicians (and their left-liberal counterparts) face dilemmas similar to those of US political elites. If they seek to form and campaign through third parties, their electoral potential may remain low unless they can successfully dislodge one of the established parties. By contrast, they may find it more promising to seek influence within one of the established parties and thus to transform it into a high authoritarian or low authoritarian party. If so, the worldview evolution could unfold through a realignment of the positions and voter bases of the two main parties. The difficulties of either strategy could hinder a potential worldview evolution.

In short, there is reason to believe that the worldview evolution in Western Europe is similar in its core conflict (i.e. protecting social cohesion versus promoting individual autonomy) to that described in the United States, and that similar developments may unfold in other advanced democracies that face similar social and cultural developments. In this sense, it is part of a broader series of developments, and scholars should examine these common developments. However, differences in the local contexts will also have important effects in whether and how such a worldview evolution occurs in each state. Finally, political elites' strategic choices matter. By choosing whether to emphasize the threat posed by developments such as immigration or values change to social cohesion, political elites contribute to the activation or minimization of authoritarian attitudes (Stenner 2005).

The Future of West European Politics?

Though this book contributes to our understanding of West European electoral politics, it leaves various questions open for continuing research. Going further, what does this book's argument suggest about the future of West European politics? This final section offers some directions for future research.

One important question concerns the relationship between authoritarianism and changing socio-economic structures. Chapter 3 shows that authoritarianism correlates negatively with educational attainment; high authoritarians are less likely to complete university education. The reasons for this are not clear. One possibility is that higher education has a liberalizing effect on individuals, reducing their levels of intolerance. Thus, higher education might reduce authoritarianism. The problem with this argument is that authoritarianism is theorized to be a dispositional trait reflecting basic orientations towards society. It is unlikely that several years of education could reduce one's level of authoritarianism. It is more plausible that university education reinforces normative social values opposing prejudice, which could result in high authoritarians being more likely to embrace individual autonomy as a normative value. However, threats to social cohesion would likely trigger authoritarian attitudes among high authoritarians, and there is little reason to expect that authoritarianism as a predisposition will vanish as a result of increasing educational attainment. A further concern is that selection effects influence who pursues higher education (Lancee and Sarrasin 2015). Because university education typically promotes greater autonomy, ambiguity, and complexity, high authoritarians may be reluctant to pursue higher education. As a result, the apparent liberalizing effect of higher education may reflect self-selection more than typically imagined. This selection effect may be magnified if elite messages describe universities as 'bastions' of liberal or multicultural thought that threatens the authoritarian worldview. This study has not examined the broader effects of this negative association between education and authoritarianism. The growing importance of higher education in the post-industrial economy means that low authoritarians may have greater access to well-paying and prestigious jobs. Many of these jobs are located in metropolitan areas, leading to a clustering of low authoritarians in growing, expensive metropolitan centres, while high authoritarians may reside more in smaller cities and towns with fewer job opportunities. The effects of these educational, occupational, and residential patterns on political attitudes and behaviour merits further research.

Another question suggested by this book's analysis is how high authoritarians change their attitudes in response to the evolving social and political environment. Theories of authoritarianism claim that high authoritarians feel a strong attachment to the normative social order, provoking authoritarian responses when that order is under threat (Stenner 2005). But the normative social order evolves over time, as attitudes about acceptable morality, culture, identity, and politics change. The evidence presented in Chapter 3 illustrated high authoritarians' changing attitudes. On questions concerning same-sex marriage and traditional gender roles, low authoritarians had almost universally adopted the normative positions approving of same-sex marriage and rejecting traditional gender roles. High authoritarians were mixed as a group, illustrating change mixed with greater resistance. Generational replacement may be an important factor as younger high authoritarians have been socialized into a world of greater gender equality and acceptance of same-sex marriage. But it is also likely that some older high authoritarians adjust their own beliefs in response to elite messages. While the authoritarian predisposition may be stable, the normative social order to which high authoritarians attend is dynamic, so we need to understand better how their own understanding of the normative order evolves.

This discussion of the normative order highlights the importance of elite messages. Strategic political elites have an incentive to shift the dimensions of political conflict in order to gain new support at the expense of established parties (Riker 1982; Carmines and Stimson 1989; de Vries and Hobolt 2012). In doing so, they bring new attention to neglected political issues, encourage voters to understand their political identities differently, and potentially trigger electoral realignments. In Western Europe, enterprising political elites found receptive voters among high authoritarians by adopting a radical right message. As mainstream parties converged around liberal positions on European integration, immigration, and value change, radical right parties were able to peel away high authoritarian voters. This worldview evolution resulted from strategic elite behaviour; it was not inevitable. Thus, the future of West European electoral politics will depend on the strategic choices of political elites.

Two party groupings stand out as being particularly important in shaping the future of the worldview evolution. The first are social democratic parties. The discussion in Chapter 9 noted that PRR parties' threat to social democratic parties has been overstated; PRR parties have drawn high authoritarian voters from across the established party spectrum. In fact, social democratic parties have uniquely faced a challenge in that they have lost high authoritarians to PRR parties and low authoritarians to left-liberal parties. This analysis suggests that social democratic parties face a difficult choice in the current political environment, as they can seek to win back either group of voters but not both. In other words, social democratic parties could pursue a 'left-authoritarian' strategy that combines a defence of the welfare state with exclusionary socio-cultural policies. Doing so would represent a form of welfare chauvinism that promoted a generous welfare state accessible only to natives, which may appeal to high authoritarians but would repel low authoritarian voters. Alternatively, social democratic parties could pursue a more aggressive left-liberal strategy consistent with an emphasis on individual autonomy and multiculturalism, which would appeal to low authoritarians. It is not the purpose of this book to recommend either strategy, but it seems unlikely that social democratic parties could success-fully pursue both groups of voters.

Mainstream centre-right parties face a different dilemma. The choice for such parties is whether to emulate and cooperate with PRR parties or whether to isolate and reject them. The temptation to emulate PRR parties by offering a sort of 'radical right light' message is understandable as a means of preventing vote losses. However, this strategy may come at a longer-term cost of further normalizing PRR party messages, and high authoritarians may still view PRR parties as being more credible on their core socio-cultural issues. However, isolation may contribute to PRR parties' message that they are the only authentic voice of high authoritarian voters, and that the mainstream parties are working against their interests. In addition, strategies of forming grand coalition governments with centre-left parties may succeed in the short term by keeping PRR parties out of power, but they also leave PRR parties as a leading alternative for voters dissatisfied with performance of the government.[2] In short, both the centre-left and centre-right will face dilemmas when considering how to respond to the radical right and the worldview evolution.

Considering the future of West European politics more generally, this book posits that the worldview evolution is ongoing and has progressed at different speeds across each state. As a result, West European politics may continue to shift towards an axis of conflict concerning individual autonomy versus social conformity (expressed in a broader national-cosmopolitan or integration-demarcation dimension), in which culture and identity will be central. Traditional class-based economic conflict may face unique challenges, as the interests of low authoritarians—who tend to be educated and urban—are not the same as those of the working class. Similarly, high authoritarians, who are represented more in less educated and less urban settings, do not necessarily share traditional centre-right economic interests. There is no consistent empirical relationship between authoritarianism and economic attitudes (Malka et al. 2014; Johnston et al. 2017; Federico and Malka 2018), so it is uncertain how radical right and left-liberal parties may pursue economic issues in the future. Nonetheless, older parties based around class interests may struggle to balance the economic interests of evolving constituencies.

This book's findings also speak to the potential and limits of this worldview evolution. One cannot attribute the rise of the radical right simply to a revolt of left-behind, older voters. High authoritarians exist in numbers among all generations, and Chapter 8 shows that the relationship between authoritarianism and PRR party support is stronger among younger voters. Therefore, it would be wrong to expect generational replacement to undermine the long-term viability of the radical right. However, this book's findings also suggest that there are limits to the potential electoral support of the radical right, as high authoritarians do

---

[2] Grand coalition governments also fit PRR narratives that the centre-left and the centre-right are indistinguishable on their core political issues, further contributing to a worldview evolution.

not comprise a majority in West European societies. Given that most West European states use proportional electoral systems, it is more likely that PRR parties will consolidate a core of high authoritarian voters without becoming the largest party or being able to control the executive. Conversely, the same will be true for left-liberal parties that attract low authoritarian voters, which means that those voters scoring near the midpoint of the authoritarianism scale will play an important role in election outcomes. Given the demonstrated importance of economic conditions in shaping incumbent support and of elite messages in shaping political behaviour, the future shape of West European politics will depend on the ability of governing elites to deliver economic prosperity while finding a balance between inclusion and security.

Wording of Control and Treatment Conditions in Survey Experiment

Radical Right Treatment

The Irish People's Party: A New Choice for Voters?

The Irish People's Party promises to put citizens first and make government work better for the people of Ireland. They pledge to reform the tax system to ensure that everyone pays a fair share, and to reduce the burden on Irish households while ensuring greater funding for schools and healthcare. The party is also committed to promoting rural development so that the economy works for all citizens. To protect Ireland's cities and families, the party pledges to increase Garda numbers by 10 per cent and to implement mandatory tougher sentences for serious crimes.

The Irish People's Party believes that mass immigration poses a threat to Ireland's economy and society, so it will implement reforms to ensure that only those immigrants who bring scarce skills that benefit the economy and who will assimilate into Irish society are allowed. They reject multiculturalism, and they pledge to make it easier to deport immigrants who have committed serious crimes. They believe that the European Union holds too much power, so they will renegotiate with EU partners to restore a Europe of cooperating, sovereign states.

Mainstream Control

The Irish People's Party: A New Choice for Voters?

The Irish People's Party promises to put citizens first and make government work better for the people of Ireland. They pledge to reform the tax system to ensure that everyone pays a fair share, and to reduce the burden on Irish households while ensuring greater funding for schools and healthcare. The party is also committed to promoting rural development so that the economy works for all citizens. To protect Ireland's cities and families, the party pledges to increase Garda numbers by 10 per cent and to implement mandatory tougher sentences for serious crimes.

The Irish People's Party believes that Ireland's economy and society benefit from the skills and energy that immigrants bring, so it will work to keep Ireland open and welcoming. They believe that Irish society gains as new residents incorporate their own customs into Irish culture and traditions. The party believes that Ireland must remain an active member of the European Union, and it will work with EU partners to continue building a democratic and inclusive Europe.

Party Support by Authoritarianism (Alternative Measure), 1990–2017

Austria

Year	Voters	Greens	SPÖ	ÖVP	FPÖ
1990	High Authoritarians	2.4	43.8	42.0	11.9
	Low Authoritarians	15.7	40.1	27.0	17.2
1999	High Authoritarians	2.8	33.5	42.7	20.6
	Low Authoritarians	15.3	33.7	25.0	19.3
2008	High Authoritarians	10.3	40.5	31.8	11.3
	Low Authoritarians	25.4	30.0	22.4	15.1
2017	High Authoritarians	3.4	32.6	39.1	23.6
	Low Authoritarians	10.7	32.1	32.4	18.5
Change 1990–2017	*High Authoritarians*	*1.0*	*−11.2*	*−2.9*	*11.7*
	Low Authoritarians	*−5.0*	*−8.0*	*5.4*	*1.3*

Denmark

Year	Voters	SPP	Red–Green	SDP	Venstre	Cons	DF
1990	High Authoritarians	7.1	–	38.4	20.2	19.2	10.1
	Low Authoritarians	22.4	–	33.3	12.7	15.1	5.6
1999	High Authoritarians	8.6	–	30.0	40.0	14.3	7.1
	Low Authoritarians	16.5	–	28.2	35.5	8.1	4.7
2008	High Authoritarians	11.0	0.9	22.8	37.3	8.9	15.1
	Low Authoritarians	23.7	2.2	22.5	27.6	8.2	6.4
2017	High Authoritarians	3.7	3.7	28.7	28.2	7.4	20.4
	Low Authoritarians	7.6	8.3	31.5	22.1	5.5	10.8
Change 1990–2017	*High Authoritarians*	*−3.4*	*3.7*	*−9.7*	*8.0*	*−11.8*	*10.3*
	Low Authoritarians	*−17.8*	*8.3*	*−1.8*	*9.4*	*−9.6*	*5.2*

Finland

Year	Voters	Left	Greens	SDP	KESK	KOK	PS
1990	High Authoritarians	2.9	5.8	25.2	33.0	32.0	–
	Low Authoritarians	5.0	18.2	26.0	26.0	27.1	–
1999	High Authoritarians	5.2	5.8	32.4	39.3	17.3	–
	Low Authoritarians	12.9	20.6	22.6	23.1	20.9	–
2008	High Authoritarians	5.4	4.8	20.4	24.5	26.5	18.4
	Low Authoritarians	6.5	24.3	21.3	10.6	26.4	10.9
2017	High Authoritarians	4.7	4.2	17.2	26.0	24.0	14.1
	Low Authoritarians	9.8	24.2	16.7	17.3	25.3	5.8
Change 1990–2017	*High Authoritarians*	*1.8*	*−1.6*	*−8.0*	*−7.0*	*−8.0*	*14.1*
	Low Authoritarians	*4.8*	*6.0*	*−9.3*	*−9.7*	*−1.8*	*5.8*

France

Year	Voters	PG	Greens	Socialists	LREM	Republicans	RN
1990	High Authoritarians	2.0	14.1	45.0	–	28.8	10.1
	Low Authoritarians	8.8	22.8	53.4	–	11.2	3.6
1999	High Authoritarians	4.6	10.4	38.2	–	35.5	8.5
	Low Authoritarians	4.3	22.5	49.5	–	16.9	4.1
2008	High Authoritarians	4.7	4.1	36.6	–	33.1	6.4
	Low Authoritarians	9.7	10.0	38.2	–	21.5	1.1
2017	High Authoritarians	4.6	5.0	26.9	15.3	18.6	28.5
	Low Authoritarians	12.7	11.9	27.9	25.5	9.6	7.8
Change 1990–2017	*High Authoritarians*	*2.6*	*−9.1*	*−18.1*	*15.3*	*−10.2*	*18.4*
	Low Authoritarians	*3.9*	*−10.9*	*−25.5*	*25.5*	*−1.6*	*4.2*

Germany

Year	Voters	Left	Greens	SPD	CDU	FDP	AfD
1990	High Authoritarians	5.6	2.2	29.9	54.8	7.5	–
	Low Authoritarians	1.9	10.4	45.4	33.3	9.0	–
1999	High Authoritarians	6.6	2.4	29.4	59.7	1.9	–
	Low Authoritarians	14.5	8.2	28.8	45.8	2.7	–
2008	High Authoritarians	6.2	9.9	19.9	57.1	6.8	–
	Low Authoritarians	23.4	12.2	24.2	29.5	10.8	–
2017	High Authoritarians	3.4	3.9	26.1	52.2	3.9	10.6
	Low Authoritarians	10.6	19.5	24.5	32.2	8.0	5.3
Change 1990–2017	*High Authoritarians*	*−2.2*	*1.7*	*−3.8*	*−2.6*	*−3.6*	*10.6*
	Low Authoritarians	*8.7*	*9.1*	*−19.9*	*−1.1*	*−1.0*	*5.3*

Great Britain

Year	Voters	Greens	Labour	Lib Dems	Tories	UKIP
1990	High Authoritarians	–	54.7	5.8	39.6	–
	Low Authoritarians	–	54.1	6.3	39.6	–
1999	High Authoritarians	2.3	52.2	16.1	31.7	–
	Low Authoritarians	7.3	56.7	19.1	24.4	–
2008	High Authoritarians	4.9	36.1	15.6	43.4	–
	Low Authoritarians	9.4	32.1	17.5	41.1	–
2017	High Authoritarians	3.4	46.7	6.2	39.2	4.5
	Low Authoritarians	9.9	41.1	12.0	33.7	3.4
Change 1990–2017	*High Authoritarians*	*3.4*	*–10.0*	*0.4*	*–0.4*	*4.5*
	Low Authoritarians	*9.9*	*–13.0*	*5.7*	*–5.9*	*3.4*

The Netherlands

Year	Voters	SP	GL	PvdA	D66	CDA	VVD	PVV
1990	High Authoritarians	0.7	2.3	29.3	8.6	50.5	9.5	–
	Low Authoritarians	0.2	13.8	23.9	27.6	22.4	12.3	–
1999	High Authoritarians	4.5	14.2	20.0	4.5	34.2	22.6	–
	Low Authoritarians	4.7	25.0	28.4	11.2	8.9	21.9	–
2008	High Authoritarians	9.8	1.0	14.3	2.5	37.8	9.2	13.7
	Low Authoritarians	13.5	10.8	17.3	13.7	16.7	17.3	8.5
2017	High Authoritarians	9.2	4.9	7.7	6.1	21.5	16.6	11.7
	Low Authoritarians	9.2	16.4	11.7	17.0	10.0	17.8	4.9
Change 1990–2017	*High Authoritarians*	*8.5*	*2.6*	*–21.6*	*–2.5*	*–28.5*	*7.1*	*11.7*
	Low Authoritarians	*9.0*	*2.6*	*–11.2*	*–10.6*	*–12.4*	*5.5*	*4.9*

Sweden

Year	Voters	Left	Greens	SAP	Liberals	Moderates	SD
1990	High Authoritarians	6.6	6.6	40.4	14.5	21.7	–
	Low Authoritarians	9.5	11.1	23.7	20.5	26.3	–
1999	High Authoritarians	8.0	5.3	32.0	2.7	29.3	–
	Low Authoritarians	16.8	10.1	25.7	11.4	25.0	–
2008	High Authoritarians	8.9	4.4	51.1	3.3	21.1	–
	Low Authoritarians	8.5	11.7	29.9	11.3	30.6	–
2017	High Authoritarians	2.0	2.0	36.0	2.0	24.0	20.0
	Low Authoritarians	9.4	7.8	32.3	9.6	24.0	5.8
Change 1990–2017	*High Authoritarians*	*–4.4*	*–4.4*	*–4.4*	*–12.5*	*2.3*	*20.0*
	Low Authoritarians	*–0.1*	*–3.3*	*8.4*	*–10.9*	*–2.2*	*5.8*

Note: Low authoritarians are those scoring –0.33 or lower on the –1 to +1 scale of authoritarianism, and high authoritarians are those scoring 0.33 or higher.

References

Aarts, Kess, and Henk van der Kolk, 2006. 'Understanding the Dutch "No": The Euro, the East, and the Elite'. *PS: Political Science and Politics* 39(2): 243–6.

Abramowitz, Alan I., and Steven Webster, 2016. 'The Rise of Negative Partisanship and the Nationalization of U.S. Elections in the 21st Century'. *Electoral Studies* 41(1): 12–22.

Abramowitz, Alan I., and Steven W. Webster, 2017. 'Taking it to a New Level: Partisanship, Voter Anger and the 2016 Presidential Election'. Paper presented at the State of the Parties Conference, University of Akron, 9–10 November.

Adorno, Theodor, Else Frankel-Brunswick, Daniel J. Levinson, and Nevitt Sanford, 1950. *The Authoritarian Personality*. New York: Wiley.

Altemeyer, Robert, 1981. *Right-Wing Authoritarianism.* Winnipeg, Canada: University of Manitoba Press.

Altemeyer, Robert, 1996. *The Authoritarian Spectre.* Cambridge, MA: Harvard University Press.

Althaus, Scott, 2003. *Collective Preferences in Democratic Politics: Opinion Surveys and the Will of the People.* New York: Cambridge University Press.

Anderson, Christopher J., 1998. 'When In Doubt, Use Proxies: Attitudes toward Domestic Politics and Support for European Integration'. *Comparative Political Studies* 31(5): 569–601.

Arzheimer, Kai, 2009. 'Contextual Factors and the Extreme Right Vote in Western Europe, 1980–2002'. *American Journal of Political Science* 53(2): 259–75.

Arzheimer, Kai, and Elisabeth Carter, 2009. 'Christian Religiosity and Voting for West European Radical Right Parties'. *West European Politics* 32(5): 985–1011.

Azrout, Rachid, Joost van Spanje, and Claes de Vreese, 2011. 'Talking Turkey: Anti-Immigrant Attitudes and their Effect on Support for Turkish Membership of the EU'. *European Union Politics* 12(1): 3–19.

Bakker, Bert N., and Claese H. de Vreese, 2016. 'Personality and European Union Attitudes: Relationship across European Union Attitudes'. *European Union Politics* 17(1): 25–45.

Bakker, Bert N., David Nicolas Hopmann, and Mikael Persson, 2015a. 'Personality Traits and Party Identification over Time'. *European Journal of Political Research* 54: 197–215.

Bakker, Bert N., Robert Klemmensen, Asbjørn Sonne Nørgard, and Gijs Schumacher, 2016a. 'Stay Loyal or Exit the Party? How Openness to Experience and Extraversion Explain Vote Switching'. *Political Psychology* 37(3): 419–29.

Bakker, Bert N., Mattijs Rooduijn, and Gijs Schumacher, 2016b. 'The Psychological Roots of Populist Voting: Evidence from the United States, the Netherlands, and Germany'. *European Journal of Political Research* 55: 302–20.

Bakker, Ryan, Catherine de Vries, Erica Edwards, Liesbet Hooghe, Seth Jolly, Gary Marks, Jonathan Polk, Jan Rovny, Marco Steenbergen, and Milada Vachudova, 2015b. 'Measuring Party Positions in Europe: The Chapel Hill Expert Survey Trend File, 1999–2010'. *Party Politics* 21(1): 143–52.

Barbaranelli, Claudio, Gian Vittorio Caprara, Michele Vecchione, and Chris R. Fraley, 2006. 'Voters' Personality Traits in Presidential Elections'. *Personality and Individual Differences* 42: 1199–208.

Barrett, David, 2016. 'Irish general election 2016 report: whither the party system?' *Irish Political Studies* 31(3): 418–31.

Berning, Carl C., 2017. 'Alternative für Deutschland: Germany's New Radical Right-Wing Populist Party'. München: Ifo DICE Report, ISSN 2511-7823, ifo Institut-Leibniz Institut für Wirtschaftsforschung an der Universität München 15(4): 16–19.

Betz, Hans-Georg, 1993. 'The New Politics of Resentment: Radical Right-Wing Populist Parties in Western Europe'. *European Journal of Political Research* 22(1): 3–34.

Bornschier, Simon, 2010. *Cleavage Politics and the Populist Right*. Philadelphia, PA: Temple University Press.

Bowler, Shaun, and David M. Farrell, 2017. 'The Lack of Party System Change in Ireland in 2011'. In *A Conservative Revolution? Electoral Change in Twenty-First Century Ireland*. Edited by Michael Marsh, David M. Farrell, and Gail McElroy, 83–101. Oxford: Oxford University Press.

Brady, Henry E., Sidney Verba, and Kay Lehman Schlozman, 1995. 'Beyond SES: A Resource Model of Political Participation'. *American Political Science Review* 89(2): 271–94.

Brambor, Thomas, William Roberts Clark, and Matt Golder, 2006. 'Understanding Interaction Models: Improving Empirical Analyses'. *Political Analysis* 14(1): 63–82.

Brandt, Mark J., John R. Chambers, Jarret T. Crawford, Geoffrey Wetherell, and Christine Reyna, 2015. 'Bounded Openness: The Effect of Openness to Experience on Intolerance is Moderated by Target Group Conventionality'. *Journal of Personality and Social Psychology* 109: 549–68.

Brandt, Mark J., Christine Reyna, John R. Chambers, Jarret T. Crawford, and Geoffrey Wetherell, 2014. 'The Ideological-Conflict Hypothesis: Intolerance Among Both Liberals and Conservatives'. *Current Directions in Psychological Science* 23(1): 27–34.

Butler, David, and Donald Stokes, 1969. *Political Change in Britain*. New York: St. Martin's Press.

Campbell, Angus, Phillip E. Converse, Warren E. Miller, and Donald E. Stokes, 1960. *The American Voter*. Chicago, IL: University of Chicago Press.

Carey, Sean, 2002. 'Undivided Loyalties? Is National Identity an Obstacle to European Integration?' *European Union Politics* 3(4): 387–413.

Carmines, Edward G., and James A. Stimson, 1980. 'The Two Faces of Issue Voting'. *American Political Science Review* 74(1): 78–91.

Carmines, Edward C., and James A. Stimson, 1989. *Issue Evolution: Race and the Transformation of American Politics*. Princeton, NJ: Princeton University Press.

Carty, R. Kenneth, 1983. *Party and Parish Pump: Electoral Politics in Ireland*. Waterloo, Ontario: Wilfrid Laurier University Press.

Christin, Thomas, and Alexander Trechsel, 2002. 'Joining the EU? Explaining Public Opinion in Switzerland'. *European Union Politics* 3(4): 415–43.

Cizmar, Anne M., Geoffrey C. Layman, John McTague, Shanna Pearson-Merkowitz, and Michael Spivey, 2014. 'Authoritarianism and American Political Behavior from 1952 to 2008'. *Political Research Quarterly* 67(1): 71–83.

Clarke, Harold D., and Nitish Dutt, 1991. 'Measuring Value Change in Western Industrialized Societies: The Impact of Unemployment'. *American Political Science Review* 85(3): 905–20.

Clarke, Harold D., Matthew Goodwin, and Paul Whiteley, 2017. *Brexit: Why Britain Voted to Leave the European Union*. Cambridge: Cambridge University Press.

Converse, Phillip, 1964. 'The Nature of Belief Systems in Mass Publics'. In *Ideology and Discontent*. Edited by David E. Apter. Glencoe, IL: Free Press.

Costello, Rory, 2017. 'The Ideological Space in Irish Politics: Comparing Voters and Parties'. *Irish Political Studies* 32(3): 404–31.

Cramer, Katherine J., 2016. *The Politics of Resentment: Rural Consciousness in Wisconsin and the Rise of Scott Walker.* Chicago, IL: University of Chicago Press.

Crawford, Jarret T., and Jane M. Pilanski, 2014. 'Political Intolerance, Right *and* Left'. *Political Psychology* 35(6): 841–51.

Dalton, Russell J., 2018. *Political Realignment: Economics, Culture, and Electoral Change.* Oxford: Oxford University Press.

Dalton, Russell J., Scott E. Flanagan, and Paul Allen Beck, 1984. *Electoral Change in Advanced Industrial Democracies: Realignment or Dealignment.* Princeton, NJ: Princeton University Press.

De Lange, Sarah L., 2007. 'A New Winning Formula? The Programmatic Appeal of the Radical Right'. *Party Politics* 13(4): 411–35.

De Lange, Sarah L., 2012. 'New Alliances: Why Mainstream Parties Govern with Radical Right-Wing Populist Parties'. *Political Studies* 60(4): 899–918.

De Vreese, Claes, and Hajo Boomgaarden, 2005. 'Projecting European Referendums: Fear of Immigration and Support for European Integration'. *European Union Politics* 6(1): 59–82.

De Vreese, Claes, Wouter van der Brug, and Sara Hobolt, 2012. 'Turkey in the EU? How Cultural and Economic Frames Affect Support for Turkish Accession'. *Comparative European Politics* 10(2): 218–35.

De Vries, Catherine E., 2007. 'Sleeping Giant: Fact or Fairytale? How European Integration Affects National Elections'. *European Union Politics* 8(3): 363–85.

De Vries, Catherine E., and Sara B. Hobolt, 2012. 'When Dimensions Collide: The Electoral Success of Issue Entrepreneurs'. *European Union Politics* 13(2): 246–68.

Downes, James, and Edward Chan, 2018. 'The Electoral Decline of Social Democratic Parties and the Rise of the Radical Right in Europe during the Refugee Crisis'. *Democratic Audit.* Available at: http://www.democraticaudit.com/2018/08/06/the-electoral-decline-of-social-democratic-parties-and-the-rise-of-the-radical-right-in-europe-during-the-refugee-crisis/.

Downs, Anthony, 1957. *An Economic Theory of Democracy.* New York: Harper & Row.

Duch, Raymond M., and Michaell A. Taylor, 1993. 'Postmaterialism and the Economic Condition'. *American Journal of Political Science* 37(3): 747–79.

Duckitt, John, 1989. 'Authoritarianism and Group Conflict: A New View of an Old Construct'. *Political Psychology* 10(1): 63–84.

Dunn, Kris, 2015. 'Preference for Radical Right-Wing Populist Parties Among Exclusive-Nationalists and Authoritarians'. *Party Politics* 21(3): 367–80.

Eger, Maureen A., and Sarah Valdez, 2015. 'Neo-nationalism in Western Europe'. *European Sociological Review* 31(1): 115–30.

Eichenberg, Richard C., and Russell J. Dalton, 1993. 'Europeans and the European Community: The Dynamics of Public Support for European Integration'. *International Organization* 47(4): 507–34.

Elgün, Özlem, and Erik R. Tillman, 2007. 'Exposure to European Union Policies and Support for Membership in the Candidate Countries'. *Political Research Quarterly* 60(3): 391–400.

European Commission, 2020. *Standard Eurobarometer 53-90.* Eurobarometer Surveys [online]. Available at: https://ec.europa.eu/commfrontoffice/publicopinion/index.cfm/Chart/index.

EVS, 2011a. European Values Survey 1990: Integrated Dataset. GESIS Data Archive, Cologne. ZA4460 Data file Version 3.0.0, doi:10.4232/1.10790.

EVS, 2011b. European Values Study 1999: Integrated Dataset. GESIS Data Archive, Cologne. ZA3811 Data file Version 3.0.0, doi:10.4232/1.10789.

EVS, 2016. European Values Study 2008: Integrated Dataset (EVS 2008). GESIS Data Archive, Cologne. ZA4800 Data File Version 4.0.0, doi:10.4232/1.12458.

EVS, 2019. European Values Study 2017: Integrated Dataset (EVS 2017). GESIS Data Archive, Cologne. ZA7500 Data File Version 2.0.0, doi:10.4232/1.13314.

Eysenck, Hans, 1954. *The Psychology of Politics.* London: Routledge.

Federico, Christopher M., Emily L. Fisher, and Grace Deason, 2011. 'Political Expertise and the Link between the Authoritarian Predisposition and Conservatism'. *Public Opinion Quarterly* 75: 686–708.

Federico, Christopher M., and Ariel Malka, 2018. 'The Contingent, Contextual Nature of the Relationship between Needs for Security and Certainty and Political Preferences: Evidence and Implications'. *Advances in Political Psychology* 39(1): 3–48.

Feldman, Stanley, 2003. 'Enforcing Social Conformity: A Theory of Authoritarianism'. *Political Psychology* 24(1): 41–74.

Feldman, Stanley, and Karen Stenner, 1997. 'Perceived Threat and Authoritarianism'. *Political Psychology* 18: 741–70.

Fieldhouse, Ed, Jane Green, Geoffrey Evans, Hermann Schmitt, Cees van der Eijk, Jon Mellon, and Chris Prosser, 2019. British Election Study Internet Panel Waves 1–16. DOI: 10.15127/1.293723.

Finnish National Election Study [2011 codebook], 2015. Tampere: Finnish Social Science Data Archive [producer and distributor].

Finnish National Election Study [2015 codebook], 2018. Tampere: Finnish Social Science Data Archive [producer and distributor].

Foa, Roberto Stefan, and Yascha Mounk, 2016. 'The Danger of Deconsolidation: The Democratic Disconnect'. *Journal of Democracy* 27(3): 5–17.

Ford, Robert, and Matthew Goodwin, 2014. *Revolt on the Right: Explaining Support for the Radical Right in Britain.* New York: Routledge.

Franklin, Mark, 2004. *Voter Turnout and the Dynamics of Electoral Competition in Established Democracies since 1945.* New York: Cambridge University Press.

Franklin, Mark, Thomas Mackie, and Henry Valen, 2009. *Electoral Change: Responses to Evolving Social and Attitudinal Structures in Western Countries.* London: ECPR Press.

Gabel, Matthew J., 1998. *Interests and Integration: Market Liberalization, Public Opinion, and European Union.* Ann Arbor: University of Michigan Press.

Gabel, Matthew, and Harvey D. Palmer, 1995. 'Understanding Variation in Public Support for European Integration'. *European Journal of Political Research* 27(1): 3–19.

Gelman, Andrew, and Jennifer Hill, 2007. *Data Analysis Using Regression and Multilevel/ Hierarchical Models.* New York: Cambridge University Press.

Gerber, Alan S., Gregory A. Huber, David Doherty, Conor M. Dowling, and Shang E. Ha, 2010. 'Personality and Political Attitudes: Relationships across Issue Domains and Political Contexts'. *American Political Science Review* 104(1): 111–33.

Gest, Justin, 2016. *The New Minority: White Working Class Politics in an Age of Immigration and Inequality.* New York: Oxford University Press.

Gest, Justin, Tyler Reny, and Jeremy Mayer, 2018. 'Roots of the Radical Right: Nostalgic Deprivation in the United States and Britain'. *Comparative Political Studies* 51(13): 1694–719.

Gidron, Noam, and Peter A. Hall, 2020. 'Populism as a Problem of Social Integration'. *Comparative Political Studies* 53(7): 1027–59.

Givens, Terri, 2005. *Voting Radical Right in Western Europe.* New York: Cambridge University Press.

Golder, Matt, 2003. 'Explaining Variation in the Success of Extreme Right Parties in Western Europe'. *Comparative Political Studies* 36(4): 432–66.

Goodwin, Matthew, and Roger Eatwell, 2018. *National Populism: The Revolt against Liberal Democracy.* London: Penguin UK.

Greenstein, Fred I., 1987. *Personality and Politics: Problems of Evidence, Inference, and Conceptualization.* Princeton, NJ: Princeton University Press.

Greven, Thomas, 2016. *The Rise of Right-Wing Populism in Europe and the United States: A Comparative Perspective.* Berlin: Friedrich-Ebert Stiftung.

Hainmueller, Jens, and Dominik Hangartner, 2013. 'Who Gets a Swiss Passport? A Natural Experiment in Immigrant Discrimination'. *American Political Science Review* 107(1): 159–87.

Henry, P.J., 2011. 'The Role of Stigma in Understanding Ethnicity Differences in Authoritarianism'. *Political Psychology* 32(3): 419–38.

Hetherington, Marc J., and Elizabeth Suhay, 2011. 'Authoritarianism, Threat, and Americans' Support for the War on Terror'. *American Journal of Political Science* 55(3): 546–60.

Hetherington, Marc J., and Jonathan D. Weiler, 2009. *Authoritarianism and Polarization in American Politics.* New York: Cambridge University Press.

Hibbing, John R., Kevin B. Smith, and John R. Alford, 2013. *Predisposed: Liberals, Conservatives, and the Biology of Political Differences.* London: Routledge.

Higham, John, 1955. *Strangers in the Land: Patterns of American Nativism, 1860–1925.* New Brunswick, NJ: Rutgers University Press.

Hirsh, Jacob B., Colin G. DeYoung, Xiaowen Xu, and Jordan B. Peterson, 2010. 'Compassionate Liberals and Polite Conservatives: Associations of Agreeableness with Political Ideology and Moral Values'. *Personality and Social Psychology Bulletin* 36(5): 655–64.

Hix, Simon, 2008. *What's Wrong with the European Union and How to Fix It.* London: Polity.

Hobolt, Sara Binzer, 2009. *Europe in Question: Referendums on European Integration.* New York: Oxford University Press.

Hobolt, Sara B., and Catherine E. de Vries, 2015. 'Issue Entrepreneurship and Multiparty Competition'. *Comparative Political Studies* 48(9): 1159–85.

Hobolt, Sara B., and James Tilley, 2016. 'Fleeing the Centre: The Rise of Challenger Parties in the Aftermath of the Euro Crisis'. *West European Politics* 39(5): 971–91.

Hobolt, Sara Binzer, Wouter van der Brug, Claes H. De Vreese, Hajo G. Boomgaarden, and Malte C. Hinrichsen, 2011. 'Religious Intolerance and Euroscepticism'. *European Union Politics* 12(3): 359–79.

Hooghe, Liesbet, and Gary Marks, 2005. 'Calculation, Community, and Cues: Public Opinion on European Integration'. *European Union Politics* 6(4): 419–43.

Hooghe, Liesbet, and Gary Marks, 2009. 'A Postfunctionalist Theory of European Integration: From Permissive Consensus to Constraining Dissensus'. *British Journal of Political Science* 39(1): 1–23.

Hooghe, Liesbet, and Gary Marks, 2018. 'Cleavage Theory Meets Europe's Crises: Lipset, Rokkan, and the Transnational Cleavage'. *Journal of European Public Policy* 25(1): 109–35.

Hooghe, Liesbet, Gary Marks, and Carole J. Wilson, 2002. 'Does Left/Right Structure Party Positions on European Integration?' *Comparative Political Studies* 35(8): 965–89.

Ignazi, Piero, 1992. 'The Silent Counter-Revolution: Hypotheses on the Emergence of Extreme Right-Wing Parties in Europe'. *European Journal of Political Research* 22(1): 3–34.

Ignazi, Piero, 2003. *Extreme Right Parties in Western Europe.* Oxford: Oxford University Press.

Inglehart, Ronald, 1970. 'Cognitive Mobilization and European Identity'. *Comparative Politics* 3(1): 45–70.

Inglehart, Ronald, 1977. *The Silent Revolution: Changing Values and Political Styles among Western Publics*. Princeton, NJ: Princeton University Press.

Inglehart, Ronald, 1997. *Modernization and Postmodernization*. Princeton, NJ: Princeton University Press.

Inglehart, Ronald, 2018. *Cultural Evolution*. New York: Cambridge University Press.

Inglehart, Ronald, and Christian Welzel, 2005. *Modernization, Cultural Change, and Democracy: The Human Development Sequence*. New York: Cambridge University Press.

Ivarsflaten, Elisabeth, 2005. 'The Vulnerable Populist Right Parties: No Economic Realignment Fueling their Electoral Success'. *European Journal of Political Research* 44(3): 465–92.

Ivarsflaten, Elisabeth, 2007. 'What Unites Right-Wing Populists in Western Europe? Re-Examining Grievance Mobilization Models in Seven Successful Cases'. *Comparative Political Studies* 41(1): 3–23.

Jesuit, David K., Piotr R. Paradowski, and Vincent A. Mahler, 2009. 'Electoral Support for Extreme Right-Wing Parties: A Sub-National Analysis of Western European Elections'. *Electoral Studies* 28(2): 279–90.

Johnston, Christopher D., Howard G. Lavine, and Christopher M. Federico, 2017. *Open Versus Closed: Personality, Identity, and the Politics of Redistribution*. New York: Cambridge University Press.

Johnston, Christopher D., and Julie Wronski, 2015. 'Personality Dispositions and Political Preferences across Hard and Easy Issues'. *Political Psychology* 36(1): 35–53.

Jost, John T., Christopher M. Federico, and Jaime L. Napier, 2009. 'Political Ideology: Its Structure, Functions, and Elective Affinities'. *Annual Review of Psychology* 60: 307–37.

Jost, John T., Jack Glaser, Arie W. Kruglanski, and Frank J. Sulloway, 2003. 'Political Conservatism as Motivated Social Cognition'. *Psychological Bulletin* 129(3): 339–75.

Kahneman, Daniel, 2001. *Thinking, Fast and Slow*. New York: Farrar, Straus, and Giroux.

Kemmelmeier, Markus, 2010. 'Authoritarianism and its Relationship with Intuitive-Experiential Cognitive Style and Heuristic Processing'. *Personality and Individual Differences* 48(1): 44–8.

Kinder, Donald R., and Nathan P. Kalmoe, 2017. *Neither Liberal nor Conservative: Ideological Innocence in the American Public*. Chicago, IL: University of Chicago Press.

Kitschelt, Herbert, 1994. *The Transformation of European Social Democracy*. Cambridge: Cambridge University Press.

Kitschelt, Herbert, 1997. *The Radical Right in Western Europe: A Comparative Analysis*. Ann Arbor: University of Michigan Press.

Kline, Rex B., 2011. *Principles and Practice of Structural Equation Modeling*, Third Edition. New York: Guilford Press.

Knigge, Pia, 1998. 'The Ecological Correlates of Right-Wing Extremism in Western Europe'. *European Journal of Political Research* 34(2): 249–79.

Kriesi, Hanspeter, Edgar Grande, Martin Dolezal, Marc Helbling, Dominic Höglinger, Swen Hutter, and Bruno Wüest, 2012. *Political Conflict in Western Europe*. New York: Cambridge University Press.

Kriesi, Hanspeter, Edgar Grande, Romain Lachat, Martin Dolezal, Simon Bornschier, and Timotheos Frey, 2008. *West European Politics in the Age of Globalization*. New York: Cambridge University Press.

Kritzinger, Sylvia, Eva Zeglovits, Julian Aichholzer, Konstantin Glinitzer, Christian Glantschnigg, David Johann, Kathrin Thomas, and Markus Wagner, 2014. AUTNES PRE- and POST Panel Study 2013. Edition 1.0.

Kruglanski, Arie W., 1989. *Lay Epistemics and Human Knowledge: Cognitive and Motivational Bases*. New York: Springer.

Kuhn, Theresa, 2015. *Experiencing European Integration: Transnational Lives and European Identity.* Oxford: Oxford University Press.

Lancee, Bram, and Oriane Sarrasin, 2015. 'Educated Preferences or Selection Effects? A Longitudinal Analysis of the Impact of Educational Attainment on Attitudes Towards Immigrants'. *European Sociological Review* 31(4): 490–501.

Lavine, Howard, Milton Lodge, and Kate Freitas, 2005. 'Threat, Authoritarianism, and Selective Exposure to Information'. *Political Psychology* 26(2): 219–44.

Lefkofridi, Zoe, Markus Wagner, and Johanna E. Willmann, 2014. 'Left-Authoritarians and Policy Representation in Western Europe: Electoral Choice across Ideological Dimensions'. *West European Politics* 37(1): 65–90.

Lijphart, Arend, 1999. *Patterns of Democracy: Government Forms and Performance in Thirty-Six Democracies.* New Haven, CT: Yale University Press.

Lindberg, Leon, and Stuart Scheingold, 1970. *Europe's Would-Be Polity: Patterns in the European Community.* Englewood Cliffs, NJ: Prentice-Hall.

Lipset, Seymour Martin, 1959. 'Democracy and Working-Class Authoritarianism'. *American Sociological Review* 24(4): 482–501.

Lipset, Seymour, and Stein Rokkan, 1967. 'Cleavage Structures, Party Systems, and Voter Alignments: An Introduction'. In *Party Systems and Voter Alignments: Cross-National Perspectives.* Edited by Seymour M. Lipset and Stein Rokkan, 1–64. New York: Free Press.

Lubbers, Marcel, Merove Gijsberts, and Peer Scheepers, 2002. 'Extreme Right-Wing Voting in Western Europe'. *European Journal of Political Research* 41(3): 345–78.

Lucassen, Geertje, and Marcel Lubbers, 2012. 'Who Fears What? Explaining Far-Right-Wing Preference in Europe by Distinguishing Perceived Cultural and Economic Ethnic Threats'. *Comparative Political Studies* 45(5): 547–74.

Luedtke, Adam, 2005. 'European Integration, Public Opinion, and Immigration Policy: Testing the Impact of National Identity'. *European Union Politics* 6(1): 83–112.

Lutz, Georg and Nicholas Pekari, 2015. Swiss Electoral Studies (Selects) 2015. FORS.

Lutz, Karin Gilland, 2003. 'Irish Party Competition in the New Millennium: Change, or *Plus Ca Change?*' *Irish Political Studies* 18(2): 40–59.

McCrae, Robert R. and Paul Costa, 1987. 'Validation of the Five Factor Model of Personality across Instruments and Observers'. *Journal of Personality and Social Psychology* 52(1): 81–90.

McElroy, Gail, 2017. 'Party Competition in Ireland: The Emergence of a Left-Right Dimension?' In *A Conservative Revolution? Electoral Change in Twenty-First Century Ireland.* Edited by Michael Marsh, David M. Farrell, and Gail McElroy, 61–82. Oxford: Oxford University Press.

McFarland, Sam G., Vladimir S. Ageyev, and Marina A. Abalakina-Popp, 1992. 'Authoritarianism in the Former Soviet Union'. *Journal of Personality and Social Psychology* 63(6): 1004–10.

McLaren, Lauren M., 2002. 'Public Support for the European Union: Cost/Benefit Analysis or Perceived Cultural Threat?' *Journal of Politics* 64(2): 551–66.

MacWilliams, Matthew, 2016. 'Who Decides When the Party Doesn't? Authoritarian Voters and the Rise of Donald Trump'. *PS: Politics and Society* 49(4): 716–21.

Malka, Ariel, Christopher J. Soto, Michael Inzlicht, and Yphtach Lelkes, 2014. 'Do Needs for Security and Certainty Predict Cultural and Economic Conservatism? A Cross-National Analysis'. *Journal of Personality and Social Psychology* 106: 1031–51.

Marsh, Michael, and Gail McElroy, 2017. 'Voting Behaviour: Continuing Dealignment'. In *How Ireland Voted 2016.* Edited by Michael Gallagher and Michael Marsh, 159–84. New York: Palgrave Macmillan.

Marsh, Michael, Richard Sinnott, John Garry, and Fiachra Kennedy, 2008, *The Irish Voter: The Nature of Electoral Competition in the Republic of Ireland*. Manchester: Manchester University Press.

Mayer, Nonna, 2013. 'From Jean-Marie to Marine Le Pen: Electoral Change on the Far Right'. *Parliamentary Affairs* 66(1): 160–78.

Mondak, Jeffery J., 2010. *Personality and the Foundations of Political Behavior*. New York: Cambridge University Press.

Mounk, Yascha, 2018. *The People vs. Democracy: Why Our Freedom is in Danger and How to Save It*. Cambridge, MA: Harvard University Press.

Mudde, Cas, 2007. *Populist Radical Right Parties in Europe*. New York: Cambridge University Press.

Mudde, Cas, 2017. 'Introduction to the Populist Radical Right'. In *The Populist Radical Right: A Reader*. Edited by Cas Mudde, 1–10. New York: Routledge.

Mueller, John, 1970. 'Presidential Popularity from Truman to Johnson'. *American Political Science Review* 64(1): 18–34.

Müller, Jan-Werner, 2016. *What is Populism?* Philadelphia: University of Pennsylvania Press.

Napier, Jaime L., and John T. Jost, 2008. 'The "Antidemocratic Personality" Revisited: A Cross-National Investigation of Working-Class Authoritarianism'. *Journal of Social Issues* 64(3): 595–617.

Nelsen, Brent F., James L. Guth, and Cleveland R. Fraser, 2002. 'Does Religion Matter? Christianity and Public Support for the European Union'. *European Union Politics* 2(2): 191–217.

Norris, Pippa, 2005. *Radical Right: Voters and Parties in the Electoral Market*. New York: Cambridge University Press.

Norris, Pippa, and Ronald Inglehart, 2019. *Cultural Backlash: Trump, Brexit, and Authoritarian Populism*. New York: Cambridge University Press.

Oesch, Daniel, 2008. 'Explaining Workers' Support for Right-Wing Populist Parties in Western Europe: Evidence from Austria, Belgium, France, Norway, and Switzerland'. *International Political Science Review* 29(3): 349–73.

Oesterreich, Detlef, 2005. 'Flight into Security: A New Approach and Measure of the Authoritarian Personality'. *Political Psychology* 26(2): 275–97.

O'Malley, Eoin, 2008. 'Why Is There No Radical Right Party in Ireland?' *West European Politics* 31(5): 960–77.

Oyamot, Clifton M., Jr., Emily L. Fisher, Grace Deason, and Eugene Borgida, 2012. 'Attitudes toward Immigrants: The Interactive Role of the Authoritarian Predisposition, Social Norms, and Humanitarian Values'. *Journal of Experimental Social Psychology* 48(1): 97–105.

Peffley, Mark, Marc L. Hutchison, and Michal Shamir, 2015. 'The Impact of Persistent Terrorism on Political Tolerance: Israel, 1980 to 2011'. *American Political Science Review* 109(4): 817–32.

Pollock, Philip H., Stuart A. Lilie, and M. Elliot Vittes, 1993. 'Hard Issues, Core Values, and Vertical Constraint: The Case of Nuclear Power'. *British Journal of Political Science* 23(1): 29–50.

Rattinger, Hans, Sigrid Roßteutscher, Rüdiger Schmitt-Beck, Bernhard Weßels, and Christof Wolf, 2014. Langfrist-Online-Tracking T24 (GLES). GESIS Datenarchiv, Köln: ZA5724 Datenfile Version 1.0.0, doi: 10/4232/1/11963.

Riker, William H., 1982. *Liberalism against Populism: A Confrontation between the Theory of Democracy and the Theory of Social Choice*. Long Grove, IL: Waveland Press.

Rohrschneider, Robert, 2002. 'The Democracy Deficit and Mass Support for an EU-wide Government'. *American Journal of Political Science* 46(2): 463–75.

Rosenberg, Milton J., and Carl I. Hovland, 1960. 'Cognitive, Affective, and Behavioral Components of Attitudes'. In *Attitude Organization and Change: An Analysis of Consistency among Attitude Components*. Edited by Milton J. Rosenberg and Carl I. Hovland, 1–14. New Haven, CT: Yale University Press.

Rydgren, Jens, 2013. *Class Politics and the Radical Right*. London: Routledge.

Rydgren, Jens, and Joop van Holsteyn, 2004. 'Holland and Pim Fortuyn: Deviant Case or the Beginning of Something New?' *Current Politics and Economics of Europe* 13(3): 209–38.

Sanchez-Cuenca, Ignacio, 2000. 'The Political Basis of Support for European Integration'. *European Union Politics* 1(2): 147–71.

Schoen, Harald, and Siegfried Schumann, 2007. 'Personality Traits, Partisan Attitudes, and Voting Behavior. Evidence from Germany'. *Political Psychology* 28(4): 471–98.

Schwartz, Shalom M., 1992. 'Universals in the Content and Structure of Values: Theoretical Advances and Empirical Tests in 20 Countries'. *Advances in Experimental Social Psychology* 25: 1–65.

Schwartz, Shalom M., 1994. 'Are There Universal Aspects in the Structure and Contents of Human Values?' *Journal of Social Issues* 50(4): 19–45.

Schwartz, Shalom M., and Wolfgang Bilsky, 1987. 'Toward a Universal Psychological Structure of Human Values'. *Journal of Personality and Social Psychology* 53(3): 550–62.

Sibley, Chris G., and John Duckitt, 2008. 'Personality and Prejudice: A Meta-Analysis and Theoretical Review'. *Personality and Social Psychology Review* 12(3): 248–79.

Sinnott, Richard, 1998. 'Party Attachment in Europe: Methodological Critique and Substantive Implications'. *British Journal of Political Science* 28(4): 627–50.

Steenbergen, Marco R., and Bradford S. Jones, 2002. 'Modeling Multilevel Data Structures'. *American Journal of Political Science* 46(1): 218–37.

Stenner, Karen, 2005. *The Authoritarian Dynamic*. New York: Cambridge University Press.

Stenner, Karen, 2009. 'Three Kinds of "Conservatism"'. *Psychological Inquiry* 20 (1): 142–59.

Stephens, John, 1979. 'Class Formation and Class Consciousness: A Theoretical and Empirical Analysis with Reference to Britain and Sweden'. *British Journal of Sociology* 30(4): 389–414.

Tajfel, Henri, 1978. *Differentiation between Social Groups: Studies in the Social Psychology of Intergroup Relations*. London: Academic Press.

Theiss-Morse, Elizabeth, 2009. *Who Counts as an American? The Boundaries of National Identity*. New York: Cambridge University Press.

Thorisdottir, Hulda, John T. Jost, Ido Liviatan, and Patrick E. Shrout, 2007. 'Psychological Needs and Values Underlying Left-Right Orientation: Cross-National Evidence from Eastern and Western Europe'. *Public Opinion Quarterly* 71(2): 175–203.

Tilley, James, and John Garry, 2017. 'Class Politics in Ireland: How Economic Catastrophe Realigned Irish Politics'. In *A Conservative Revolution? Electoral Change in Twenty-First Century Ireland*. Edited by Michael Marsh, David M. Farrell, and Gail McElroy, 11–27. Oxford: Oxford University Press.

Tillman, Erik R., 2004. 'The European Union at the Ballot Box? European Integration and Voting Behavior in the New Member States'. *Comparative Political Studies* 37(5): 590–610.

Tillman, Erik R., 2013. 'Authoritarianism and Citizen Attitudes toward European Integration'. *European Union Politics* 14(4): 566–89.

Tillman, Erik R., 2016. 'Has the Global Financial Crisis Changed Citizen Behaviour? A Four-Country Study'. In *Globalization and Domestic Politics: Parties, Elections, and Public Opinion*. Edited by Jack Vowles and Georgios Xezonakis, 113–30. Oxford: Oxford University Press.

van der Brug, Wouter, and Joose van Spanje, 2009. 'Immigration, Europe, and the "new" cultural dimension'. *European Journal of Political Research* 48(3): 309–34.

Van der Eijk, Cees, Wouter van der Brug, Martin Kroh, and Mark Franklin, 2006. 'Rethinking the Dependent Variable in Voting Behavior: On the Measurement and Analysis of Electoral Utilities'. *Electoral Studies* 25(3): 424–47.

Van Spanje, Joost, 2010. 'Contagious Parties: Anti-Immigration Parties and Their Impact on Other Parties' Immigration Stances in Contemporary Western Europe'. *Party Politics* 16(5): 563–86.

Vasilopoulos, Pavlos, and Romain Lachat, 2018. 'Authoritarianism and Political Choice in France'. *Acta Politica* 53(4): 612–34.

Whyte, John H., 1974. 'Ireland: Politics without Social Bases'. In *Electoral Behavior: A Comparative Handbook*. Edited by Richard Rose. New York: Free Press.

Zaller, John R., 1992. *The Nature and Origins of Mass Opinion*. New York: Cambridge University Press.

Zandonella, Martina, and Eva Zeglovits, 2013. 'Young Men and Their Vote for the Radical Right in Austria: Can Personality Traits, Right-Wing Authoritarianism and Social Dominance Orientation Contribute to the Explanation of Radical Right Voting?' *Politics, Culture and Socialization* 3(1–2). Available at: https://www.budrich-journals.de/index.php/pcs/article/view/19761.

Index